IMAGES
*of America*

# MOUNT PLEASANT

**On the Cover:** Morris and Herman Lilienstern opened their dry goods store in Mount Pleasant in 1881 after their train broke down in the city. (Courtesy of Mount Pleasant Public Library and Historical Museum.)

IMAGES
*of America*

# MOUNT PLEASANT

Melissa Weinbrenner and James McGregor

ARCADIA
PUBLISHING

ISBN 1-4671-3179-7

Published by Arcadia Publishing
Charleston, South Carolina

Printed in the United States of America

Library of Congress Control Number: 2013957658

For all general information, please contact Arcadia Publishing:
Telephone 843-853-2070
Fax 843-853-0044
E-mail sales@arcadiapublishing.com
For customer service and orders:
Toll-Free 1-888-313-2665

Visit us on the Internet at www.arcadiapublishing.com

*To Traylor Russell, Titus County's original historian and scholar, whose extensive research both inspired and supported our work.*

# Contents

# Acknowledgments

A number of organizations and individuals contributed research, photographs, stories, anecdotes, information, notes, journals, and encouragement that made this book a reality. Most significant among them is the Mount Pleasant Public Library and Historical Museum, which provided access to numerous historical items and images. Its staff and resources have been immensely helpful, in particular Brenda Bynum and Helen Thompson. The library and museum preserve a significant collection of Mount Pleasant and Titus County memorabilia and also maintain a helpful local history and genealogy research section. The *East Texas Journal* furnished invaluable assistance when compiling the images and information found in this work. Hudson Old and Steven Barker proved especially helpful. When beginning this undertaking, Steven Austin and the Titus County Historical Association were helpful in directing our attention to pertinent resources. The *Mount Pleasant Tribune* and its publications provided additional information useful for this project. Northeast Texas Community College, which houses an extensive collection of Caddo pottery, provided access to its collection. In addition, specific thanks go to Jodi Weber, Jon McCullough, Nita May, and Brad Johnson for their assistance and support.

We also wish to thank several additional community members who assisted in one way or another. Barry Hamilton, owner of the oldest retail establishment in Mount Pleasant, provided photographs and information on the history of the Mount Pleasant merchant community. Longtime residents also provided assistance in varying degrees. Claude Alexander spent hours sharing stories and memories. A retired construction inspector for the city of Mount Pleasant, he served as longtime chair of the Titus County Historical Commission and member of the Mount Pleasant Main Street Board. Mount Pleasant natives Rex Allen, John Williams, and Betty Gerhart graciously provided useful images and information as well.

In addition, we want to thank the many past and present residents of Mount Pleasant who have documented the history of their families and their city. Special thanks go to Traylor Russell, who wrote extensively on Mount Pleasant, and his son Robert Traylor Russell, who later helped him in that endeavor. Robert and Mary Turner also served as unofficial historians of Titus County and Mount Pleasant.

We dedicate this work to our families, who have endured our distraction and preoccupation with the past with grace and patience: Heather and Katie McGregor and Brian, Arthur, and Eric Taylor.

# Introduction

"Come and sleep where the red man slept, and drink of the waters that the red man drank," invited Iridescent Springs promoter Jessie Reed, encouraging visitors to come to Mount Pleasant in the 1890s.

Native cultures settled in what is now Mount Pleasant because food, water, and shelter were readily available in the mixed hardwood forests of the area. The waters, unusual in that they bubbled up in colors—red, clear, and blue—attracted natives to a very popular gathering site atop a hill the Caddo called "pleasant mound."

One reason Native Americans remained in this area so long is because it was unclear which European nation actually owned it. At one time both France and Spain laid claim to the region but mostly ignored it as long as the other country was not an immediate threat. In both the 1820 and 1830 US Census, Miller County, Arkansas, laid claim to the area, although it was actually still a part of Spain and later Mexico. Most of the confusion dealt with ambiguity regarding the boundary line running between the Sabine and Red Rivers. Spanish and American officials hoped they had negotiated an amicable settlement to the boundary dispute with the 1819 Adams-Onis Treaty. However, even after the successful Texas Revolution in 1836, the confusion remained. In 1840, for example, individuals living in Northeast Texas elected representatives to serve them in both the legislature of the Republic of Texas and the Arkansas state legislature.

The first permanent white settlers came as a result of circumstances surrounding the movement of tribes from the southeastern United States during the Trail of Tears. However, it was only after boundaries (and thus land titles) were clearly established following annexation that Anglo settlement began in earnest. The first Texas legislature carved a new county out of Red River County in 1846 and named it after an early settler in the area, Andrew Jackson Titus. In part because of its central location, Mount Pleasant was then chosen to serve as the seat of Titus County. Mount Pleasant sat astride several pre-existing native trails and therefore was an early transportation hub for the residents of Northeast Texas.

A road connecting the community to the port city of Jefferson made it an ideal location for trading and freighting. Cotton, which grew well in the creek-fed area, and native hardwood timber were the economic mainstays in the early years. Churches and schools and other trappings of an increasingly settled community quickly developed in the years prior to the Civil War.

Once the Civil War began, Mount Pleasant supported the effort by sending men to fight in the conflict and using its burgeoning economic resources on behalf of the Confederate government. During the war, Mount Pleasant had nine sawmills, eight gristmills, tanneries, and a steam-powered distillery. The city also founded a pottery to help sustain the war effort. In addition, Mount Pleasant supported the Confederacy with a transportation depot that employed blacksmiths, carpenters, harness makers, and wheelwrights.

When the war ended, Mount Pleasant initially fell upon difficult times. The area was ravaged by violence in what the media at the time called the "New Rebellion." Union troops called into the area to enforce Reconstruction clashed with frustrated former Confederates, while lawless men hoped to take advantage of the chaos for their own benefit. However, authorities worked hard to restore order, and when Reconstruction ended, Mount Pleasant emerged more confident than ever.

In large part that confidence came from the increasing availability of transportation that linked Mount Pleasant to other cities. The railroad reached the city in the 1870s and with it came an increase in the city's influence and economic opportunity. The 1890s were a prosperous decade for the city. And as a new century dawned, the citizens decided that it was time for the town to become an incorporated city.

The plentiful water supply that made the location an inviting spot for early settlers provided both economic opportunity and travel difficulties. First Jesse Reed and then the developers of the Dellwood Hotel and Resort sought to transform those colored mineral waters into a tourist attraction. For a few brief years, Mount Pleasant positioned itself as a travel destination for people hoping to benefit from the recuperative and healing powers of the local mineral waters. Unfortunately, the rest of the nation was beginning to doubt the health benefits of mineral springs at the same time. So the Dellwood, despite an opulent and optimistic start, faltered and succumbed to financial disaster.

The many creeks that kept the area well watered and forested flooded frequently and made roads impassable at times. Residents could make money renting out rooms to stranded travelers, but it would hardly help the city become a commercial and entrepreneurial success if travel were so unpredictable. While several ferries and toll bridges did operate in the area, it was not until the 20th century that far-sighted city administrators and county officials began to deal with the city's transportation issues in earnest.

One advantage Mount Pleasant historically enjoyed was its natural location as a travel hub. The nation's first attempt at a transcontinental road, the Bankhead Highway, came through the city. However, the initial promise of prosperity faded when the highway quickly proved obsolete and unable to meet the nation's ever-increasing demand for new roads. The Eisenhower Interstate Highway System would eventually replace the Bankhead Highway, but Mount Pleasant would not reap the benefits of the new transcontinental system until much later. The section of Interstate 30 that runs through Mount Pleasant was one of the very last sections of the interstate built. In the meantime, the city developed a variety of industries that have helped it prosper and have earned it a number of nicknames, such as the "Sweetest City in Texas" and the "Trailer Manufacturing Capital of the United States." With over 17,000 acres of navigable water in the area, Mount Pleasant has also been called the "Bass Capital of Texas." Because of the numerous transportation options available to the city, it is often referred to as "the Hub of East Texas." Wal-Mart, the nation's leading retailer, chose Mount Pleasant as its first Texas location, and more recently, the city successfully campaigned for a new state community college.

Hopefully the images herein depicting Mount Pleasant's colorful past can inspire its citizens to preserve that unique heritage while also looking optimistically forward to the future.

# *One*

# Beginnings

In a shady, tree-covered area with a plentiful water supply, Native Americans and other settlers found a welcoming home. Natural mineral springs bubbled up red, white, and blue waters in a popular gathering site atop what the Caddo called a "pleasant mound." Being in a disputed area alternately ignored or claimed by, at one time or another, Spain, France, Mexico, the Republic of Texas, and the United States (Arkansas in particular), the natives remained in the area of Mount Pleasant longer than other areas in Northeast Texas. The first white settlers arrived following the relocation of natives known as the Trail of Tears.

Once Texas became the 28th state and created Titus County, the search began for a site for its county seat. The chosen location lay at the convergence of several native trails along the road to the port city of Jefferson. With cotton and hardwood timber as the economic mainstays, churches, schools, and other trappings of an organized community quickly developed in the years before the Civil War.

When in 1861 the Civil War broke out, the men of Mount Pleasant did what they would always do—support the war effort and fight valiantly. Most citizens of Mount Pleasant voted in favor of secession, although one of the eight delegates against secession at the Texas Secession Convention came from this area. At the time of the war Mount Pleasant had sawmills, gristmills, tanneries, a steam-powered distillery, and a pottery. In addition, Mount Pleasant housed a transportation depot that employed blacksmiths, carpenters, harness makers, and wheelwrights.

In the years immediately following the Civil War, Mount Pleasant suffered the fate of many who lose a conflict—upheaval, exploitation, and a rise in criminal activity. The city was located in the midst of what historians would call the "Devil's Triangle," but vigorous efforts by law enforcement eventually stabilized things, and the community prospered more than ever. Railroad connections helped the economy continue to grow. By 1900, Mount Pleasant had grown sufficiently to seek incorporation.

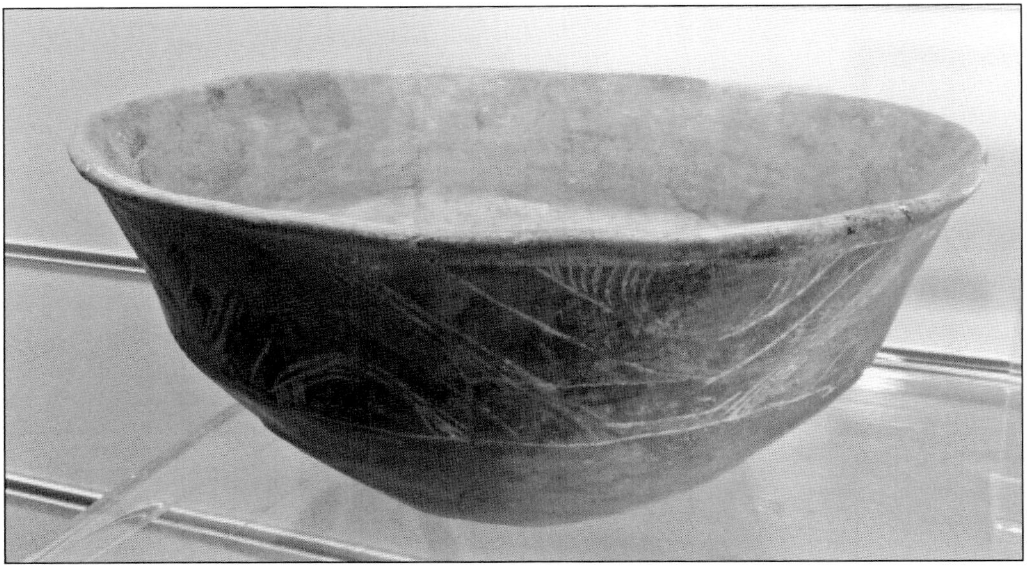

Significant findings in the area around present-day Dellwood Park, where natural mineral springs of red, white, and blue colored waters can be found, indicate that it was a popular gathering location for the natives. Mound builders as well as excellent potters, the Caddo made a variety of items such as plates, water jugs, pots, and decorative items, some of them quite large. Plentiful pottery artifacts suggest a thriving, peaceful native society in the area, although disrupted by the incoming tribes from farther east. The patterned carving on the bowl above is representative of the artwork found on Caddo pottery. The arrangement of arrowheads below is a portion of the collection of Native American artifacts currently housed at Northeast Texas Community College. (Both, courtesy of Northeast Texas Community College.)

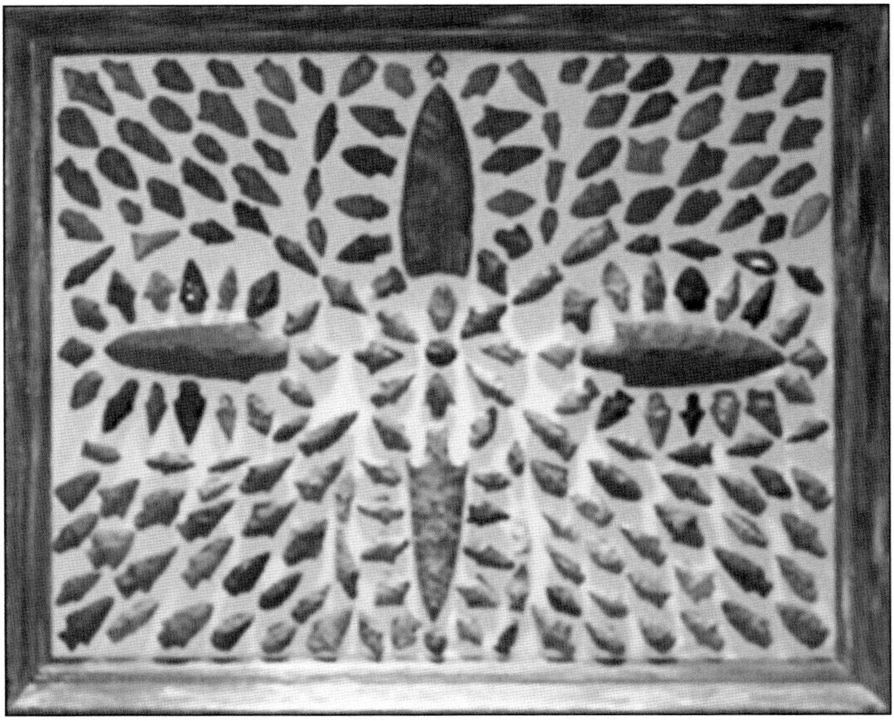

Kendall Lewis, apparently the first permanent white settler in the region, moved into the area in 1835 as a result of Georgia's relocation of natives. Like many pioneers, Kendall moved around frequently. Originally from Maryland, he owned a successful tavern and became a captain in the Alabama militia. He married one of the daughters of Chief Big Warrior. While in Alabama, he befriended Sam Houston, who would play a significant role in the settlement of Texas. In 1828, he and his wife, Kizzie, migrated with the Creek to the Indian Territory (present-day Oklahoma) along what would become known as the Trail of Tears. In 1835, he moved into the area surrounding Mount Pleasant (to the east, along the Swannano Creek) and owned the first tract of land surveyed in the area. Not only did he get the "league and a labor" granted to all heads of households living in Texas at the time of the Texas Revolution, he acquired over 20,000 acres. (Courtesy of Mount Pleasant Public Library and Historical Museum.)

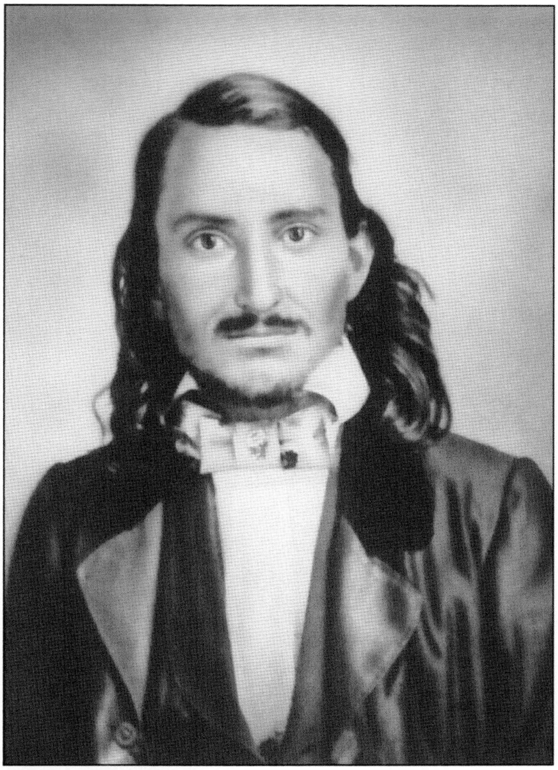

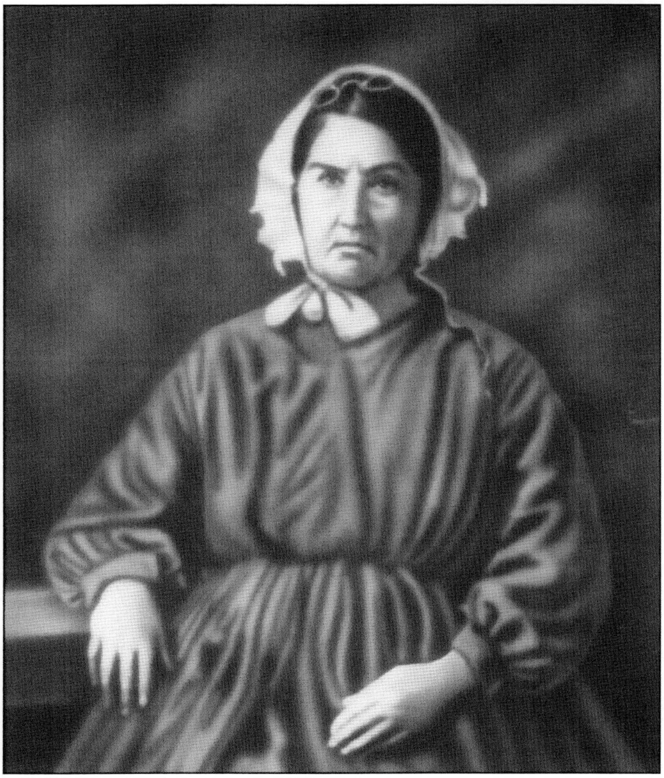

Kizzie Lewis was the daughter of Big Warrior (principal chief of the Upper Creek nation) and Kendall Lewis's wife. The Lewis household became a common stopover for white settlers and natives traveling along the Caddo Trace, also known as the Choctaw or Cherokee Trail—a trade route originally established by the native population. By 1836, several white families had moved into the area and frequented the frontier trading post. After tensions between white settlers and natives increased in the 1840s, the Lewis family returned to Indian Territory in present-day Oklahoma in 1845. (Courtesy of Mount Pleasant Public Library and Historical Museum.)

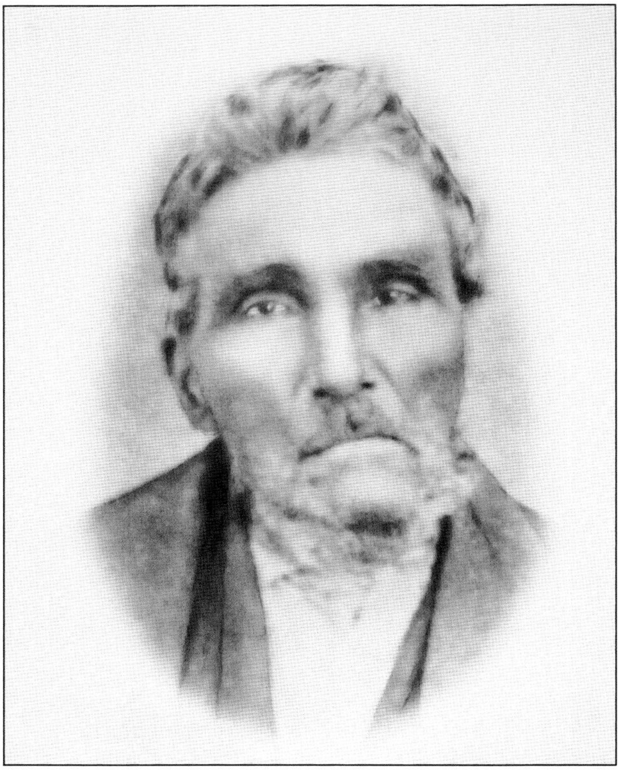

After leaving the Mount Pleasant area, Kendall Lewis appointed Benjamin Gooch as his agent and asked him to dispose of his lands in the area. In 1838, Gooch built his house on what came to be known as Gooch's Spring. (Today it is known as Town Branch and runs through Dellwood Park). Gooch also represented what was then known as Red River County in the First Texas Legislature. (Courtesy of Mount Pleasant Public Library and Historical Museum.)

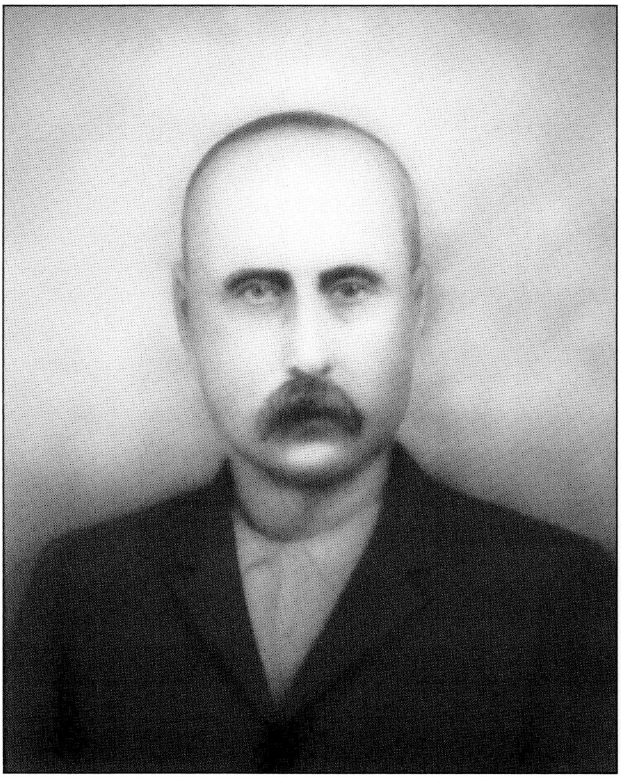

Andrew Jackson Titus's father originally came through the Mount Pleasant area as a result of his having being hired by the US government to help with the Indian removal of the late 1820s and early 1830s. Apparently, Titus became enamored with the area he had visited as a child and returned as an adult. He was active in establishing roads, including the county's first road to the port city of Jefferson, and other civic improvement projects. He served in the Fourth Legislature of the State of Texas. Titus County is named in his honor. Once Texas joined the United States in 1845, long-standing confusion caused by conflicting claims between rival nations was finally fully resolved. (Courtesy of Mount Pleasant Public Library and Historical Museum.)

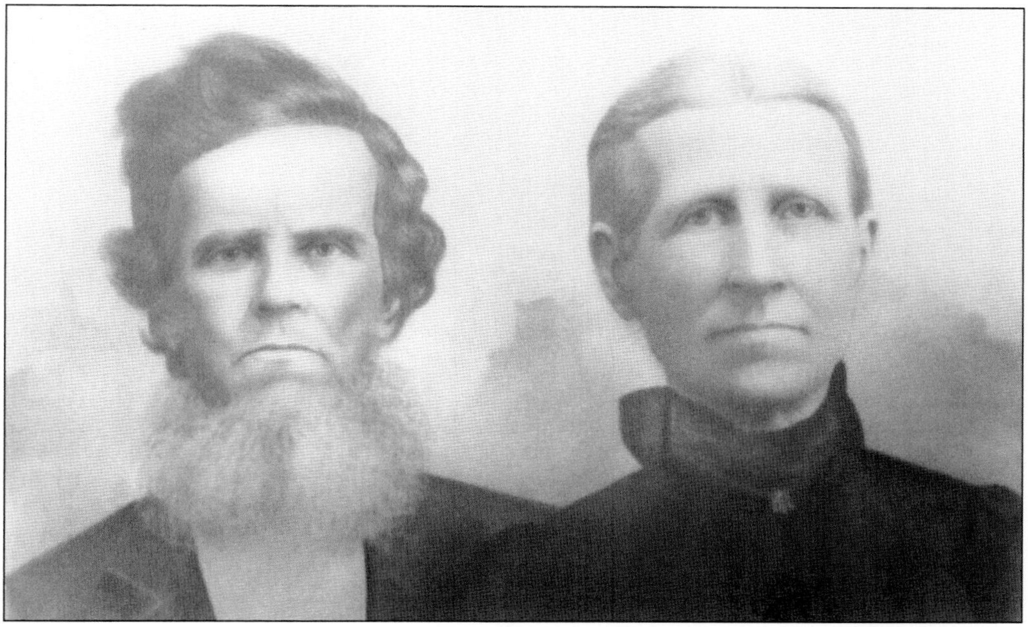

On May 11, 1846, the First Texas Legislature created Titus County by dividing Red River County into smaller sections. The county seat was to be called Mount Pleasant. John Binnion, Richard Moore, and L. Gilbert donated the land at the present location of Mount Pleasant with the courthouse square at the center. To create the downtown area, these men laid out the 48-block town site. This photograph shows Richard Moore with his wife, Nannie. (Courtesy of Mount Pleasant Public Library and Historical Museum.)

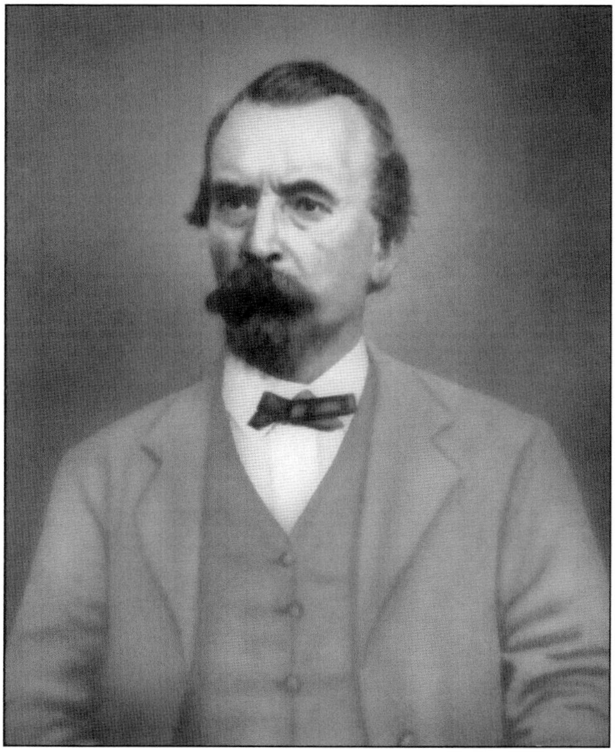

When Jacob Haynes was accused of horse theft, there was no county courthouse to hold a trial in, so Henry Jones's front porch served as the scene for the first district court in 1846. Henry Jones had arrived in Mount Pleasant in 1840 and established residence just north of present-day Dellwood Park, in the southeast corner of Mount Pleasant. He owned 1,300 acres along waterways and intersecting roads, including a ferry system and toll bridge over Hart Creek. On New Year's Day 1877, Jones was shot and killed in a saloon. Henry Jones was also the father of Dudley Jones, a respected Confederate soldier from Mount Pleasant who rose to the rank of colonel in the Civil War. (Courtesy of Mount Pleasant Public Library and Historical Museum.)

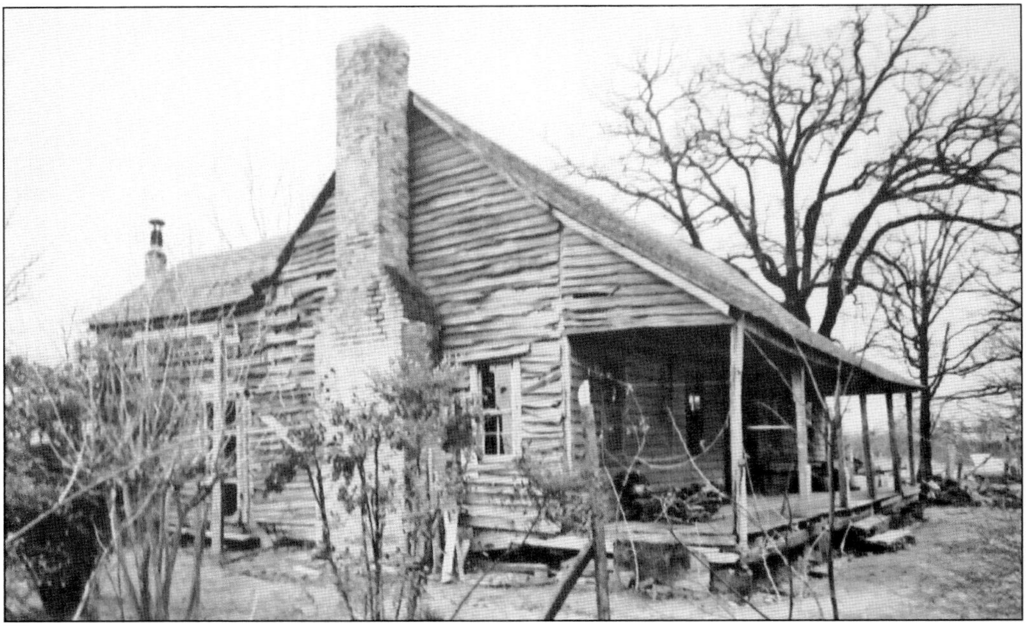

Mary Jane Riddle, one of the earliest born in Mount Pleasant, married Archibald Cameron and lived in this home. The couple had eight children and purchased 183 acres. The pioneering Riddle family arrived in 1847, and their descendants have served Mount Pleasant in a wide variety of capacities, including doctor, reverend, surveyor, farmer, postmaster, postmistress, hotelier, and businessman. (Courtesy of Mount Pleasant Public Library and Historical Museum.)

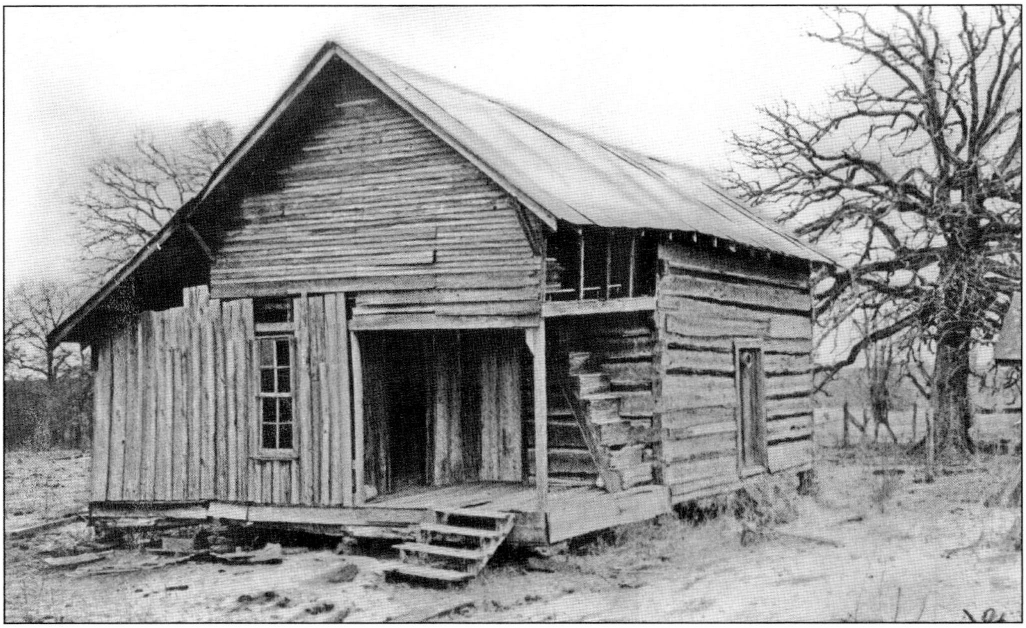

Jonathon Keith's home, pictured here, was built in 1858. Most of the structures in the area were wooden, similar to this, hence the common worry and reality of fire. This home, originally built as a two-story structure with one room on each level, had an exterior stairway to get from one floor to the next. The second floor rested on logs about nine feet above the ground. (Courtesy of Mount Pleasant Public Library and Historical Museum.)

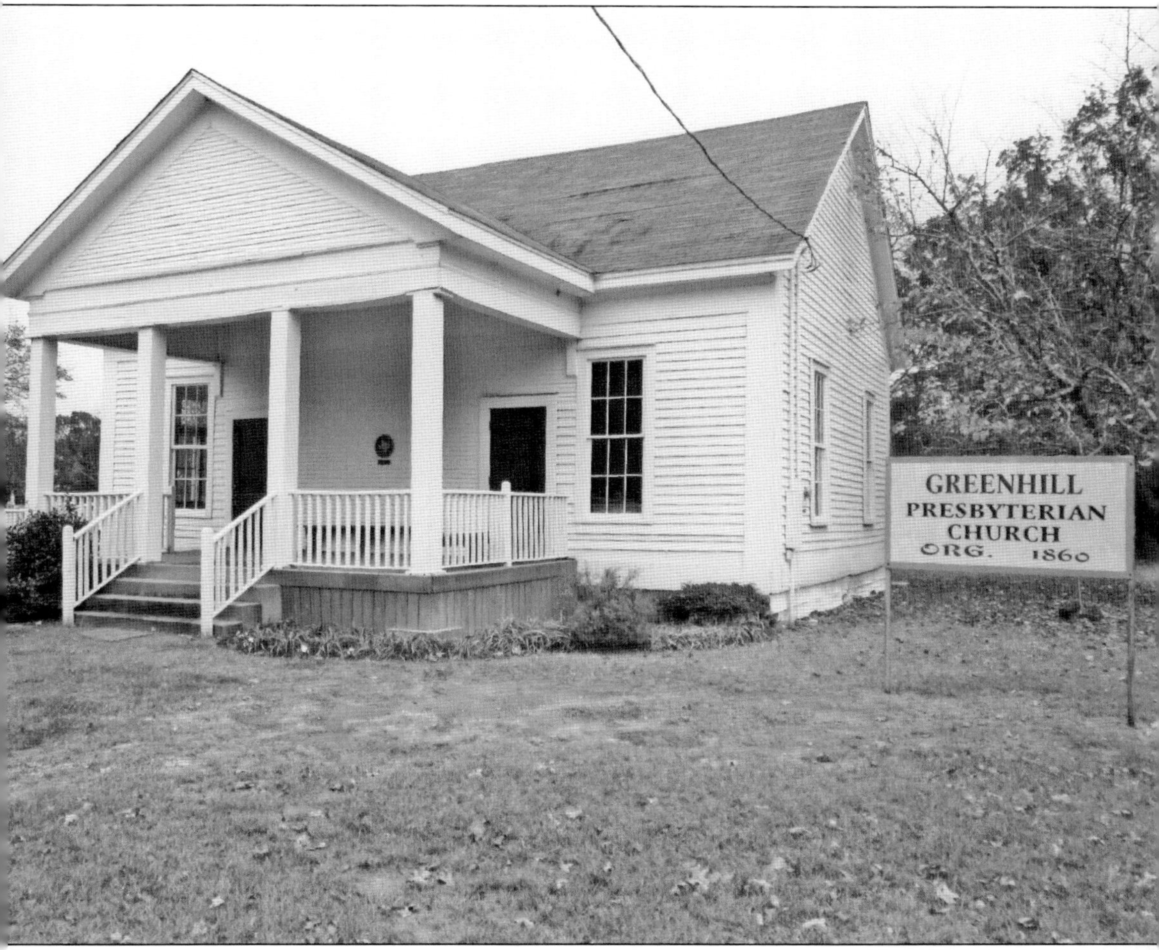


The first church built in Mount Pleasant was a Baptist church, but that structure fell during the Civil War. Greenhill Presbyterian Church, built in 1860, is the oldest church building in the Mount Pleasant area still standing today. (Authors.)

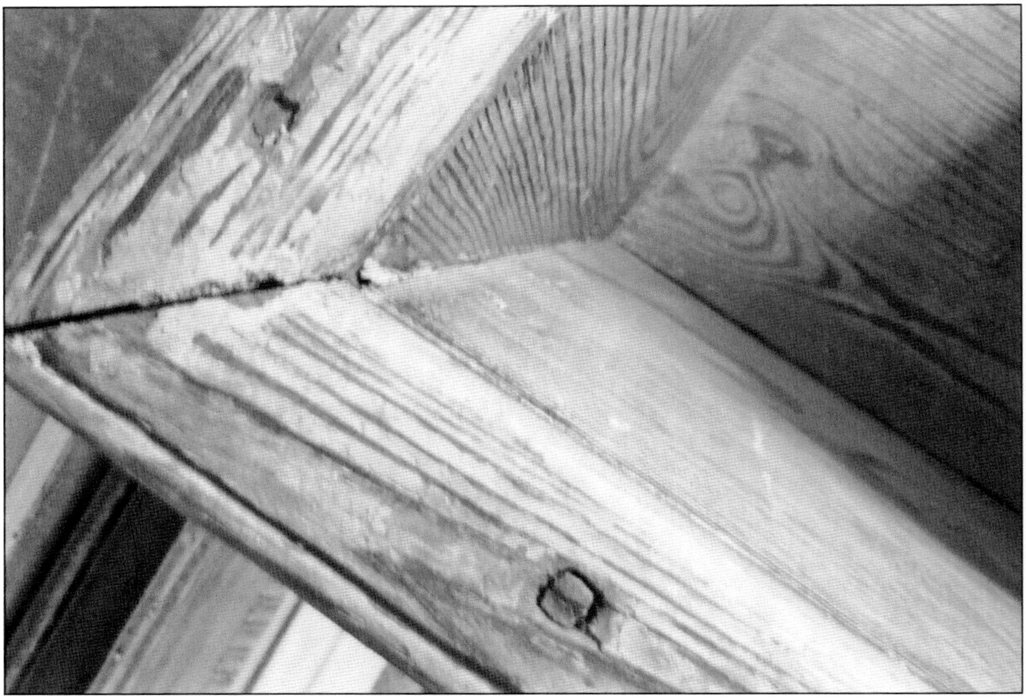

A close-up of the wrought iron cut nails used in the Greenhill church pews shows the distinctive square shape common before the widespread use of round wire nails. (Authors.)

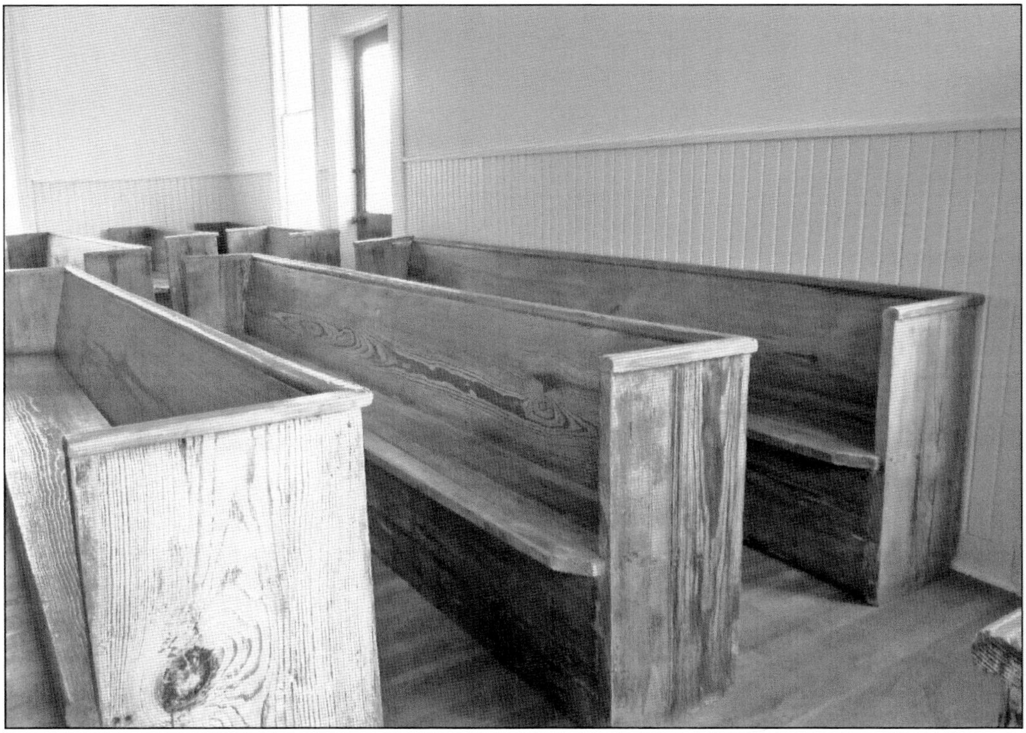

These pews, originally built in 1860 with slave labor, still provide seating inside the original structure of the Greenhill Presbyterian Church. (Authors.)

In 1860, Whitfield Russell was among those who, while fighting a group of Comanche on the Pease River with Sul Ross, captured a woman with a small girl. The woman had blue eyes and was later confirmed to be Cynthia Ann Parker, who had been taken captive by the Comanche in 1836 when only nine years old, married a Comanche chief, and gave birth to the last free Comanche chief, Quanah Parker. Whitfield enlisted and fought in the Civil War. Afterwards, he operated a freight line in the area until the railroads came to town. (Courtesy of Mount Pleasant Public Library and Historical Museum.)

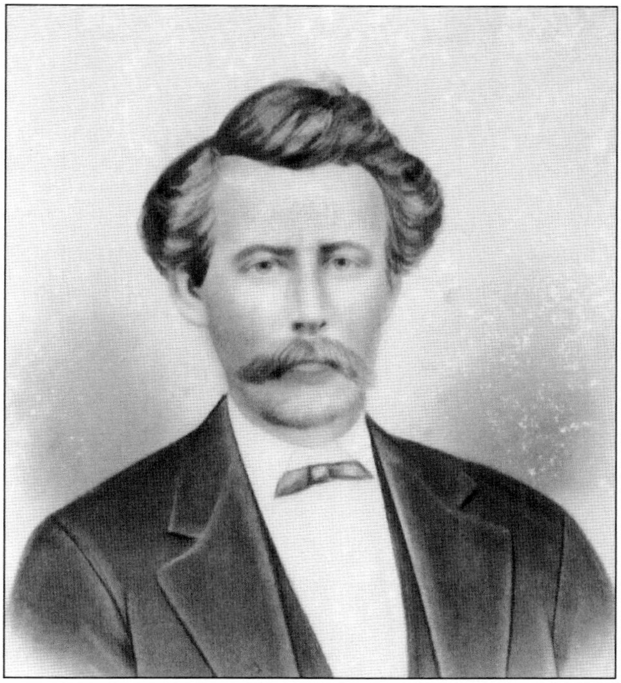

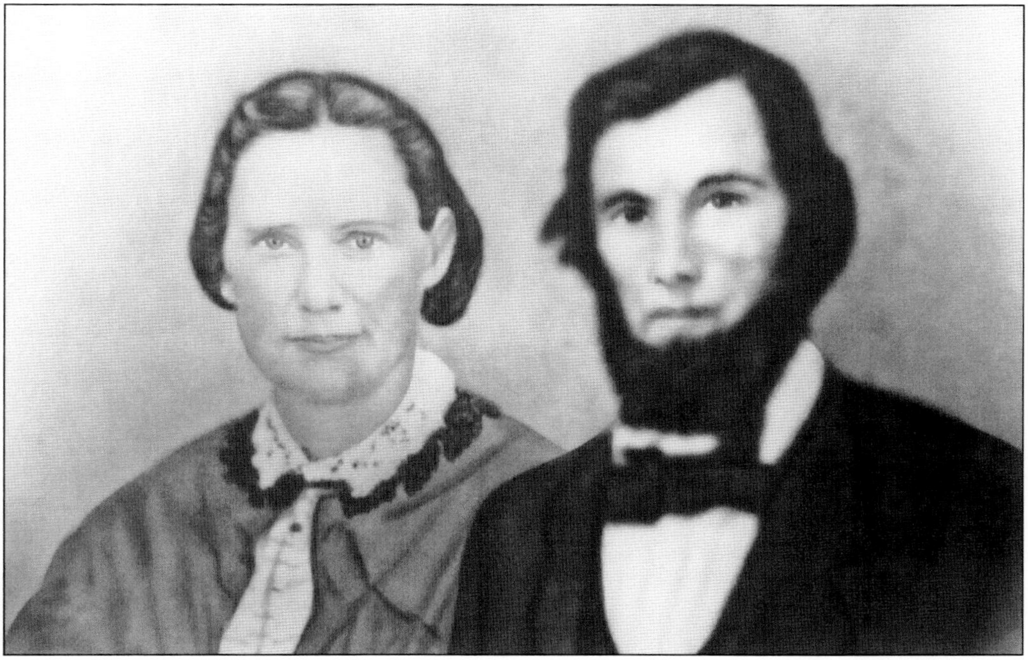

A former Titus County delegate to the Texas state legislature, Joshua Johnson represented Titus County at the secession convention in Austin in 1861, and was one of only eight members who voted against secession. He ran into some trouble with outlaws such as Tom Emmett after the Civil War and on January 13, 1869, wrote to complain about the current sheriff for failing to deal with the outlaws. He also served as a member of the Texas Constitutional Convention in 1875. When he died in 1877, Johnson (pictured here with his wife, Amanda) was the largest landowner in the area. (Courtesy of Mount Pleasant Public Library and Historical Museum.)

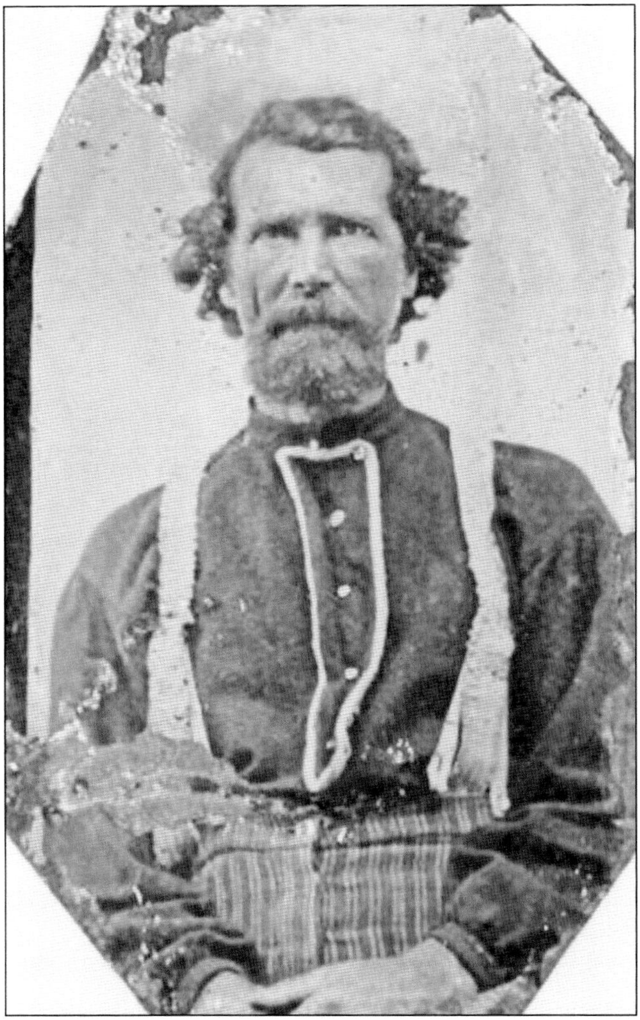

Isham Cherry moved to Mount Pleasant in 1855, and five years later, the people elected him chief justice of Titus County. He served in that capacity throughout the Civil War. After the war, Union soldiers stationed in Mount Pleasant removed Cherry from office. However, he was only temporarily out of politics and went on to be elected deputy county clerk, county treasurer, and district clerk. Cherry held that last position when, in 1880, he was killed in a saloon. (Courtesy of Mount Pleasant Public Library and Historical Museum.)

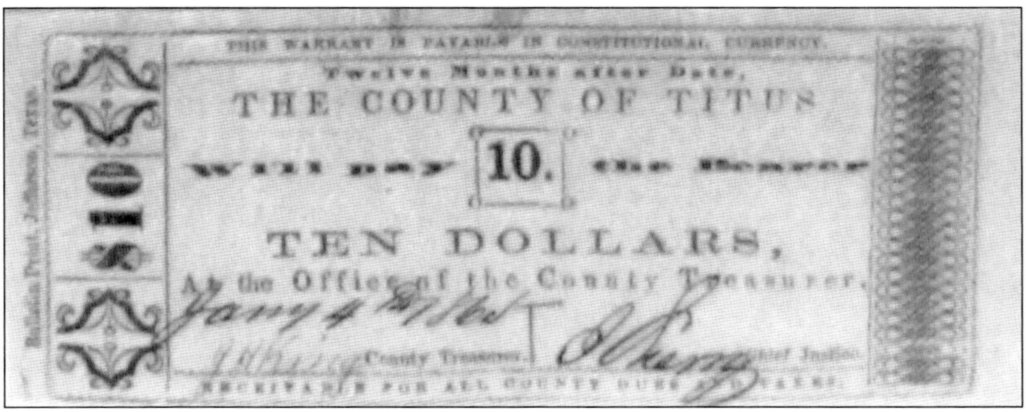


During the Civil War, money became very scarce, and some counties, such as Titus, issued their own currency. This is of a piece of Titus County scrip issued during the war and signed by the chief justice of Titus County, Isham Cherry. (Courtesy of Mount Pleasant Public Library and Historical Museum.)

A Confederate veteran with a love of music, William Taylor Presley kept a detailed diary of his time in the Civil War as well as songs that he collected while in service. A singer and a songwriter, he wrote several original pieces of music during the course of the war. (Courtesy of Mount Pleasant Public Library and Historical Museum.)

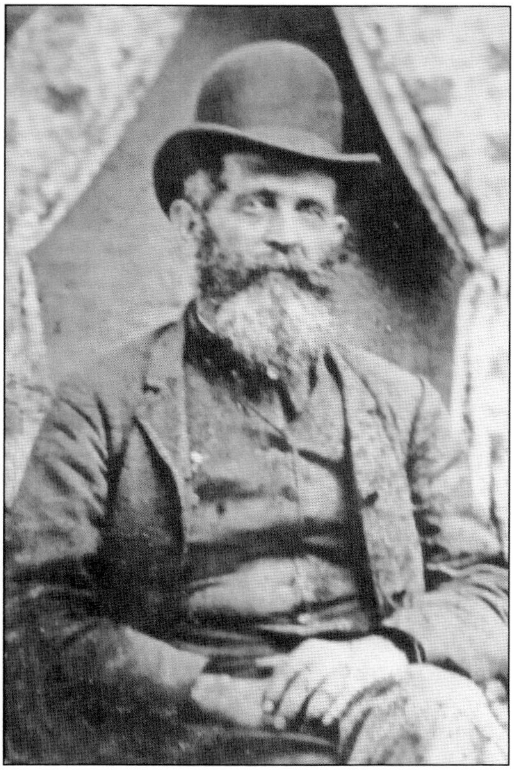

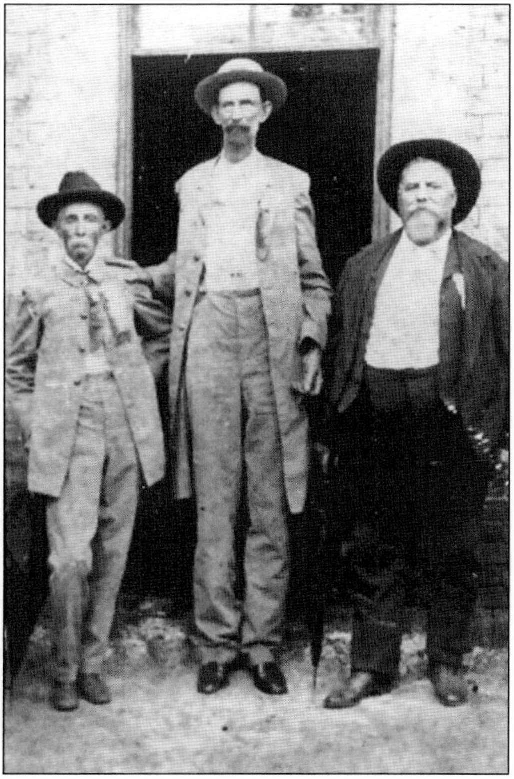

Born in South Carolina in 1833, Henry Clay Thurston moved to the Mount Pleasant area in 1870. At approximately 7 feet 7 inches tall, he was the tallest soldier in the Civil War. At one point, hostilities were ceased briefly so he and a Union soldier could stand back-to-back to see who the tallest was. After the war ended, Thurston toured with the P.T. Barnum Circus throughout America and Europe as "The World's Tallest Man." In order to accent his height, he wore a tall hat and a long coat. He is pictured here at center with H.H. Blakeley (left) and Charles McCamey Gingles. He is buried in Edwards Cemetery in Mount Pleasant. (Courtesy of Mount Pleasant Public Library and Historical Museum.)

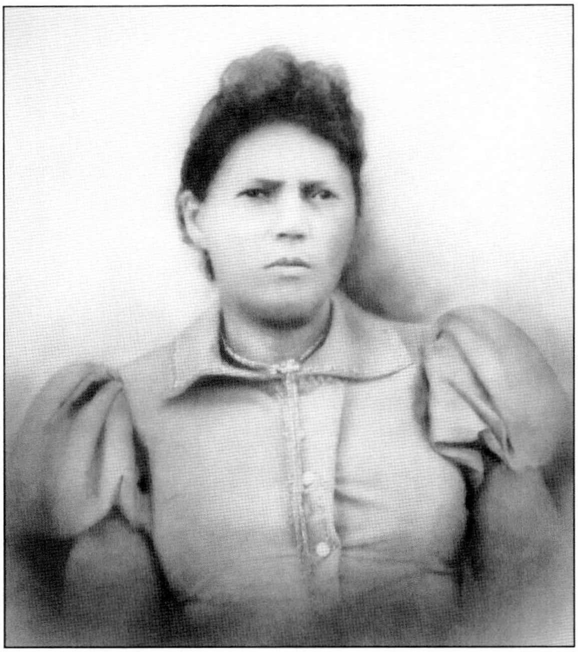

Jannie Baker, born a slave in Virginia, moved to Mount Pleasant with the Matthews family in 1856. She remained in the area after the Civil War. Her second husband was George Baker. The Bakers were highly respected and involved members of the community. They had a room in their house called the "traveler's room" for when the roads became impassable in the winter and during flooding. Her husband is pictured below. (Courtesy of Mount Pleasant Public Library and Historical Museum.)

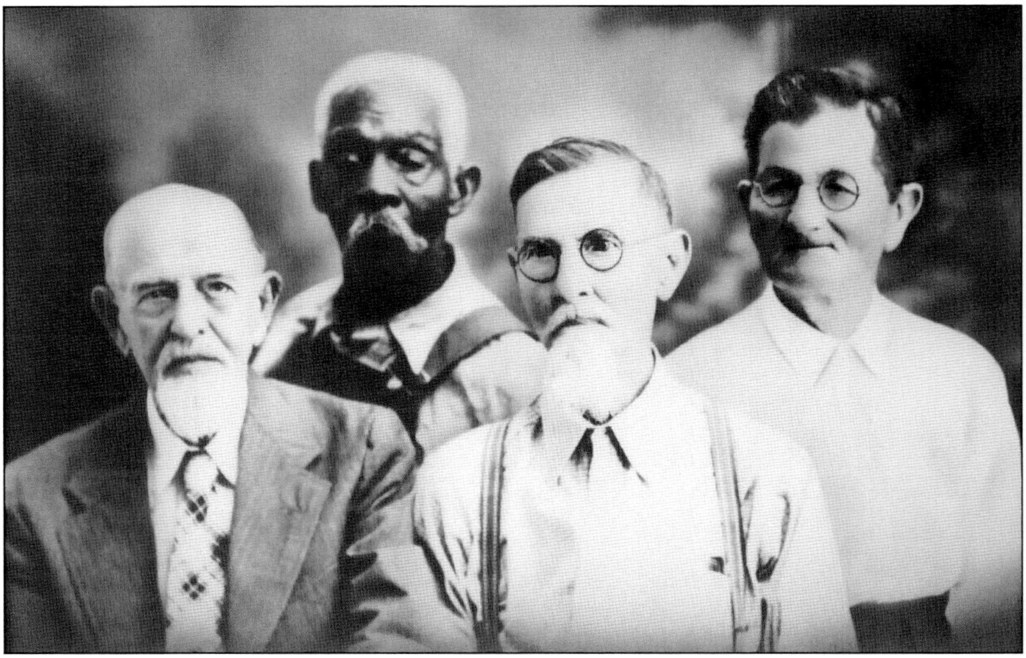

From left to right in this 1935 photograph of the four oldest citizens at the time are Green B. Dickson, George Baker, Robert C. Dale, and William Harvey. Born a slave in Mississippi in 1844, Baker moved to the Mount Pleasant area in 1867. Shortly after his arrival, he married Jannie Matthews and went on to be a significant landowner in the area. Dickson was a Confederate veteran and served as Titus County sheriff from 1882 to 1900. Dale and his siblings ended up on opposite sides in the Civil War; in fact, Dale himself seems to have begun the war fighting for the Union army, then chose to fight on behalf of the Confederacy. (Courtesy of Mount Pleasant Public Library and Historical Museum.)

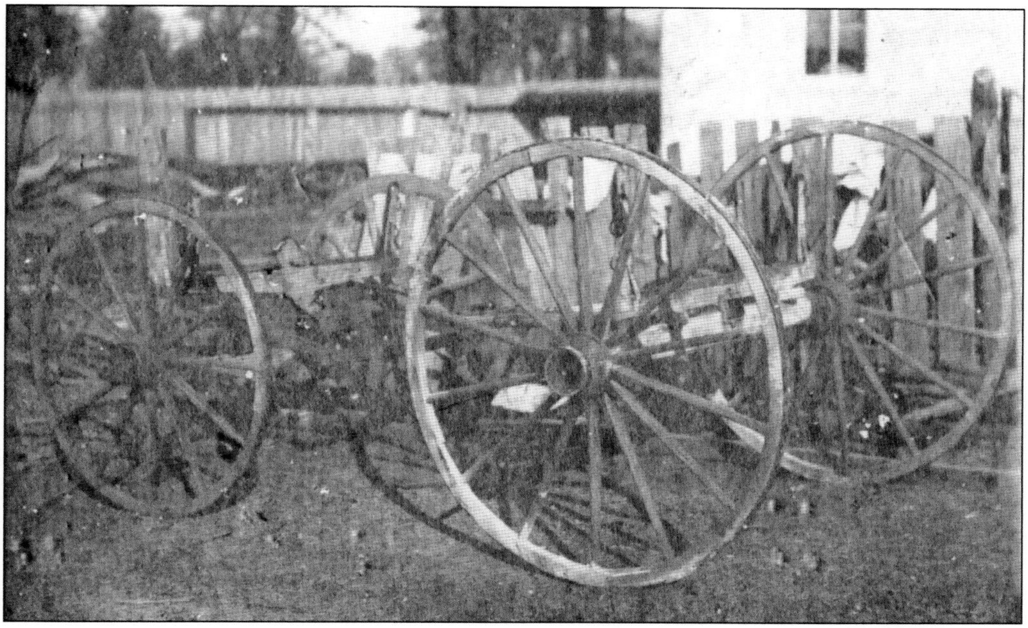

By the mid-1800s, Studebaker had become one of the world's largest manufacturers of horse-drawn vehicles. The 1867 Studebaker wagon pictured here was one of those prized vehicles. Mount Pleasant was well stationed on the Jefferson road, which served as the main thoroughfare from all of Central Texas to Jefferson, which was at that time a port city. Any farmer who had a wagon and a team could earn good money freighting between crops and throughout the summer, and many farmers sought out opportunities to do so. (Courtesy of Mount Pleasant Public Library and Historical Museum.)

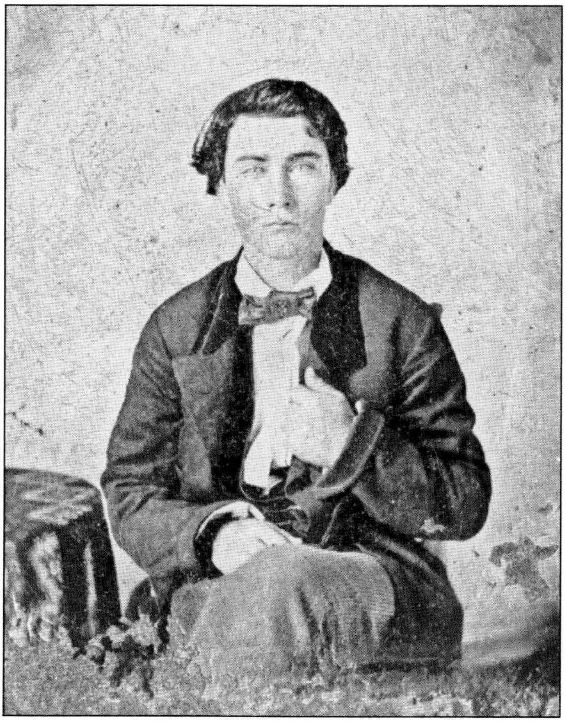

Ben Bickerstaff fought on behalf of the Confederacy during the Civil War and spent time as a prisoner of war in Union camps. After the war ended, he returned to his birthplace deeply embittered by his experiences and began causing a great deal of trouble in the area around Mount Pleasant. Media sources at the time referred to the difficulties that he and men such as Cullen Baker and Bob Lee created as the "New Rebellion." As part of Reconstruction, Federal troops moved into Mount Pleasant in 1867. Bickerstaff and his gang stole, killed, and terrorized individuals and wreaked havoc throughout the region that historians have come to call the "Devil's Triangle." He was ultimately gunned down in an ambush in Alvarado in 1869. (Courtesy of Mount Pleasant Public Library and Historical Museum.)

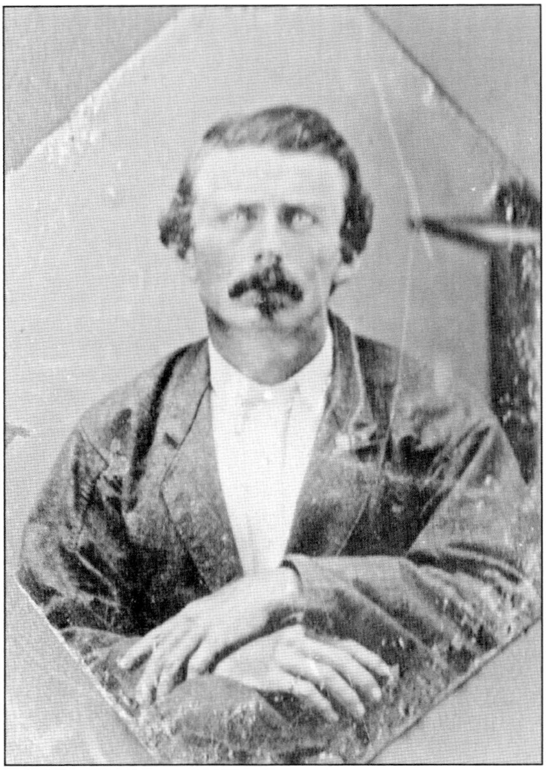

Abb Stephens began working as a bartender in a saloon in Mount Pleasant in 1870 and developed a reputation for being both a good bartender and a troublemaker. He became a horse thief and an outlaw with a four-person gang. Upon being pursued by Sheriff Bill Edwards and having one member of his gang captured and another killed, Stephens ultimately left the region, never to return. (Courtesy of Mount Pleasant Public Library and Historical Museum.)

William Riley Edwards, a music teacher and constable from Tennessee, moved to Mount Pleasant in 1858. After serving in a Texas regiment of infantry during the Civil War, Bill Edwards returned home and held various offices, most notably as sheriff from 1871 to 1882, a particularly tumultuous time in the aftermath of the war. He is credited with helping to restore law and order to the area. Edwards became an active member of various farm and labor organizations such as the Knights of Labor and the Grange when he was no longer sheriff. He is buried in Edwards Cemetery, the land for which he donated and which was at one point the main cemetery for the city. (Courtesy of Mount Pleasant Public Library and Historical Museum.)

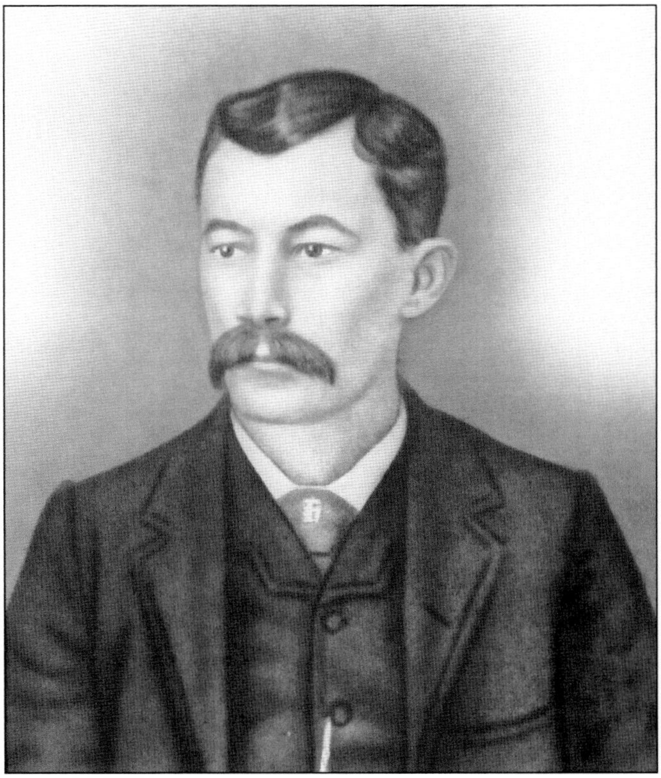

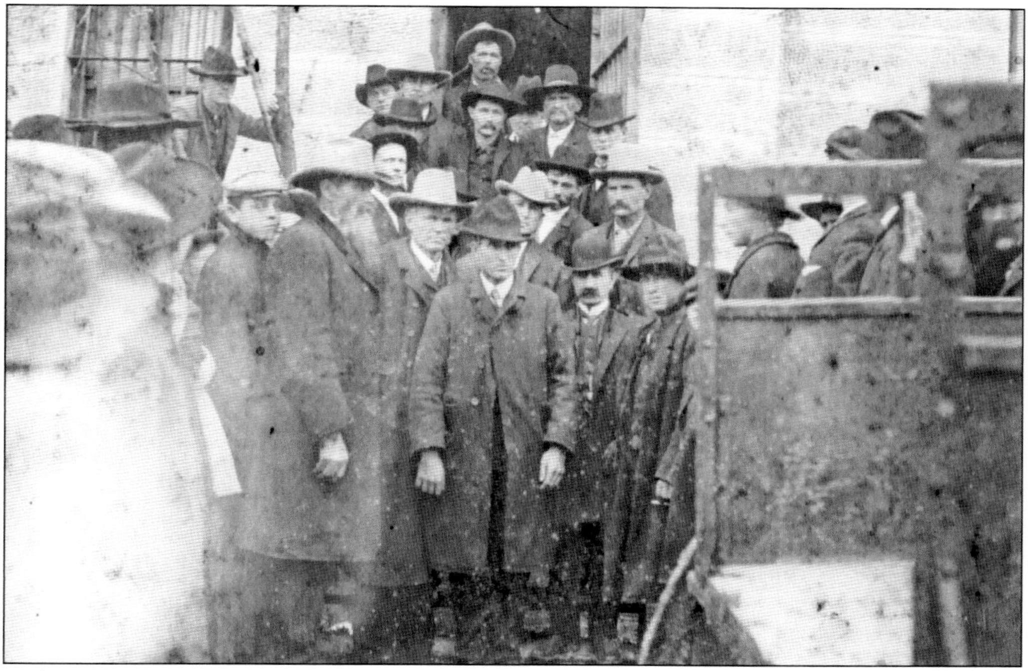

Early one morning, a visitor coming into Mount Pleasant on a wagon started to cross Town Branch when his horse began acting oddly. The visitor dismounted and found the dead body of a local peddler who frequently wandered through the area. Sheriff Edwards investigated the peddler's brutal murder and found out that the peddler had spent the night before at James C. "Sam" Rowland's house. When paying for his lodging, the peddler had pulled out a large wad of bills. Edwards found that money on Rowland. After a trial in the District Court of Titus County, a jury sentenced Rowland to be hanged, which occurred on May 3, 1872. (Both, courtesy of John Williams.)

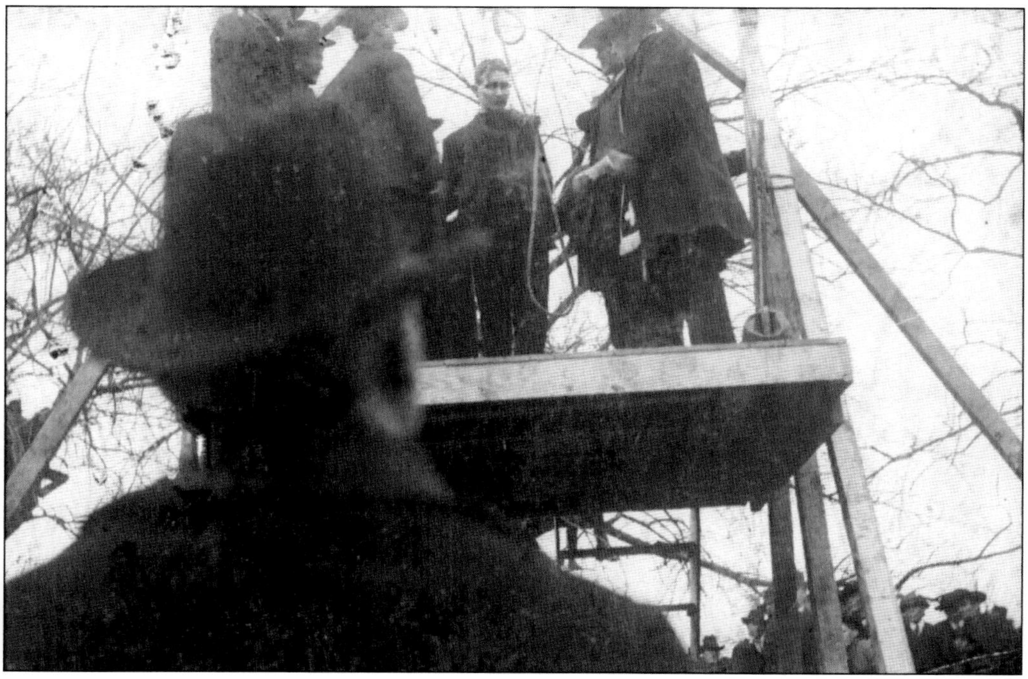

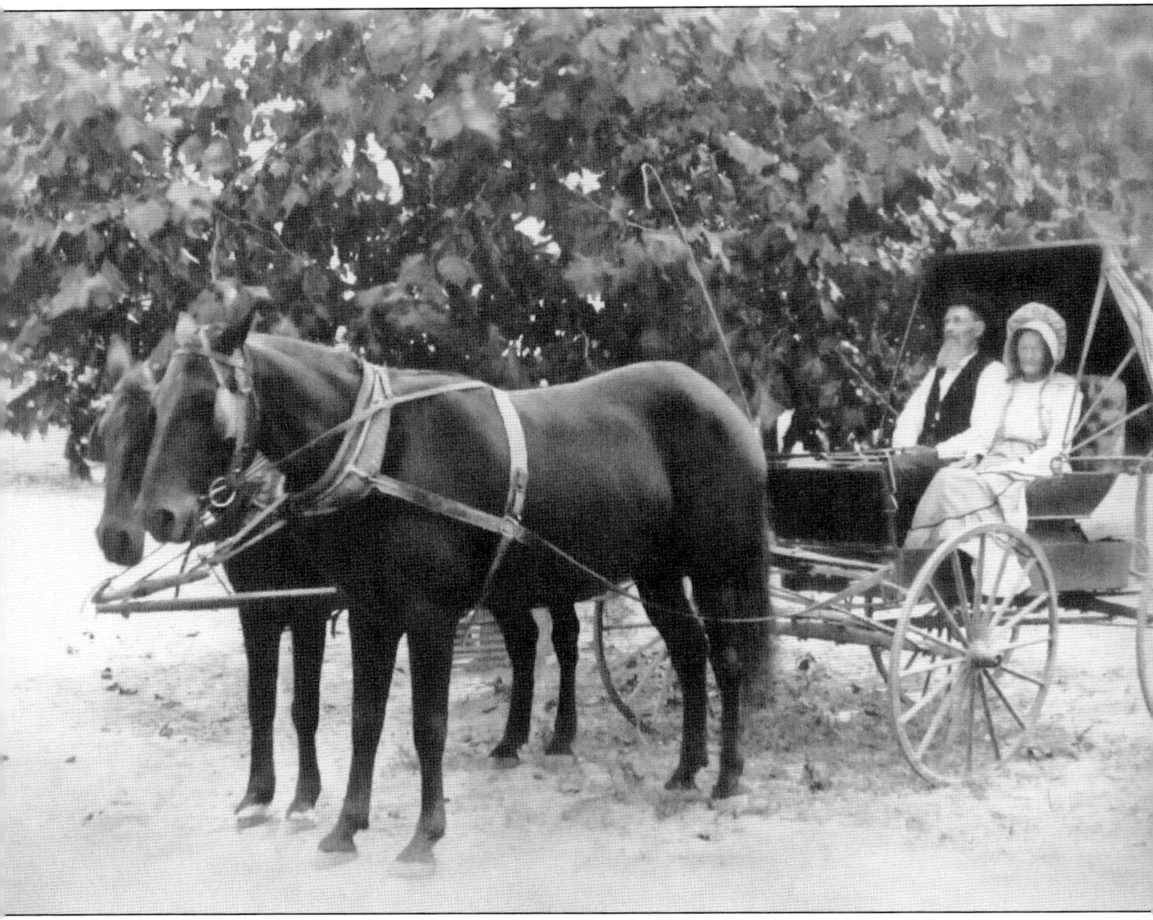

Contemporaries called Solomon Hayes Price, shown here with his wife, Bedie Barefoot, a success as "a soldier, a fighter, a drinker, a father, a farmer, and a preacher." A Confederate veteran who became a busy Baptist preacher after the war, Price served four congregations at one time. He was always quite busy riding from one location to another and could be seen around the community in his familiar buggy. (Courtesy of Mount Pleasant Public Library and Historical Museum.)

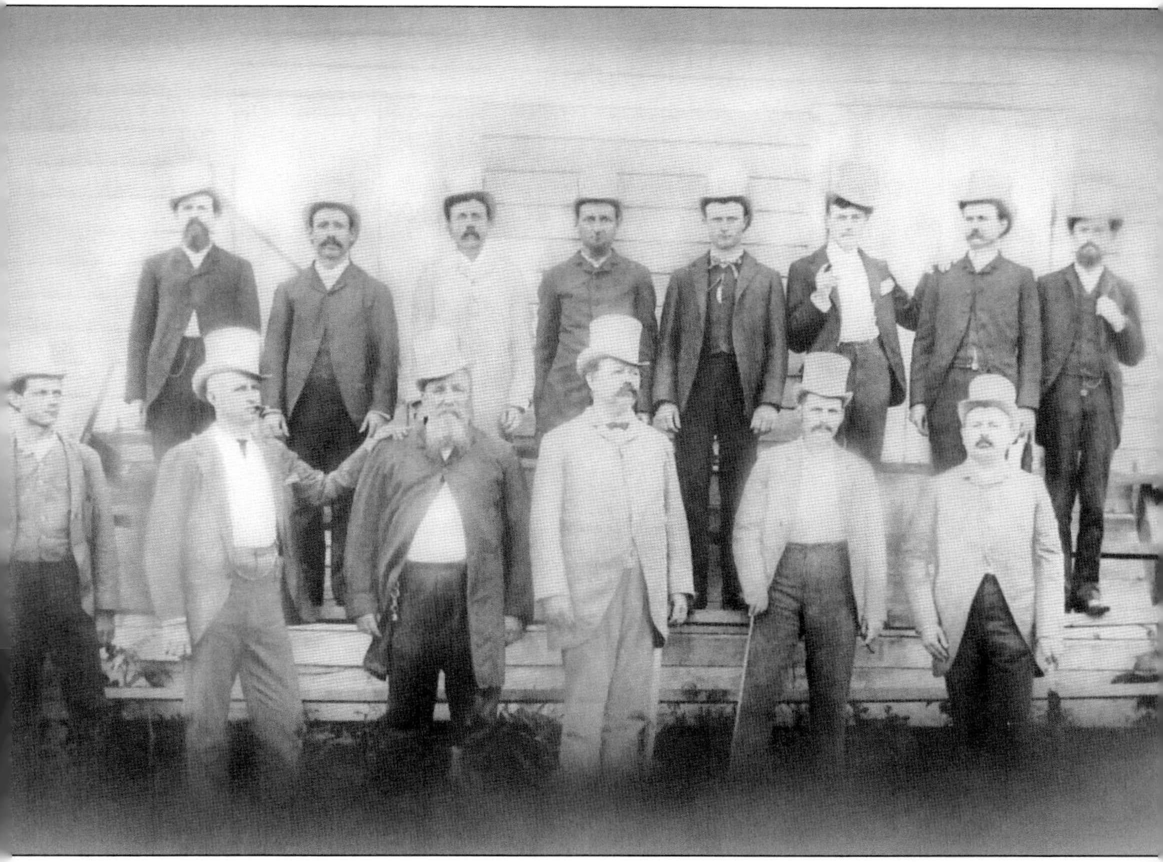

A group of supporters of Grover Cleveland posed for this picture in 1884. From left to right are (first row) Dick Smith, T.C. Morris, John Lokey, C.C. Carr, G. Hargrove, and W.J. McGee; (second row) Green B. Dickson, Joe M. Badt, George Lee Keith, Bill Johnson, Charles Lokey, Charles Dickson, Pat Griffin, and Jesse Riddle. These men were undoubtedly delighted that their presidential candidate won the election. (Courtesy of Mount Pleasant Public Library and Historical Museum.)

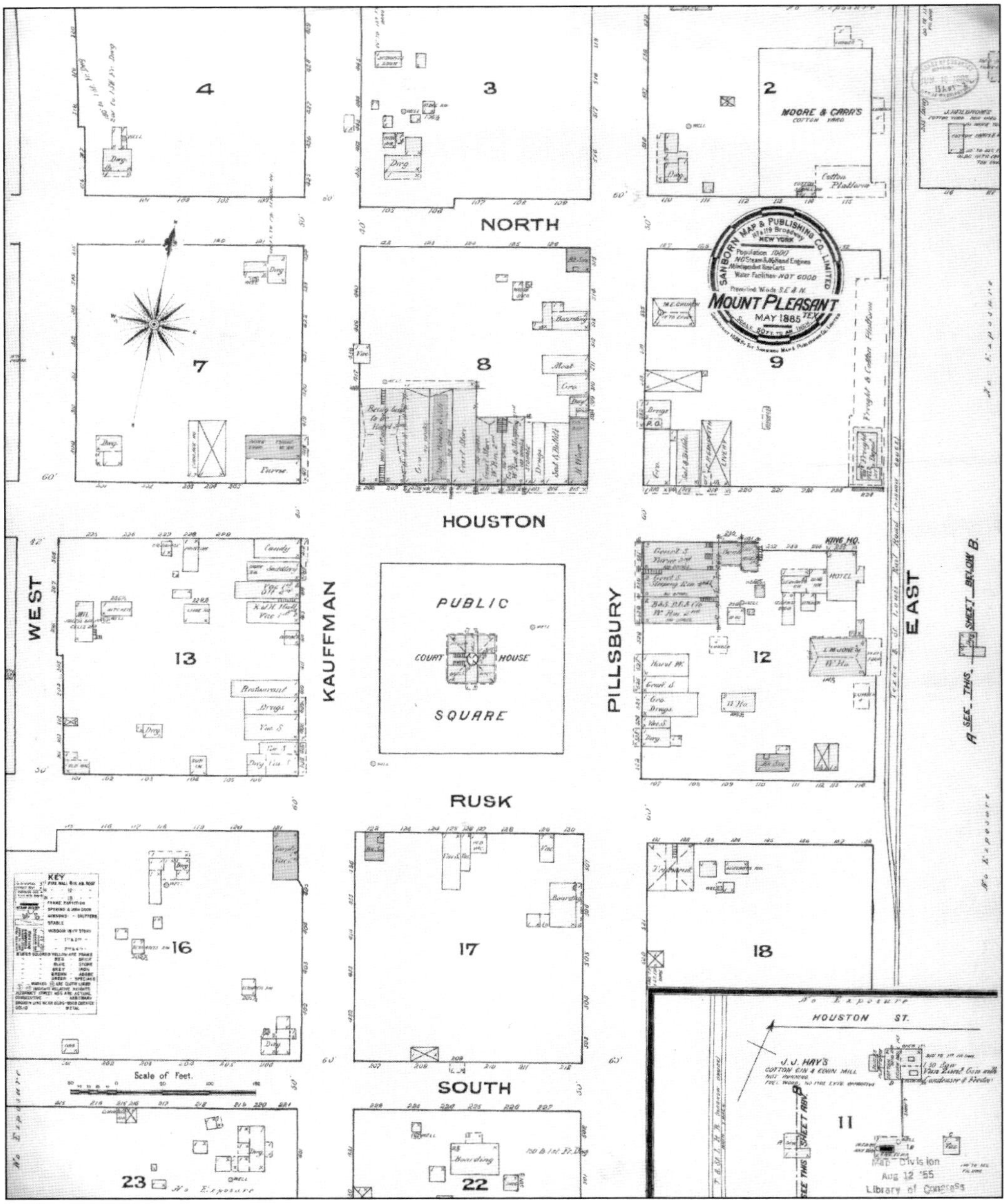


Mount Pleasant grew rapidly in the 1880s due in large part to transportation options coming into the area. The first railroad came in 1878. Known as the Tyler Tap, it was a narrow, three-foot-gauge line and offered increased transportation. Within a decade, another branch connected Mount Pleasant with Sherman. By the end of the century, Mount Pleasant became a meeting point of transportation routes, soon to be known as the "Hub of East Texas." This map of Mount Pleasant in 1885 shows the rail line connecting the town as well as the commercial development taking place downtown. Foreshadowing a future reputation as "the Sweetest Town in Texas," note the candy store marked on this early map. (Courtesy of Dolph Briscoe Center for American History, University of Texas in Austin.)

Thomas Buncombe Caldwell came to Mount Pleasant in 1870 and went on to become one of the founders of the Mount Pleasant First National Bank in 1892. He also built the first brick building in town on the east side of the square. (Courtesy of Mount Pleasant Public Library and Historical Museum.)

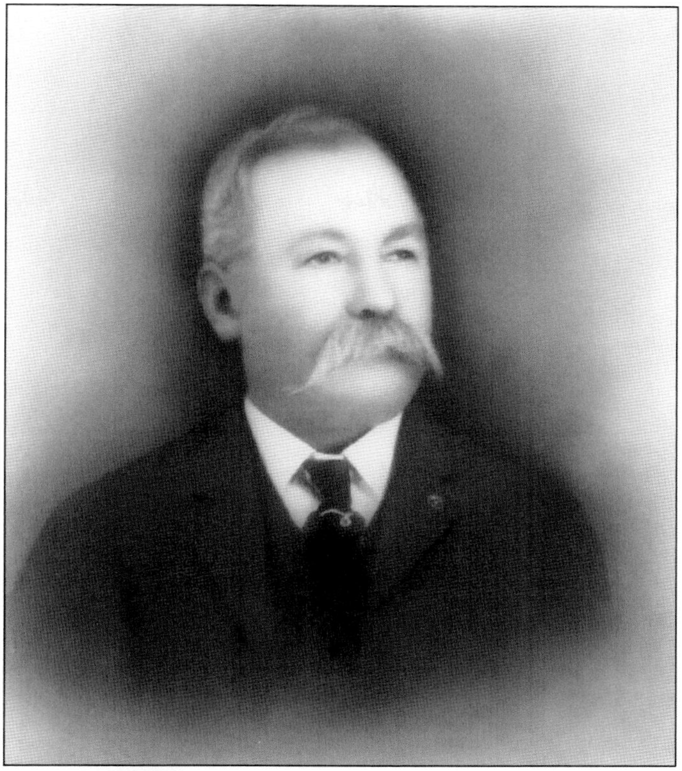

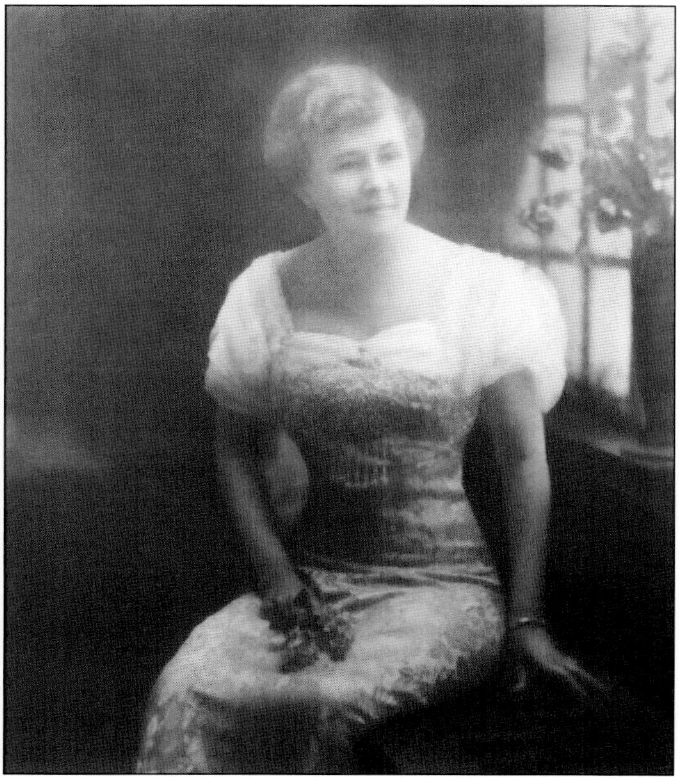

The Mount Pleasant First National Bank holds the honor of being, according to some sources, the first bank in Texas with a female president. Anne McLean Moores served alternately as president or vice president of the Mount Pleasant First National Bank from 1892 until her death in 1916. (Courtesy of Mount Pleasant Public Library and Historical Museum.)

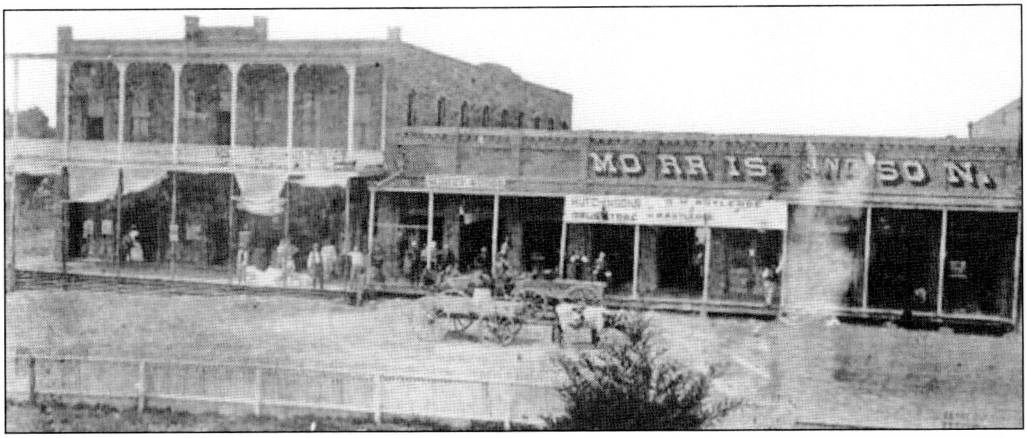

Mount Pleasant prospered in the last decade of the 19th century despite cotton's low price. The town served as a junction for rail and road travel through East Texas and thus as a convenient trade and mercantile location. At a time when Americans flocked to locations with natural mineral springs, Mount Pleasant began to advertise itself as a health resort and recreation location. Jesse Reed, who arrived in 1892, advertised those natural mineral springs of colored water as having healthful properties, calling them Iridescent Springs. (Courtesy of Mount Pleasant Public Library and Historical Museum.)

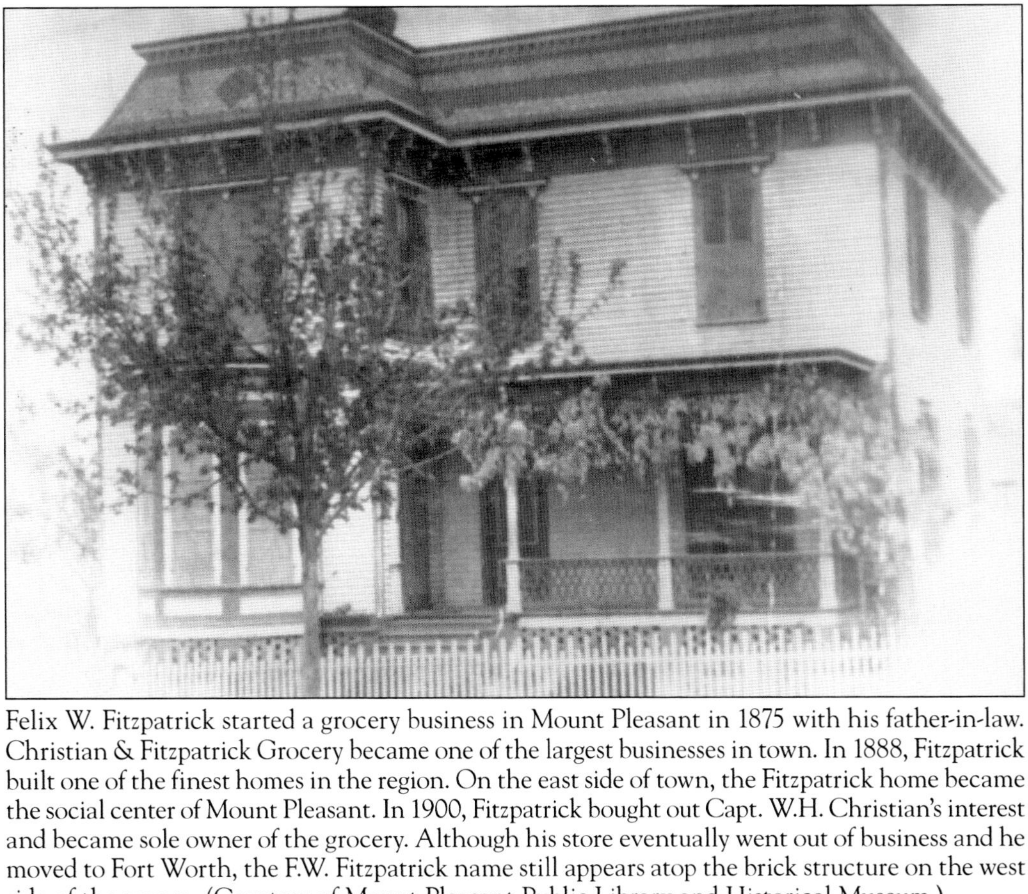

Felix W. Fitzpatrick started a grocery business in Mount Pleasant in 1875 with his father-in-law. Christian & Fitzpatrick Grocery became one of the largest businesses in town. In 1888, Fitzpatrick built one of the finest homes in the region. On the east side of town, the Fitzpatrick home became the social center of Mount Pleasant. In 1900, Fitzpatrick bought out Capt. W.H. Christian's interest and became sole owner of the grocery. Although his store eventually went out of business and he moved to Fort Worth, the F.W. Fitzpatrick name still appears atop the brick structure on the west side of the square. (Courtesy of Mount Pleasant Public Library and Historical Museum.)

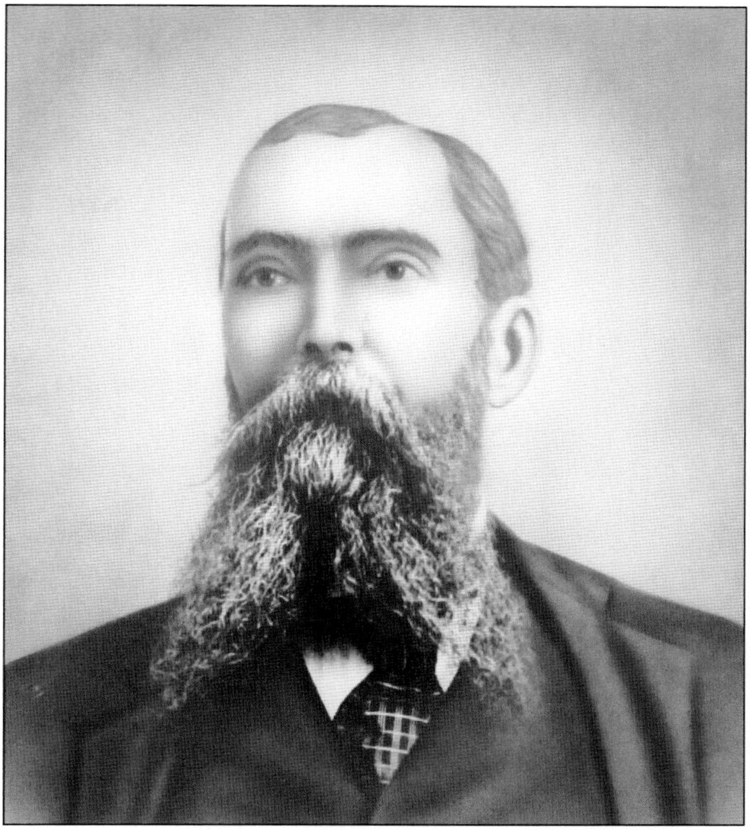

Born in Tennessee in 1838, Isaac Williams moved to Mount Pleasant in 1849. After the Civil War, he operated a mercantile business on the east side of the square. He opened Mount Pleasant's first opera house, which was in operation from 1890 to 1896. (Courtesy of Mount Pleasant Public Library and Historical Museum.)

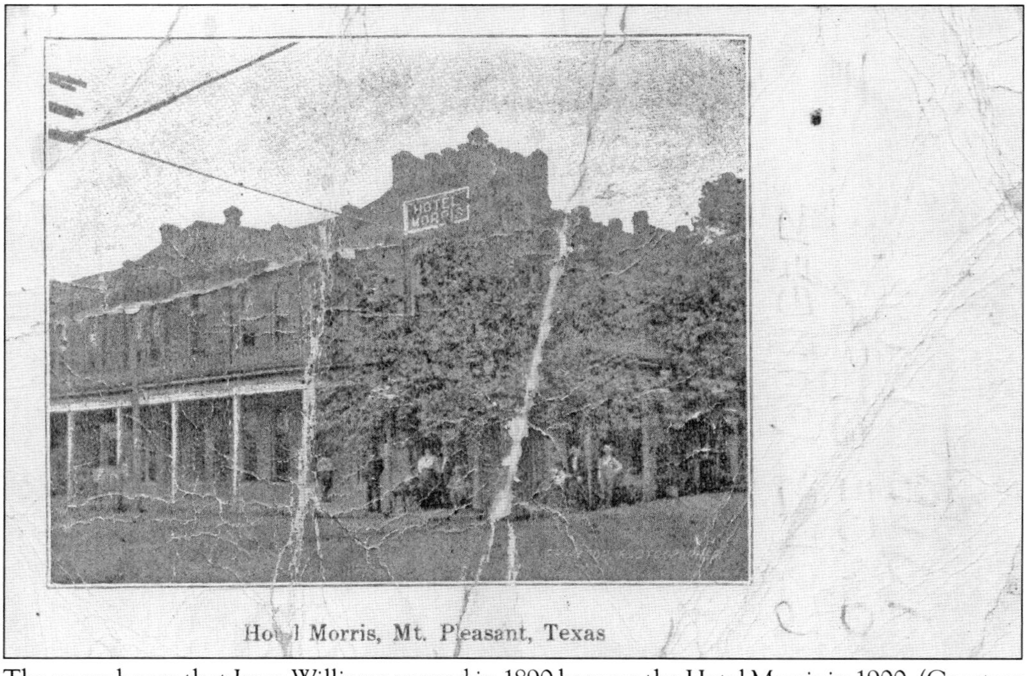


The opera house that Isaac Williams opened in 1890 became the Hotel Morris in 1900. (Courtesy of the *East Texas Journal*.)

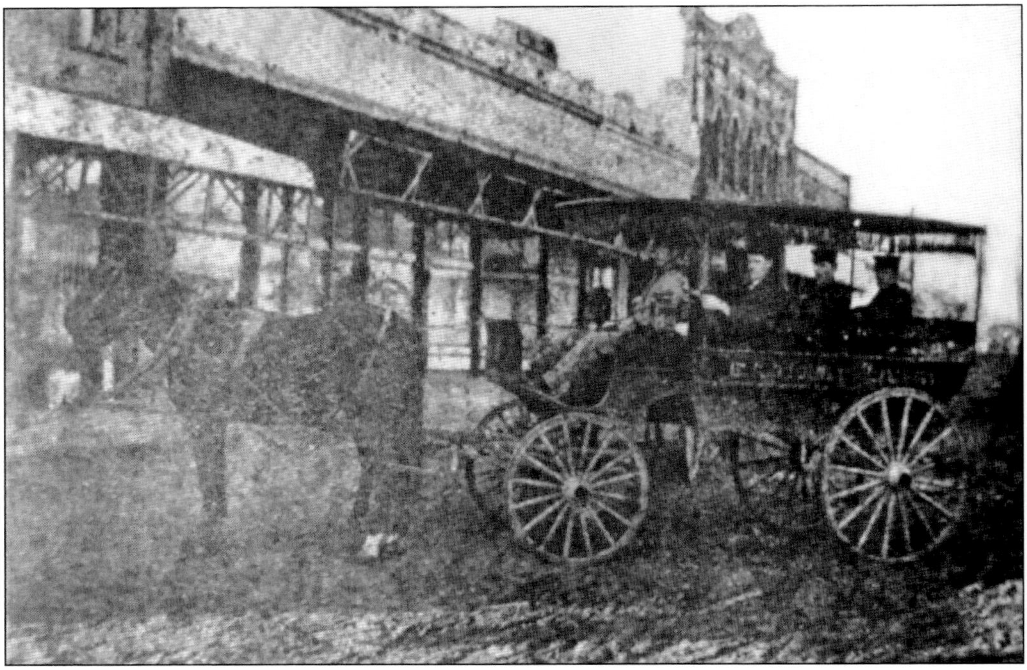

This photograph shows a scene just outside of Edmond Arthur Tigert's livery stables. (Courtesy of the *East Texas Journal.*)

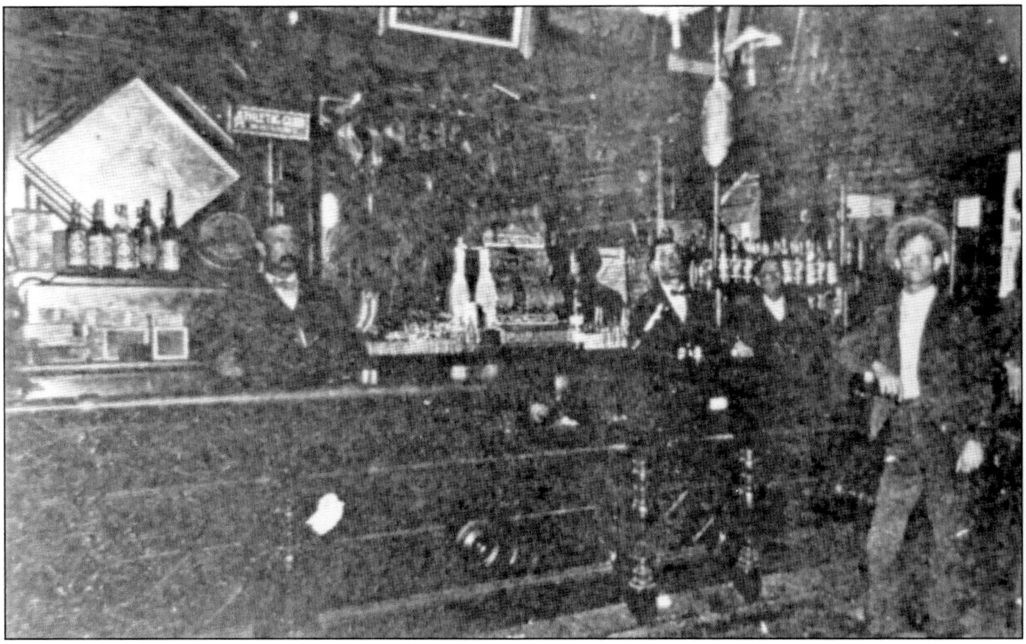

At one time, Mount Pleasant had a saloon on or near every corner. Apparently they were profitable enterprises, hence their prevalence. These facilities offered the men of the town a chance to visit, talk politics, play billiards, or just enjoy a beverage. George Russell, sporting the moustache behind the bar, owned the George Russell Saloon on the north side of the square. No women were allowed in these establishments. The sign behind the bar states that no credit was allowed either. (Courtesy of the *East Texas Journal.*)

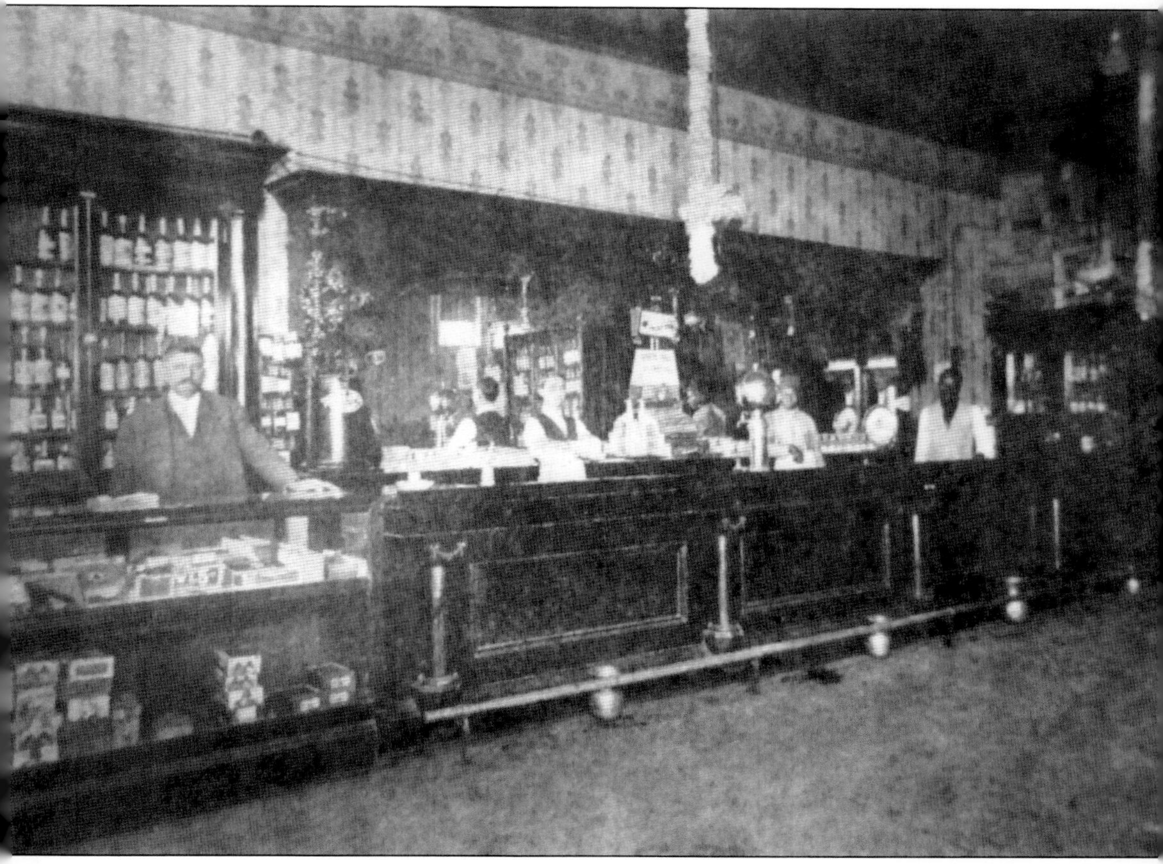

Edmond Arthur Tigert's saloon was a modern facility boasting the latest conveniences of the time. Inside the saloon, one could find shiny spittoons, a manual cash register, and even the latest technology—the telephone. Although this image shows the saloon at its finest, issues regarding alcohol production and consumption were not always so pleasant. In the late 1890s, a new licensed distillery opened up that eventually offended both the increasingly vocal prohibitionists and the saloon owners. Parker's distillery branched out into raising hogs and fed them from the residue of the distillery. The somewhat inebriated hogs smelled and elicited several complaints. The distillery ventured into retail sales and directly competed with the existing saloons. It is not known for certain who was behind the incident, but in 1900, dynamite destroyed Parker's distillery and it never reopened. Two years after that the city went dry, and the many saloons that had been a part of Mount Pleasant history from its founding disappeared from the city landscape. (Courtesy of the *East Texas Journal*.)

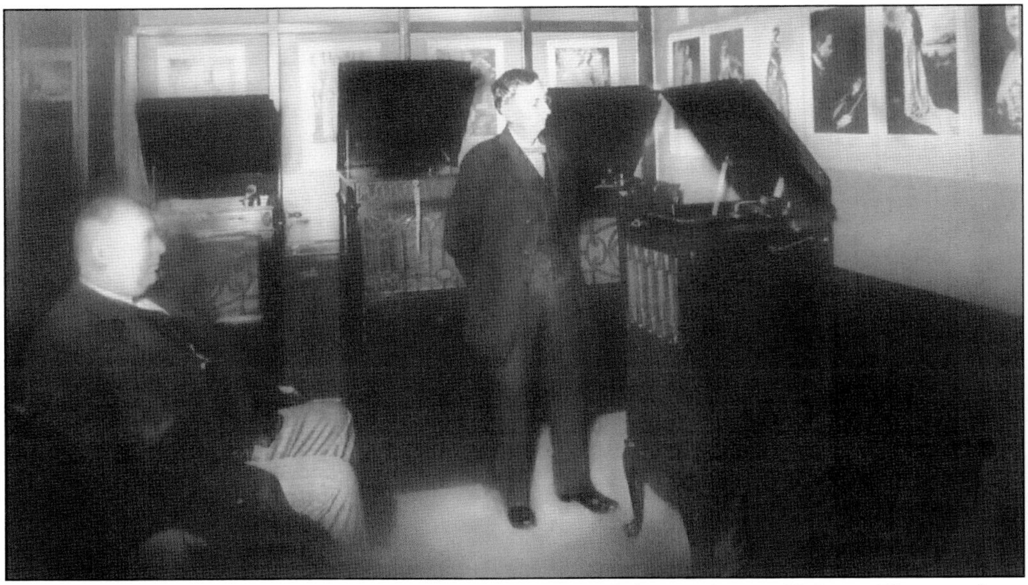

T.W. Vaughan Grocery Store, established in 1894, served the residents of Mount Pleasant from its location on the north side of the town square. Up until the year before, Vaughan had been in business with two other partners, but he struck out on his own. Like many merchants, Vaughn offered a variety of items. In this photograph, Tatum Wofford Vaughan stands in front of the latest Edison phonographs—a product offering that made his store unique. (Courtesy of Mount Pleasant Public Library and Historical Museum.)

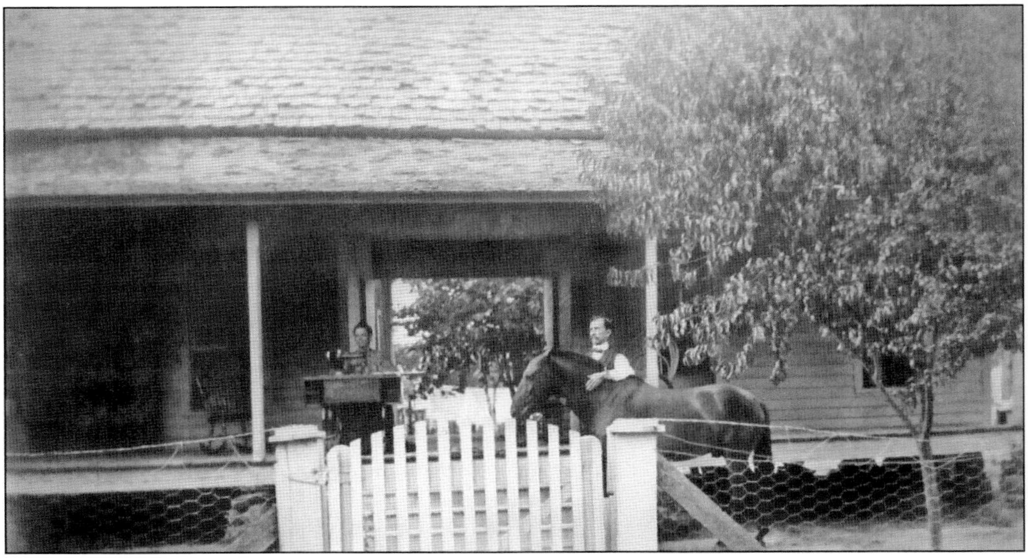

William Lafayette Hudspeth and wife Minnie L. Hudspeth pose in front of their home. This is a good example of what was known as a dogtrot house, one built with an open hall to catch the summer breezes. Because the family dog often trotted through this hall in going from one side to the other, it was called a dogtrot structure. This architectural styling, which was basically two one-room log cabins with a connecting hallway in between, generated a slightly cooler hall area to deal with the hot Texas summers. Minnie Hudspeth is sitting on the front porch using a sewing machine. Professor Hudspeth is standing in the yard with the family horse. (Courtesy of Mount Pleasant Public Library and Historical Museum.)

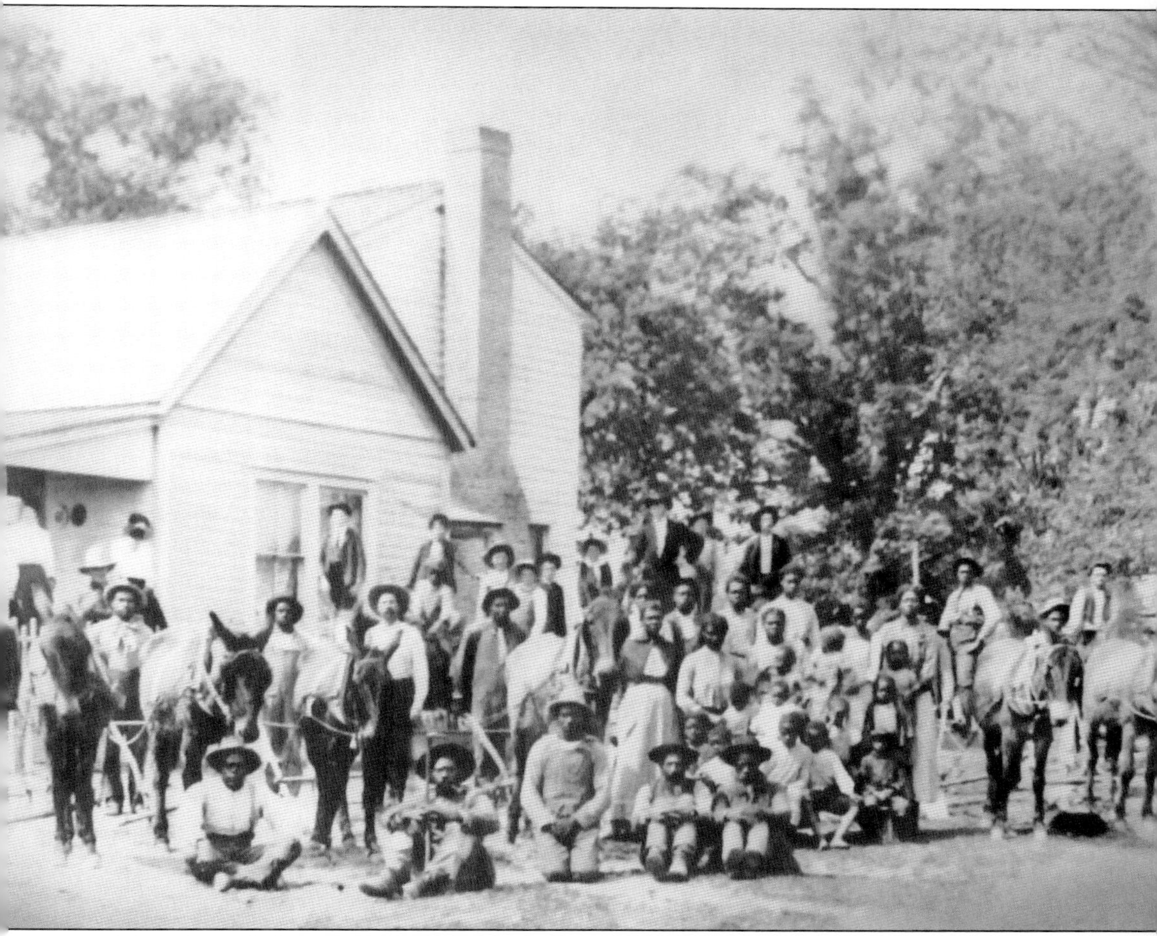

Levin H. Old farmed about 1,000 acres with 50 tenant families living on the plantation. This picture shows some of the farming implements used at the time. (Courtesy of Mount Pleasant Public Library and Historical Museum.)

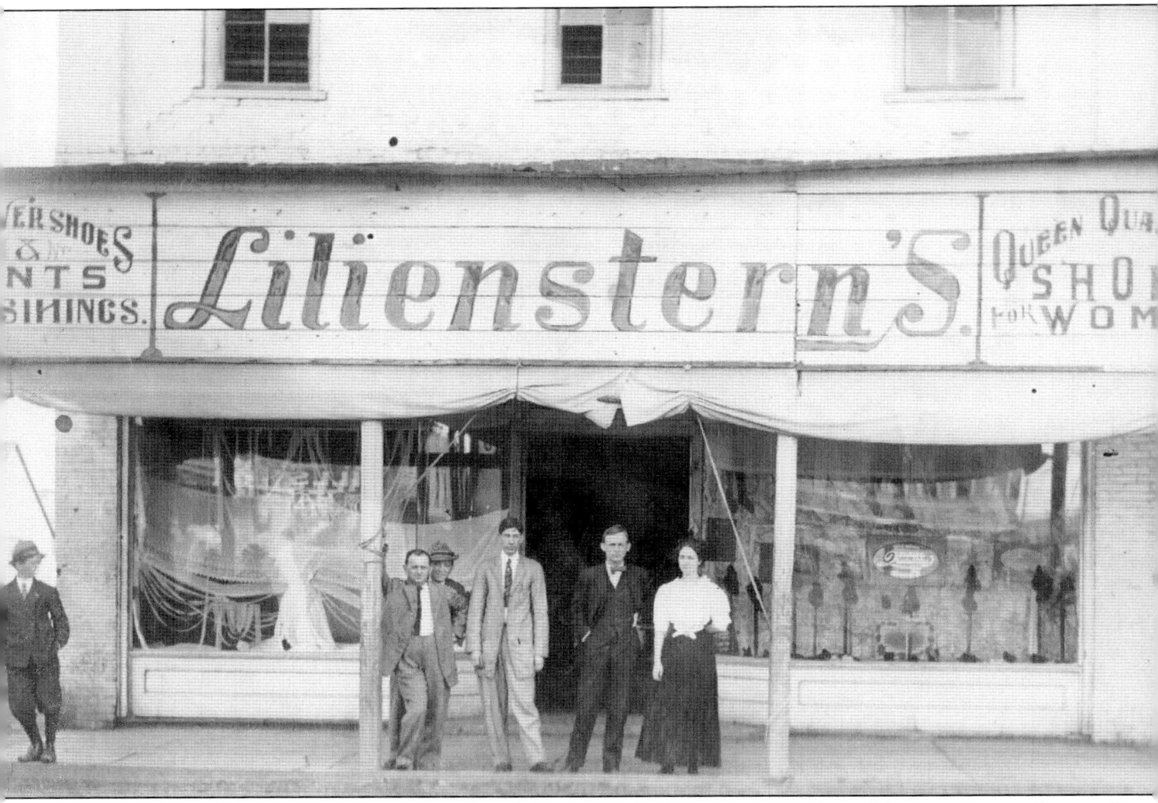


Mount Pleasant's location along the rail line resulted in some accidental business growth as well. In 1881, Morris and Herman Lilienstern were planning to relocate their store from Tennessee to Tyler. When the train engine broke down in Mount Pleasant, the brothers checked out the town and decided to open up their store in the new location rather than continuing on to Tyler. Like many family-owned stores, Lilienstern's sold a variety of dry goods and groceries but also brought in some of the latest trends and fashions in clothing. Decorative shoes were popular at a time when skirts were rising to ankle length, allowing a tantalizing glimpse of footwear. (Courtesy of Mount Pleasant Public Library and Historical Museum.)

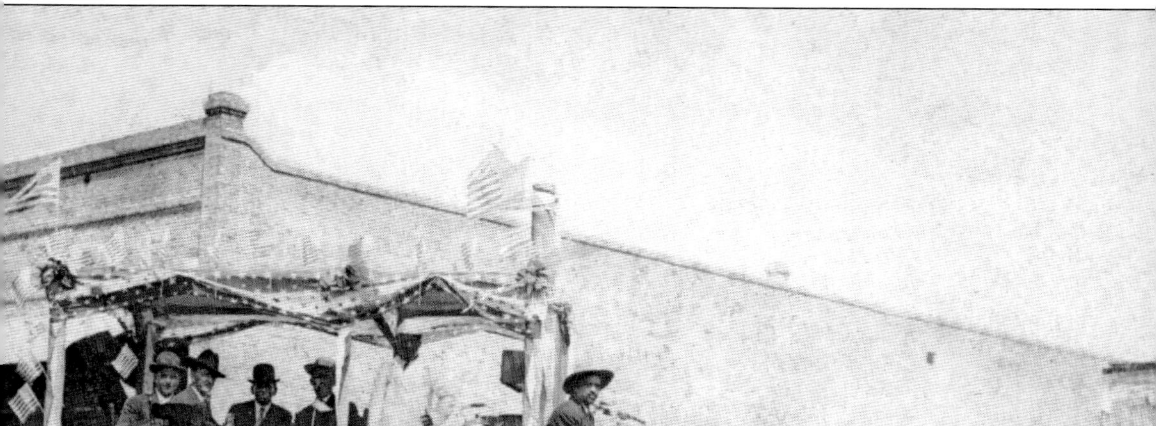


In this photograph of what appears to be a Fourth of July parade, decorated horses pull the Willson Bros. wagon complete with cook, stove, and table. Henry and Willie Willson opened Willson Bros. Hardware in the 1890s. Henry would go on to serve on the first Mount Pleasant City Council. (Courtesy of Mount Pleasant Public Library and Historical Museum.)

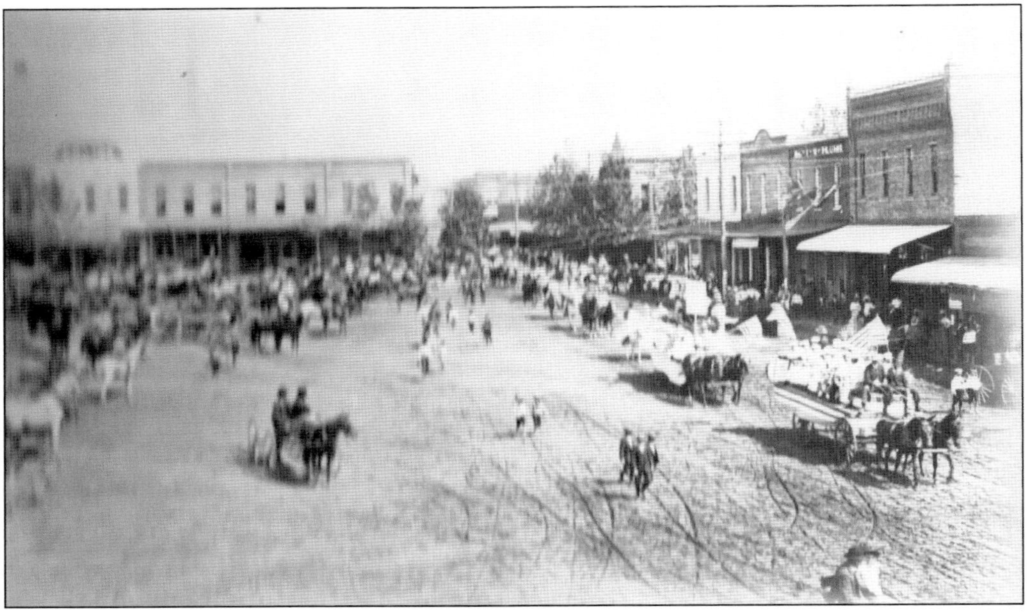

The Fourth of July was cause for great celebration in this town with red, white, and blue mineral water. In this photograph, flags fly proudly. (Courtesy of Barry Hamilton.)

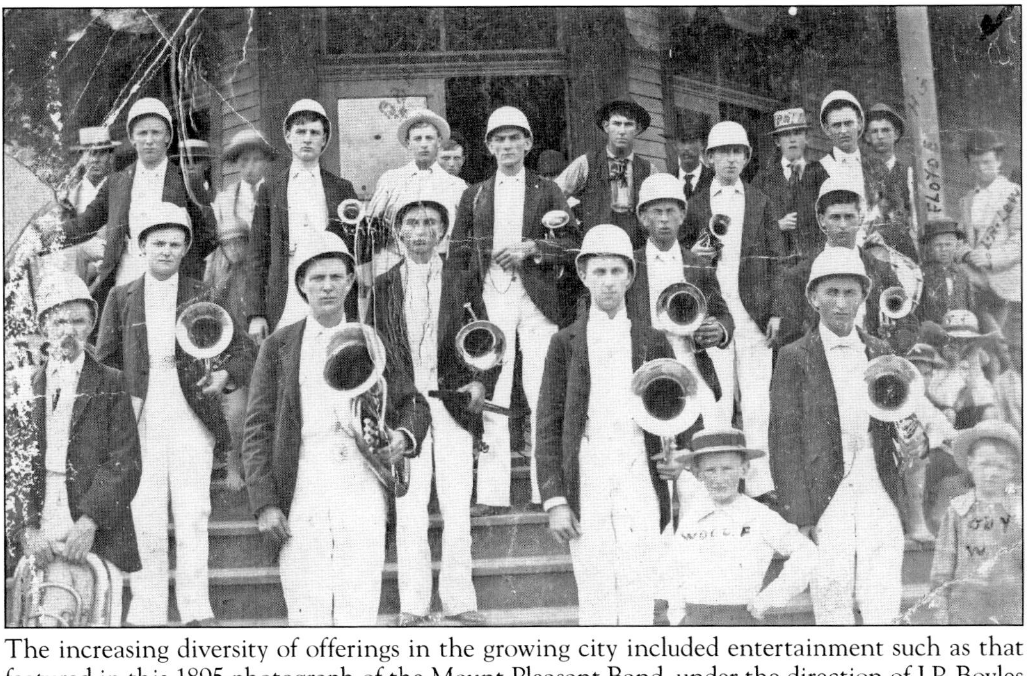

The increasing diversity of offerings in the growing city included entertainment such as that featured in this 1895 photograph of the Mount Pleasant Band, under the direction of J.P. Boyles at the time. (Courtesy of Mount Pleasant Public Library and Historical Museum.)

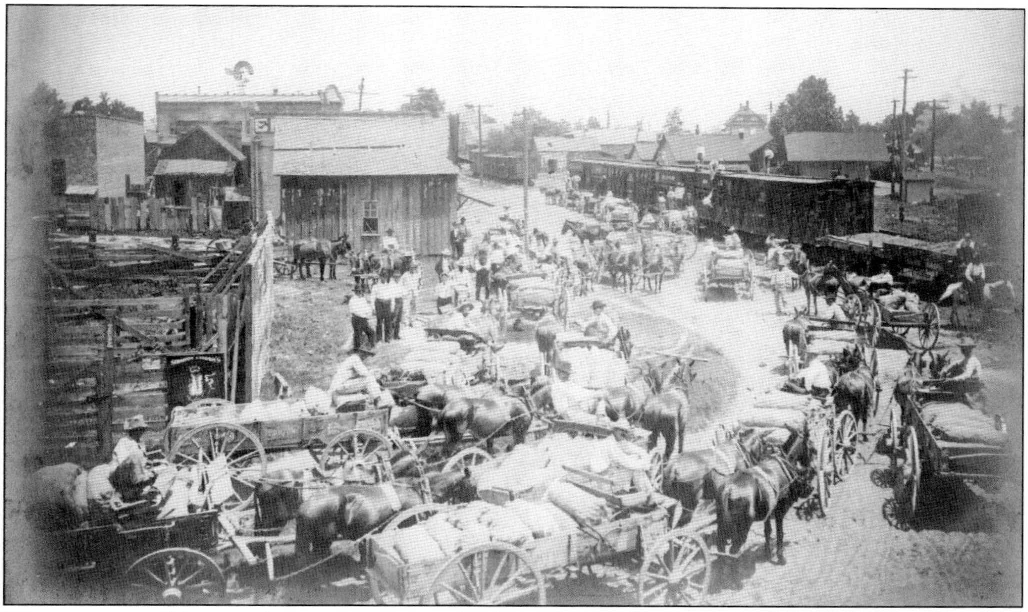

The mainstay of the town's growth continued to be its location as a transportation hub for commerce and trade throughout the Northeast Texas region. This photograph shows just how busy the town could get at certain times as farmers brought their wagons full of goods into town for a farmer's market. The farmers here are bringing in wagonloads of potatoes. (Courtesy of John Williams.)

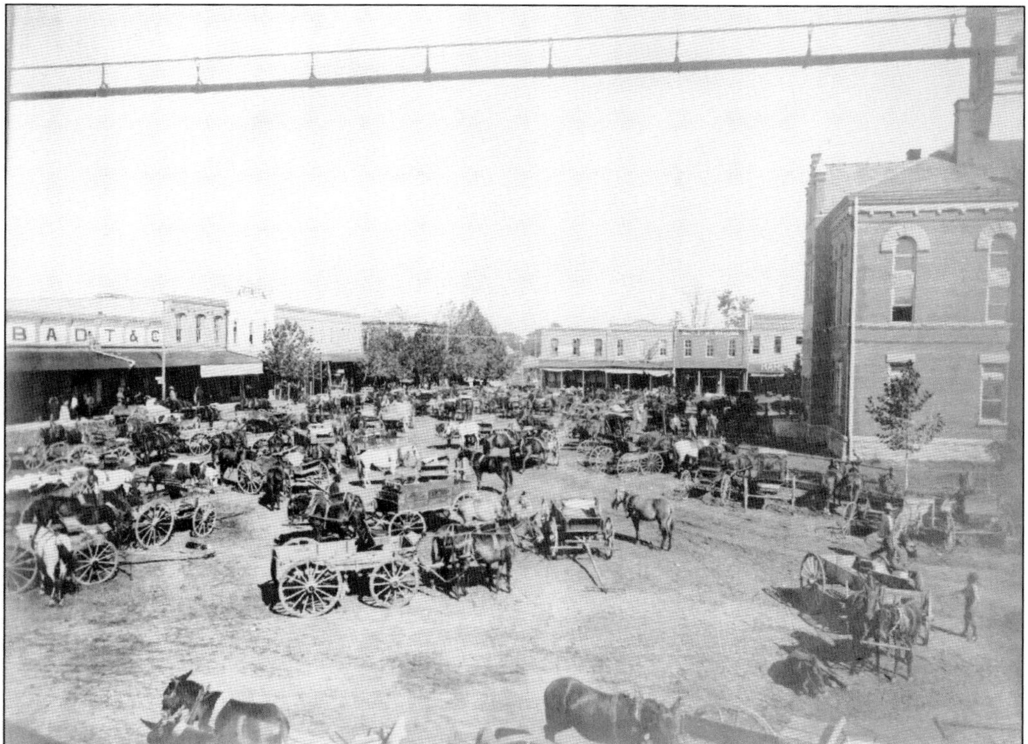

Empty wagons and horses on the crowded city square show that it has been a successful day for the farmers coming into Mount Pleasant to trade their goods. (Courtesy of Barry Hamilton.)

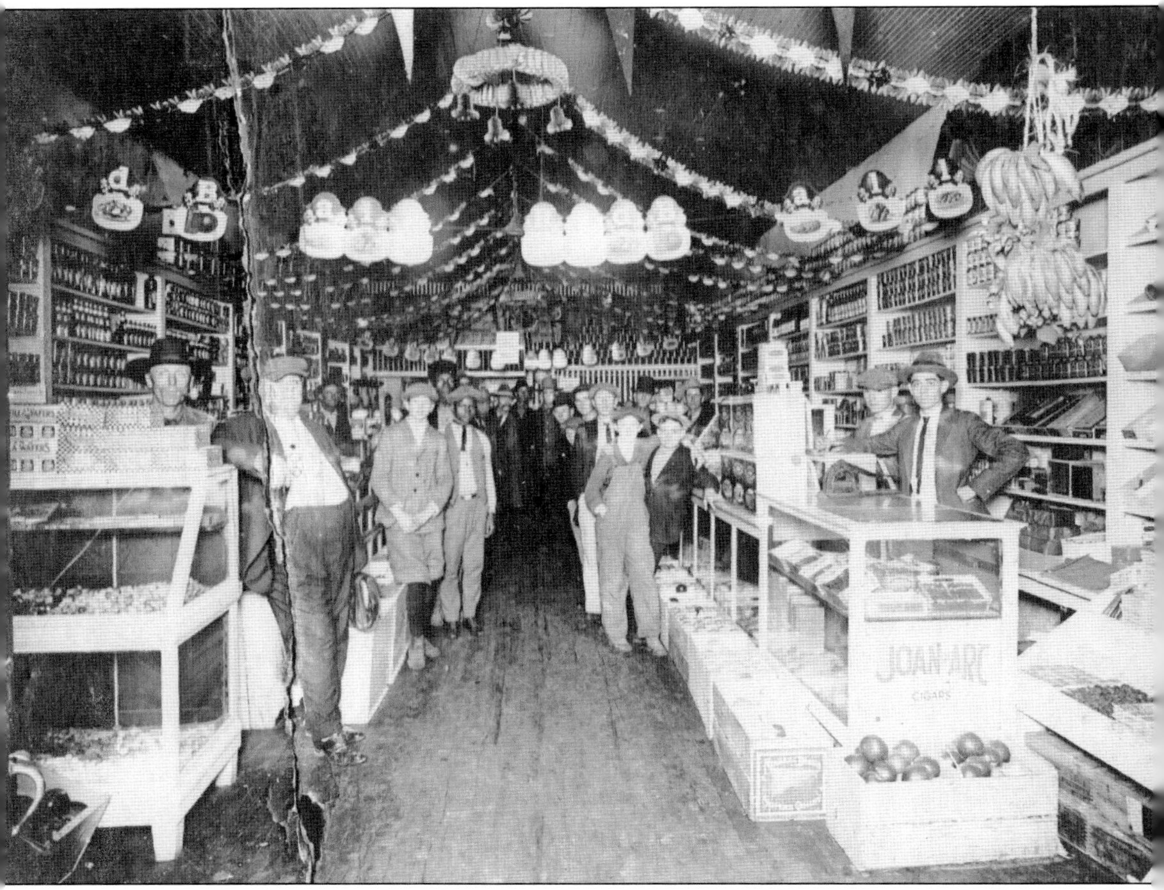

This well-stocked store catered to the expanding citizenry and visitors to Mount Pleasant. The 1890s were an excellent decade for Mount Pleasant, one of the town's best in terms of growth and prosperity. With all that expansion, the citizens finally (after an earlier failed attempt) chose to incorporate on September 17, 1900—the close of one era as a town and the beginning of another as a city. (Courtesy of Barry Hamilton.)

# *Two*

# Growth

The city began the new century with a new government. The freshly incorporated city developed municipal services and tourist attractions. The natural mineral springs, which had initially made the place an appealing spot for the natives to gather, became a resort and health spa. The Dellwood at Red Mineral Springs in Mount Pleasant boasted a grand two-story hotel in the shape of a Y. In its lobby, fountains of red, white, and blue water bubbled. The location had an electrical generating plant, an orchestra and dance pavilion, boat rentals, a herd of riding donkeys, tennis courts, a croquet field, a bowling alley, and a billiard and pool hall. As advertised, the park provided "All kinds of Amusements to add Health, Strength, and Innocent Pleasure for the Young and Old." The town also built the first movie theater between Dallas and Texarkana.

Mount Pleasant benefited from the national interest at the time in medicinal mineral waters, but it was only temporary. Americans were already doubtful of the curative power of mineral springs. With the resort facing financial difficulties, the facility was sold, and it temporarily became Speer's School for Boys. Fortunately, the town developed a variety of businesses that helped it to continue and prosper, including the Hoffman Heading and Stave Company and Libby Brick and Coal.

Increasing and improved transportation connections were key factors in the city's continued development in a location that faced chronic flooding issues from rivers and creeks. Rail lines connected Mount Pleasant initially to Tyler, but in the early 20th century, additional routes connected the area to the west towards Dallas and to the north towards Paris. The Mount Pleasant & Paris Railroad, affectionately called the "Ma and Pa," became one of the various transportation routes that earned Mount Pleasant the nickname "Hub of Northeast Texas."

As always, schools and churches grew and expanded. When war broke out, the men of Mount Pleasant—as patriotic as the red, white, and blue water that bubbled in the area—bravely served. When World War I ended, national interest in creating an American highway set the stage for the next era of the city's expansion.

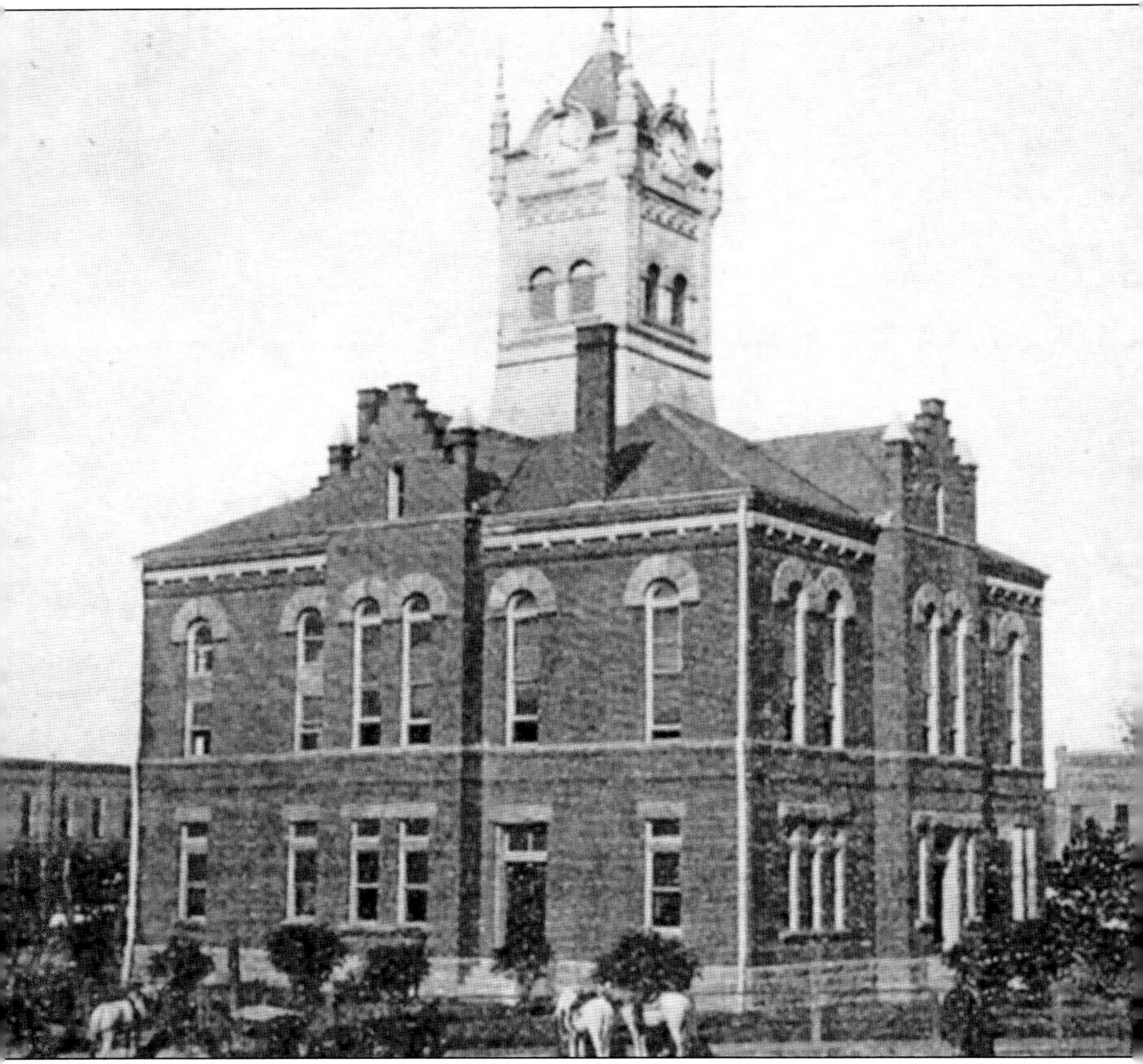

With the town having been created specifically in order to serve as the seat of Titus County, Mount Pleasant conducted its first district court on the front porch of Henry Jones's house. Its first official courthouse, a log structure built in 1847, burned a few years after being built. The second structure also burned down, and the city built a third county courthouse in 1859. In 1895, the county commissioner's court completed installation of a fireproof vault with all-steel shelves. The janitor hired extra help to move all the county records into the new two-story vault the next morning. That night, a county officer, short of county funds and concerned at being caught, sought to destroy all records that might incriminate him and in the process destroyed everything. By the next morning, the fourth county courthouse had become nothing but a pile of brick and ashes with an unused fireproof vault. The vault remained in use for the next 40 years inside the fifth (and current) courthouse. Although the courthouse looks dramatically different on the exterior now, due to being refaced several times, the original 1895 structure, as shown in this photograph, remains. (Courtesy of John Williams.)

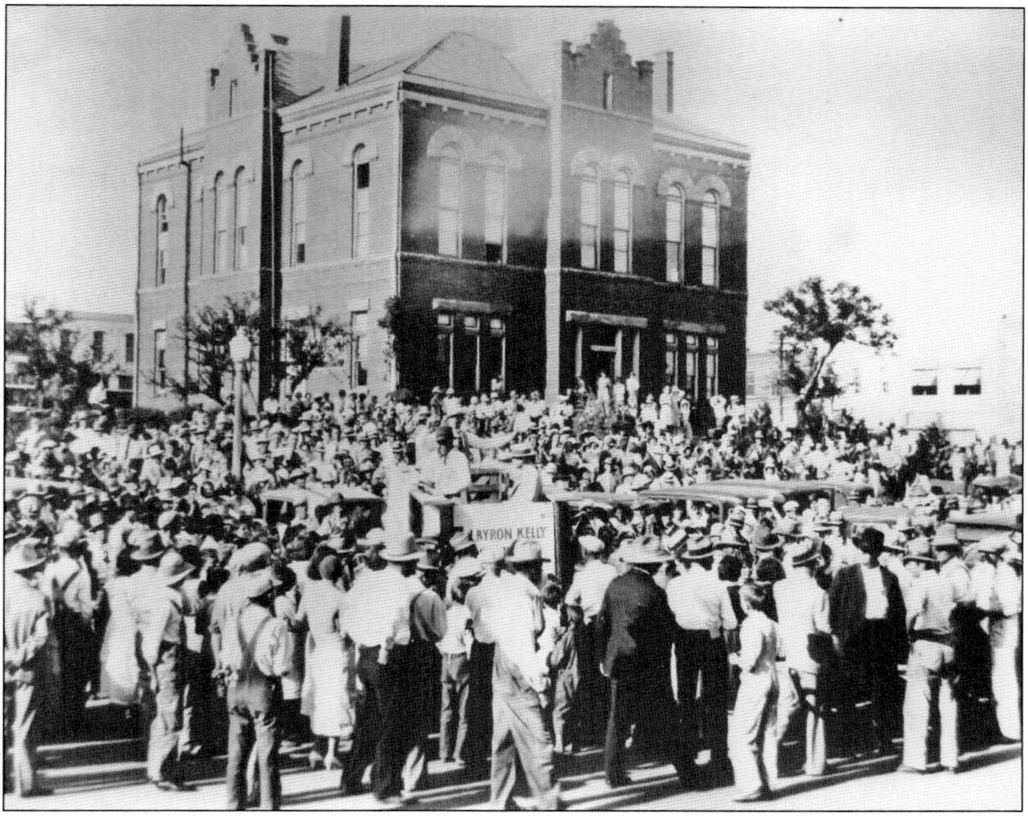


Being the county seat means that politics and political concerns always factor large in Mount Pleasant. Large crowds gathered around the Titus County Courthouse at election time during campaign rallies such as this one in the early 1930s. (Courtesy of the *East Texas Journal*.)

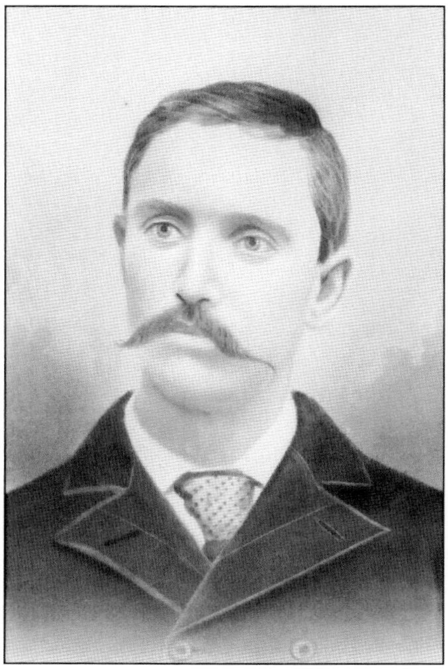

One of the first issues Mount Pleasant dealt with was the creation of a much-needed fire department. Fire had been a constant worry and fear and a somewhat frequent occurrence for the city since its founding. R. Henry Fuller owned a furniture store before organizing and becoming the first chief of the Mount Pleasant Fire Department. For the first few years, Fuller organized a group of volunteers who fought fires using buckets of water drawn from nearby wells. In 1903 Mount Pleasant completed its first waterworks system, consisting of a lake and a standpipe. The city laid water mains throughout the business and residential areas and installed fireplugs. Then the city purchased a two-wheeled hose cart that required some men to pull and others to push. Eventually, the city adopted a horse-drawn cart to fight the many fires common to a time when buildings were often constructed of wood, and gas and kerosene were common heating and lighting sources. Fuller served as fire chief for 30 years. (Courtesy of Mount Pleasant Public Library and Historical Museum.)

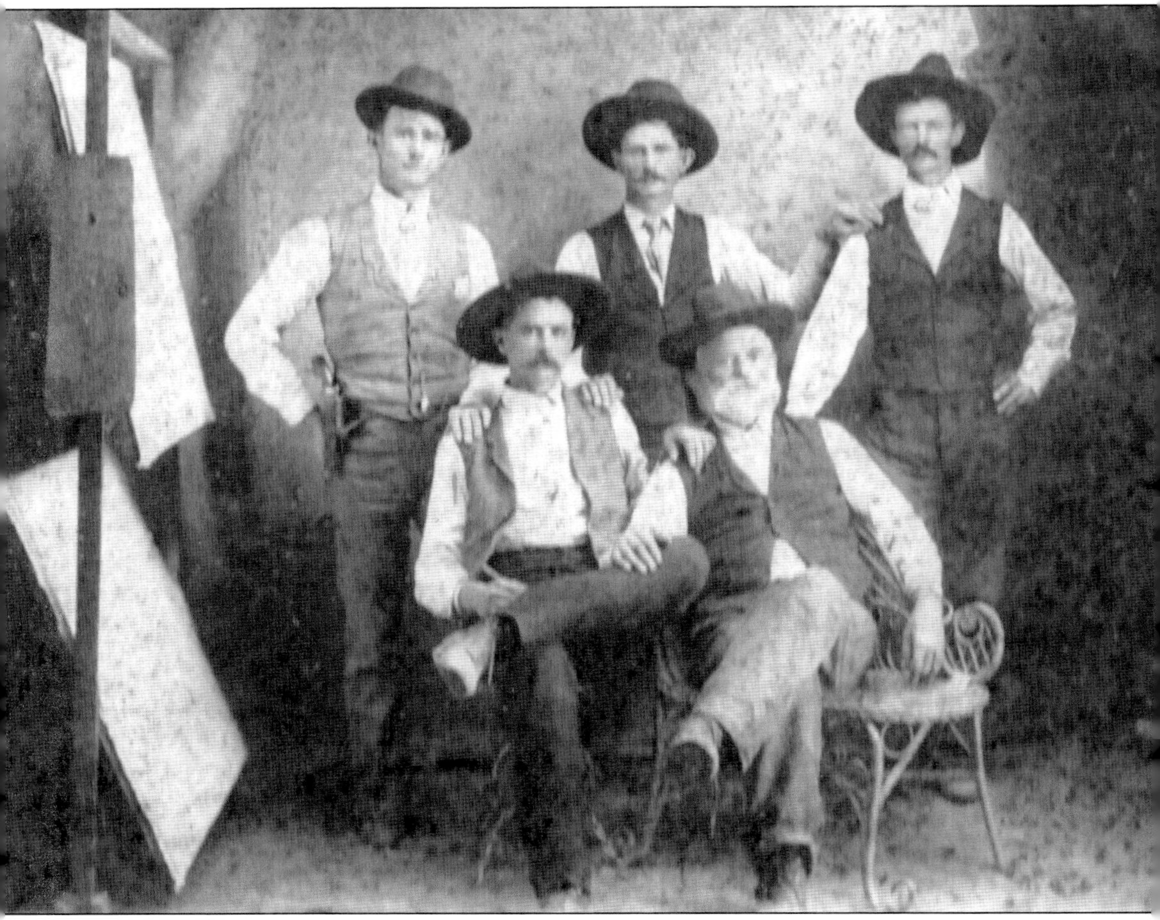

Five former Titus County sheriffs pose in this 1901 photograph. From left to right are (seated) Green B. Dickson and Sam Porter; (standing) Will Smith, John Cooper, and W.D. Sanders. (Courtesy of John Williams.)

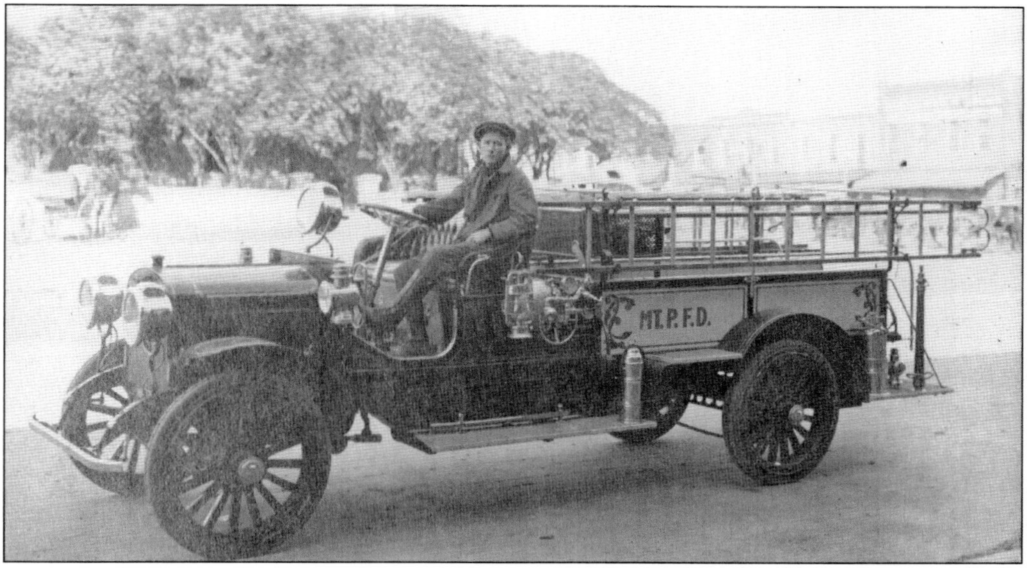


In 1915, the Mount Pleasant Fire Department purchased its first gasoline-powered fire truck. The new truck, seen above and below on Second Street in front of the Titus County Courthouse, carried men and equipment to fires but had no water tank or pump. The fire department, which consisted of volunteers until 1933, added the brass headlights and decorative paint after it purchased the truck. This Brockway truck served the department until the city purchased a new one in 1929. (Above, courtesy of Mount Pleasant Public Library and Historical Museum; below, courtesy of *East Texas Journal*.)

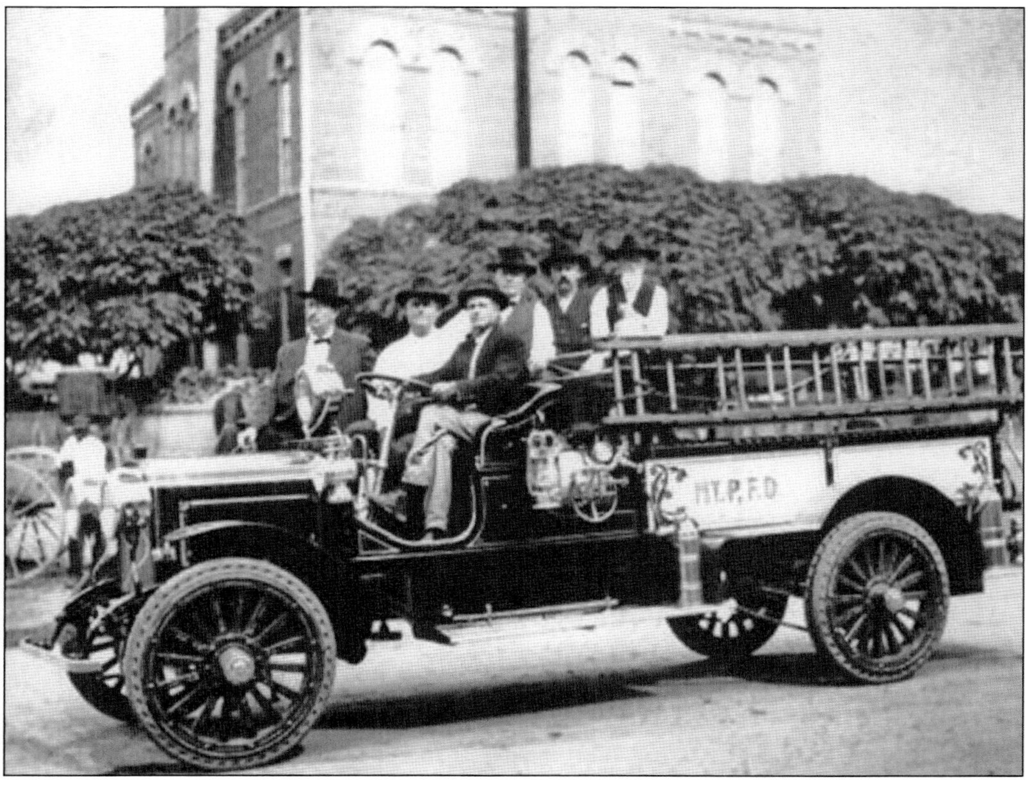

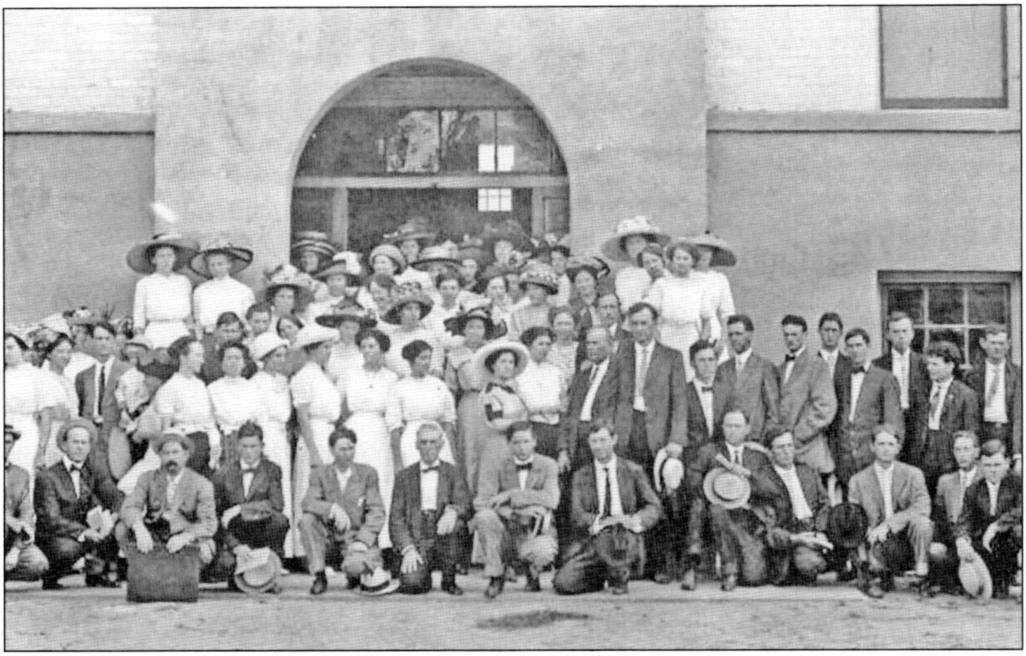

As an incorporated city, Mount Pleasant continued its tradition of supporting and expanding its local schools. This photograph shows a gathering of well-dressed teachers exhibiting pride in their chosen profession. (Courtesy of Mount Pleasant Public Library and Historical Museum.)

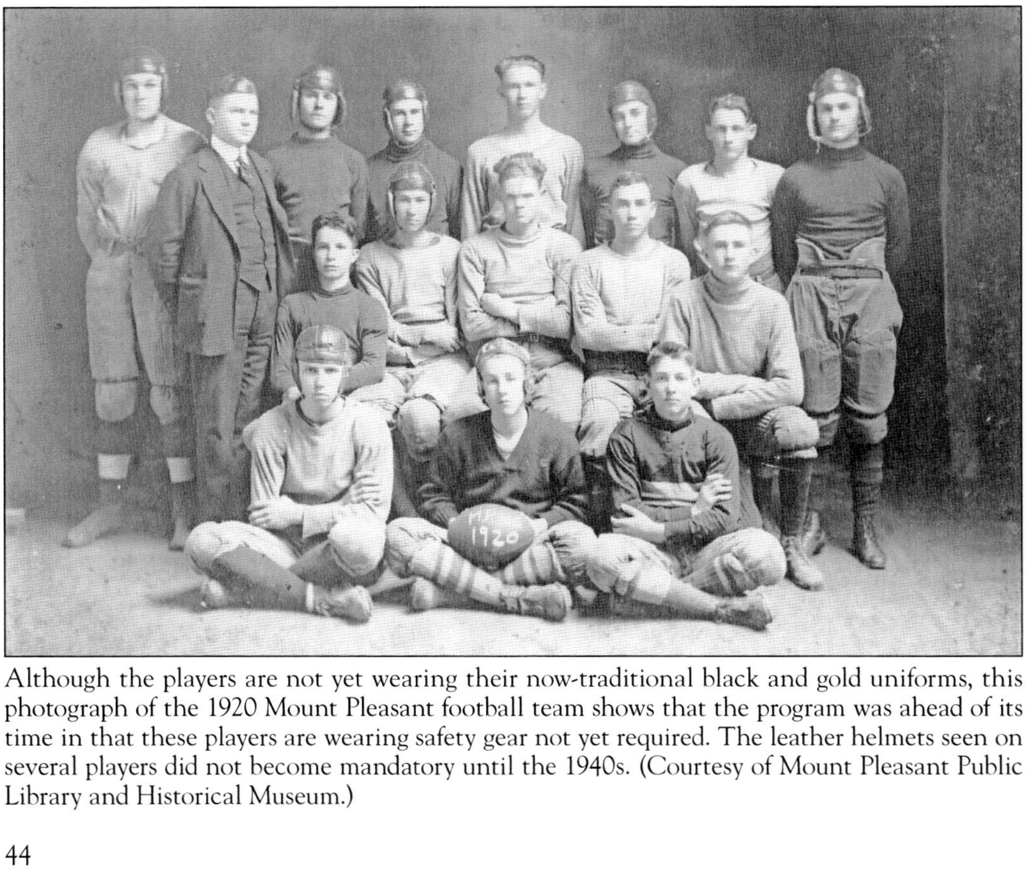


Although the players are not yet wearing their now-traditional black and gold uniforms, this photograph of the 1920 Mount Pleasant football team shows that the program was ahead of its time in that these players are wearing safety gear not yet required. The leather helmets seen on several players did not become mandatory until the 1940s. (Courtesy of Mount Pleasant Public Library and Historical Museum.)

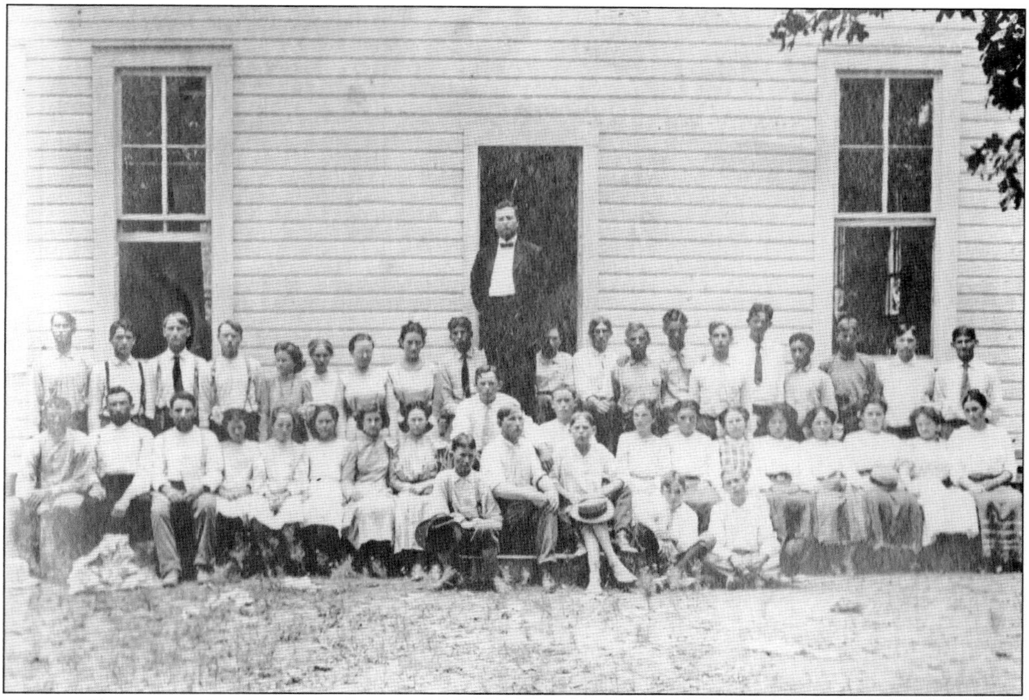

Mount Pleasant offered a variety of education options. In this 1910 photograph of the Mount Pleasant Singing School at Nevil's Chapel, the instructor, Eugene Edmunds, is standing in front of the door. (Courtesy of Mount Pleasant Public Library and Historical Museum.)

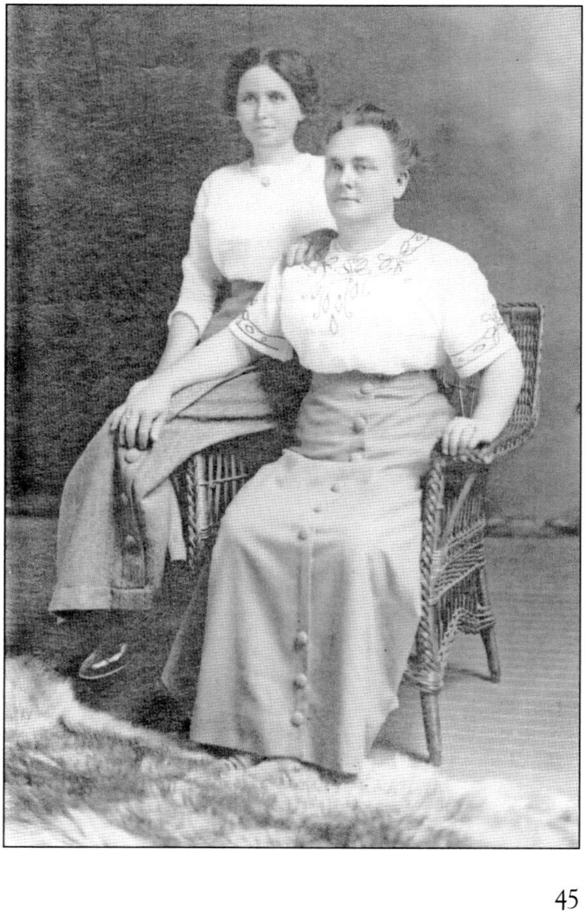

Martha Jay Herren (left), mother of Rosalee Herren, posed for this 1909 portrait with kindergarten teacher Hettie Dillyhuntie. (Courtesy of Mount Pleasant Public Library and Historical Museum.)

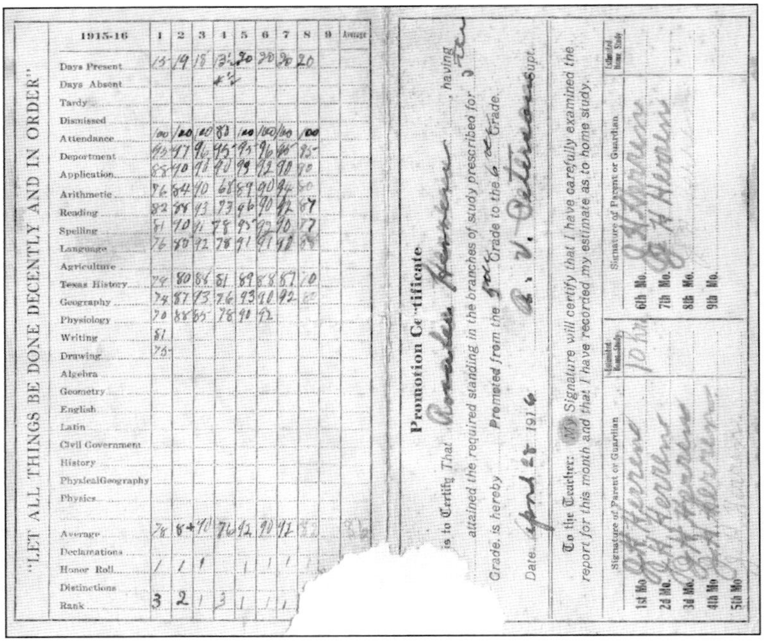

"LET ALL THINGS BE DONE DECENTLY AND IN ORDER"

1915-16

Days Present, Days Absent, Tardy, Dismissed, Attendance, Deportment, Application, Arithmetic, Reading, Spelling, Language, Agriculture, Texas History, Geography, Physiology, Writing, Drawing, Algebra, Geometry, English, Latin, Civil Government, History, PhysicalGeography, Physics, Average, Declamations, Honor Roll, Distinctions, Rank

Promotion Certificate

This is to Certify That Rosalee Herren, having attained the required standing in the branches of study prescribed for 5th Grade, is hereby Promoted from the 5th Grade to the 6th Grade.

Date April 28 1916

Supt.

To the Teacher: My Signature will certify that I have carefully examined the report for this month and that I have recorded my estimate as to home study.

Signature of Parent or Guardian

1st Mo. 2d Mo. 3d Mo. 4th Mo. 5th Mo. 6th Mo. 7th Mo. 8th Mo. 9th Mo.

This report card from Rosalee Herren, a fifth-grade student in 1916, shows that in addition to being graded on traditional subjects such as arithmetic, reading, and language, she was also evaluated on application and deportment. Rosalee attended the Eastside Public School. (Courtesy of Mount Pleasant Public Library and Historical Museum.)

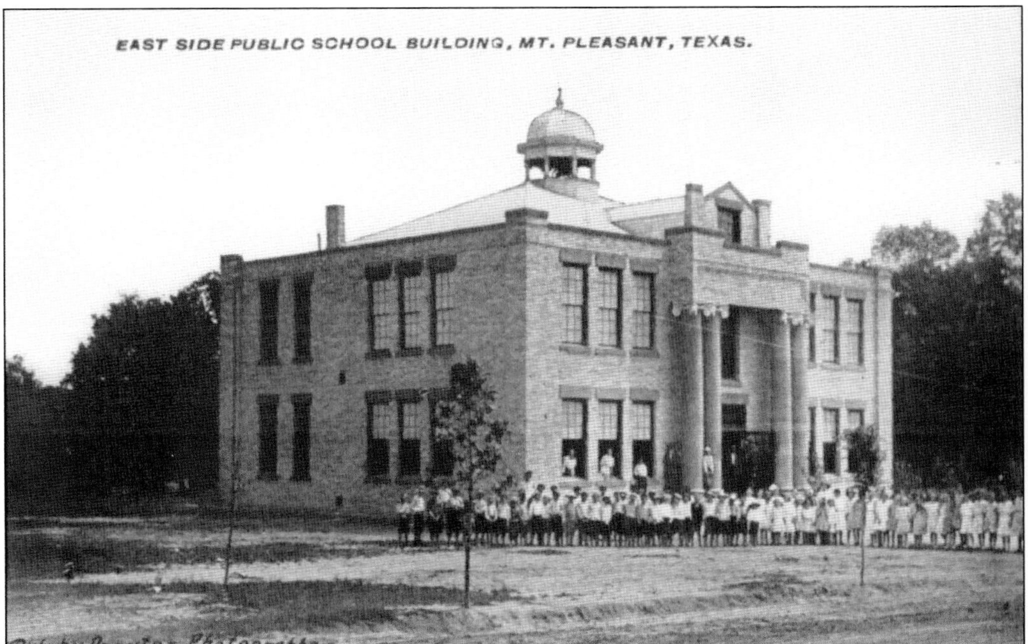


The East Ward School opened in 1911. In 1958 it was renamed in honor of Annie Sims, a teacher at the school from 1921 to 1957. (Courtesy of Mount Pleasant Public Library and Historical Museum.)

Although the congregation has roots in the Greenhill community, William Waldo Brimm organized the First Presbyterian Church in Mount Pleasant in 1881. Two years later, the congregation purchased land for the church, located on Madison Avenue and Third Street, and construction of the frame building seen in this photograph commenced soon after. The church commissioned the brick structure that now stands at the same location in 1923. (Courtesy of the First Presbyterian Church.)

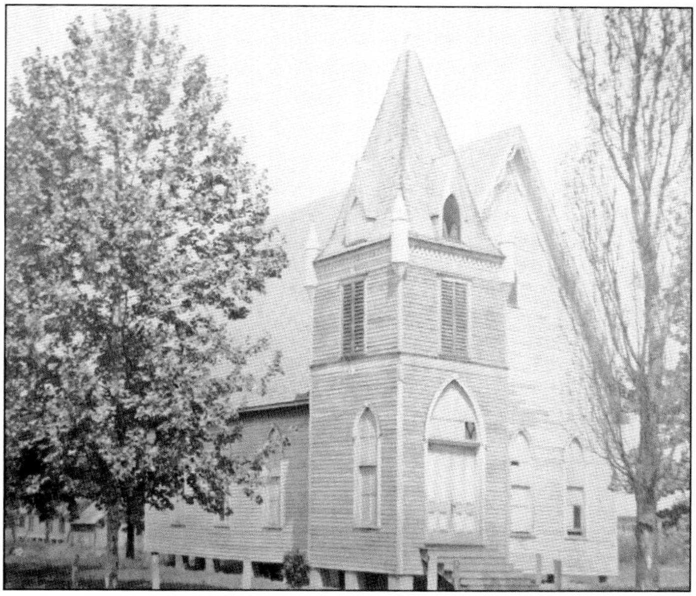

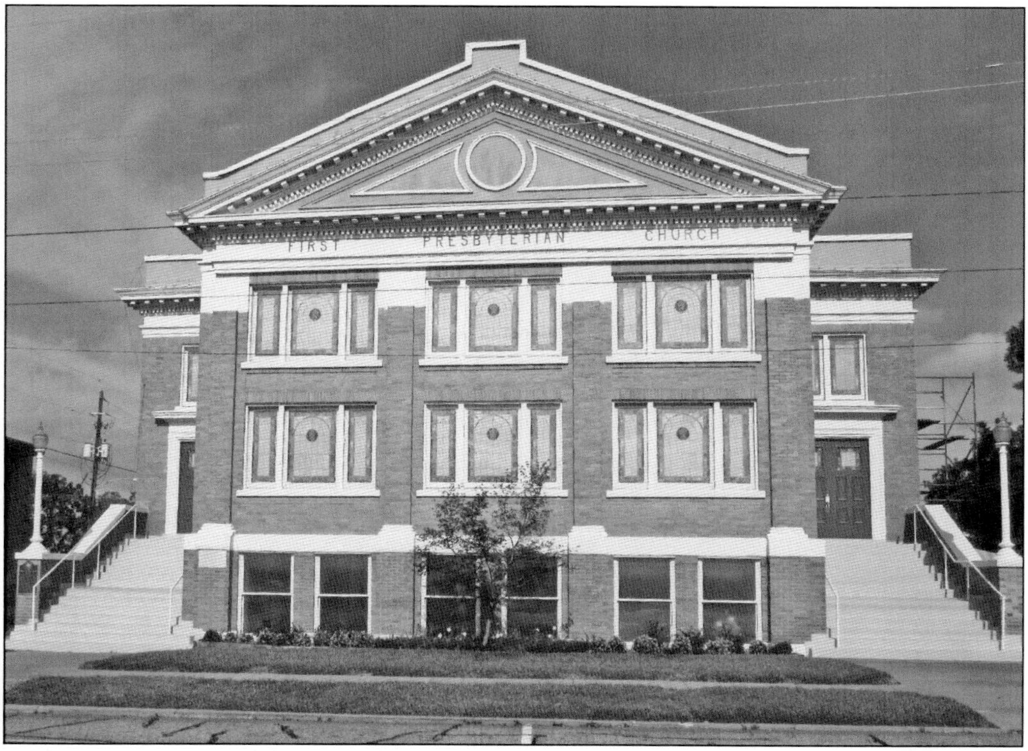


Presbyterians are one of the oldest denominations in Mount Pleasant, dating back to 1860 in the Greenhill community. The First Presbyterian Church as it presently appears was constructed in 1923, but the original wood structure at the same location was completed in 1883. (Authors.)

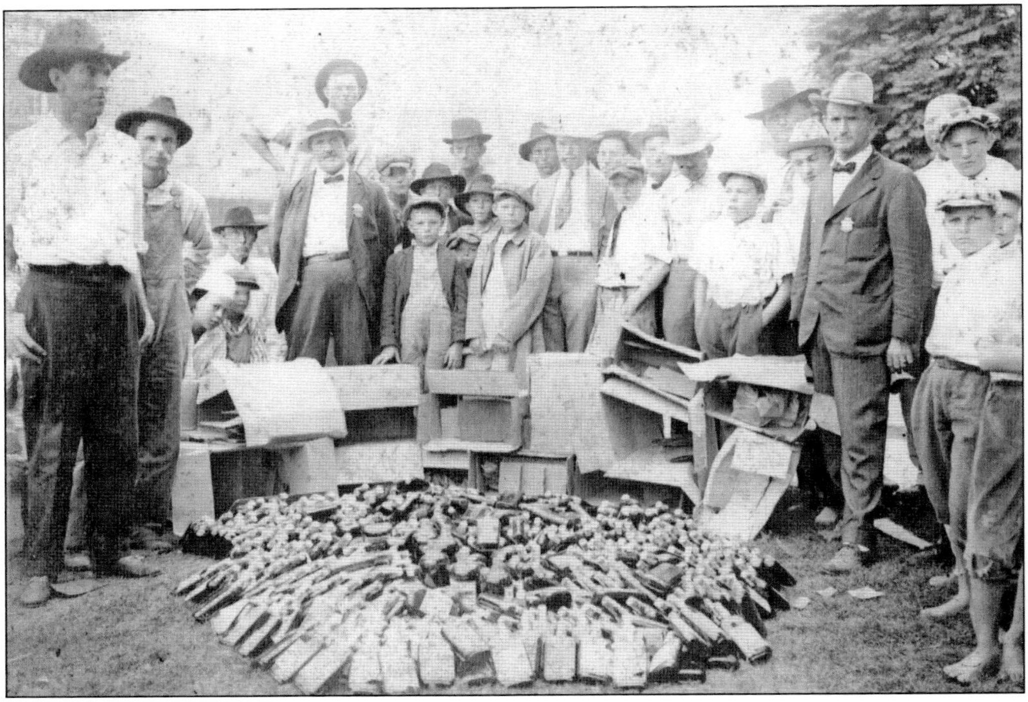

Saloons had been a staple in Mount Pleasant from its founding until the county voted itself dry in 1902. However, those opposed to Prohibition continued making moonshine on the side. As a result, liquor raids were a frequent occurrence during the early 20th century. The illegal production of alcohol was particularly persistent in rural communities such as Sugar Hill, just north of Mount Pleasant, which received its name from the large amounts of sugar its residents used to produce moonshine. (Courtesy of Mount Pleasant Public Library and Historical Museum.)

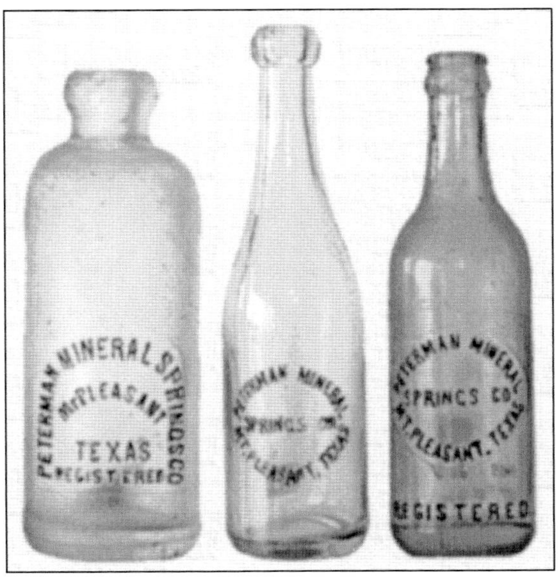


Moonshine was not the only liquid made and sold in Mount Pleasant. The mineral water that attracted the earliest settlers was bottled and sold by the Peterman Mineral Springs Company. Congressional records indicate that Peterman reported sales for several years in the early 20th century. At one time, Americans, deeply fascinated by the potential medicinal and health value of natural mineral springs, drank mineral water for health reasons and occasionally visited sites to bathe in them. Peterman was one of 28 springs in the state of Texas reporting bottled water sales for 1906. Eight of those springs (including Peterman) also offered bathing facilities. (Courtesy of Mount Pleasant Public Library and Historical Museum.)

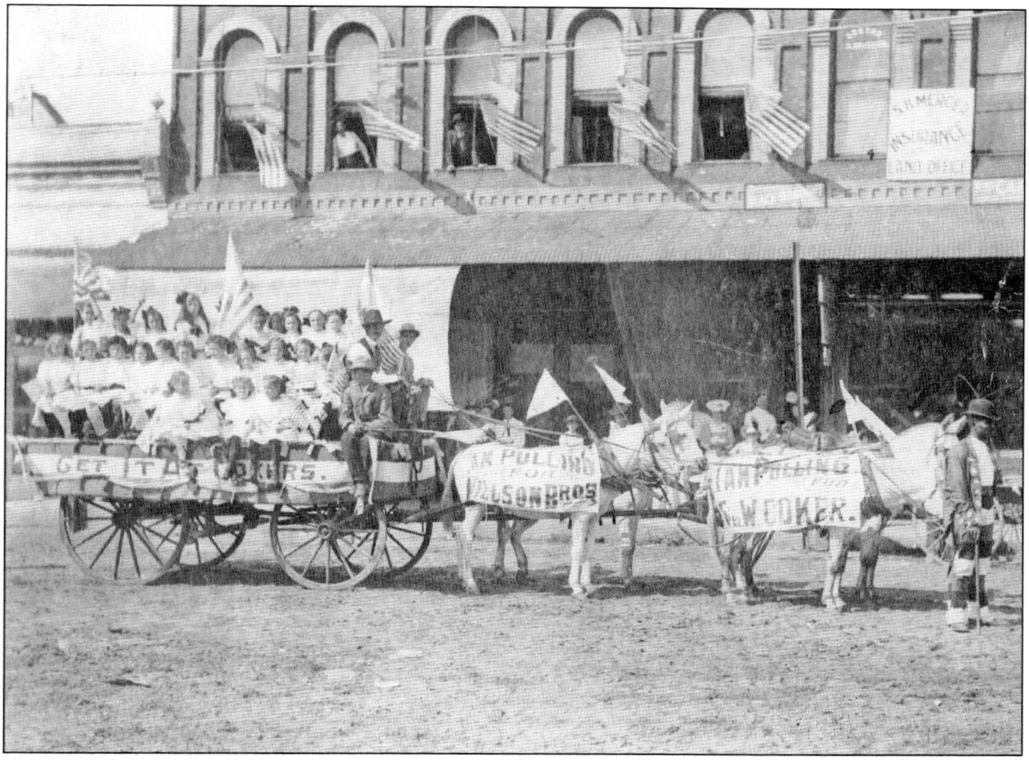


Just as in the earliest days of human settlement, the multicolored mineral water attracted large crowds and festive celebrations. Local merchants Willson Bros. and Coker's sponsored this wagon as part of an early 1900s Independence Day parade. The parade began in downtown Mount Pleasant and ended at Dellwood. (Courtesy of Mount Pleasant Public Library and Historical Museum.)

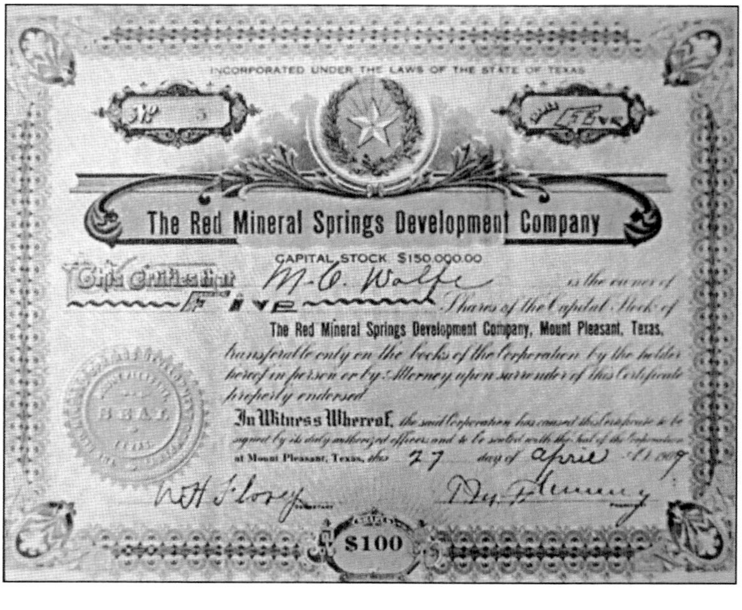


In the 1890s, Jesse Reed purchased 120 acres of spring-fed property in present-day Dellwood Park. M.C. Wolfe, T.M. Fleming, Spill Brown, and W.H. and Spencer Florey ultimately acquired the property and organized the Red Mineral Springs Development Company. The company issued stock certificates like this. (Courtesy of Mount Pleasant Public Library and Historical Museum.)

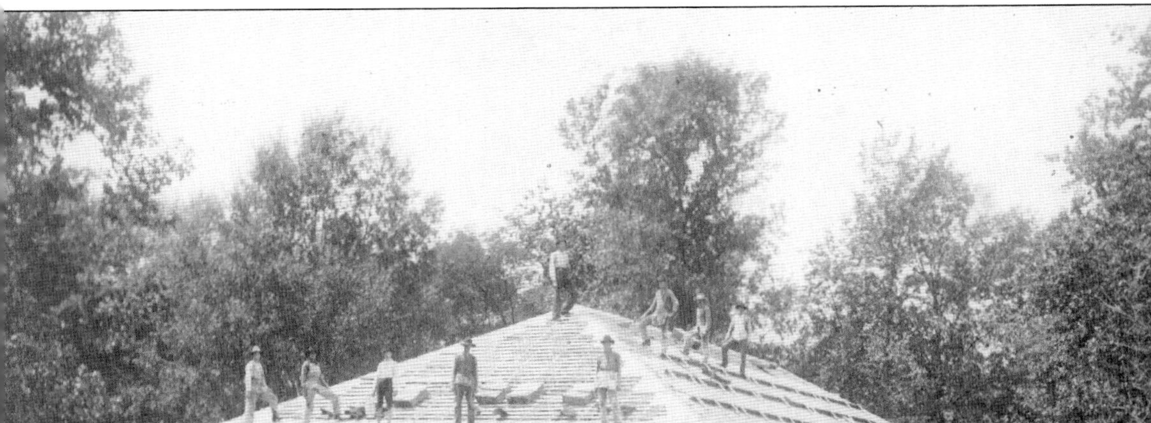

Red Mineral Springs Development Company began building the Dellwood, a resort hotel and spa complex, in 1907. While construction was underway, the developers had the mineral waters chemically analyzed by the state chemist and compiled testimonials from doctors and other individuals regarding the restorative powers of the mineral waters. One individual wrote that he had come to the springs so "lame with rheumatism that he could not step over small objects, but after using the water for one month, he was cured and able to plow all day." Advertising literature also emphasized that the waters were "three distinct colors, beautiful and attractive, soft and palatable." In this photograph, workers pose during the construction of the dance pavilion. The completed structure accommodated up to 100 couples. (Courtesy of Mount Pleasant Public Library and Historical Museum.)

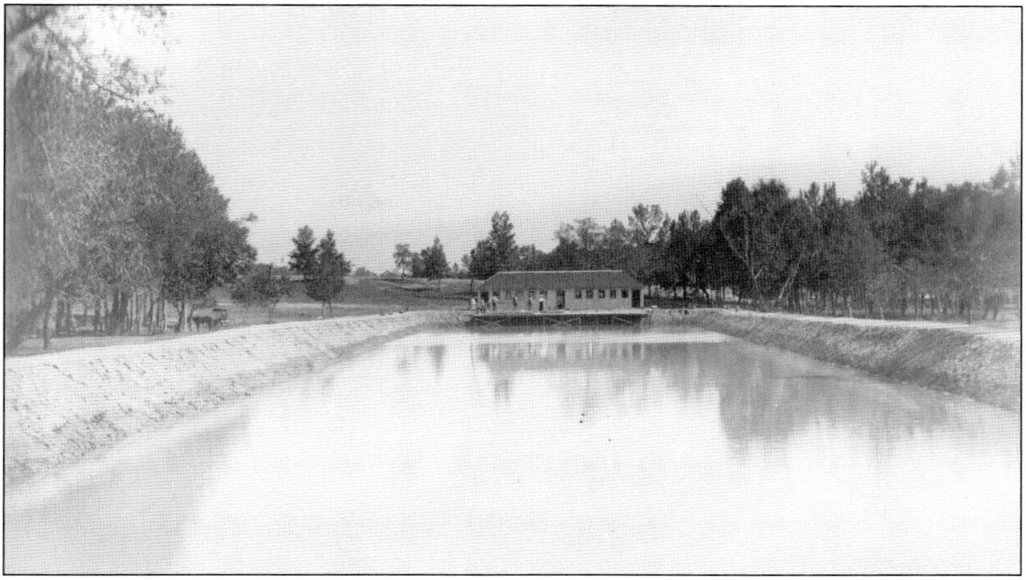

The Dellwood also boasted a large man-made pool with a cement bottom fed by natural springs. Workers assemble a large bathhouse on the far side of the lake in this photograph. Boats would be offered for rental on the man-made lake once the facilities were completed. (Courtesy of Mount Pleasant Public Library and Historical Museum.)

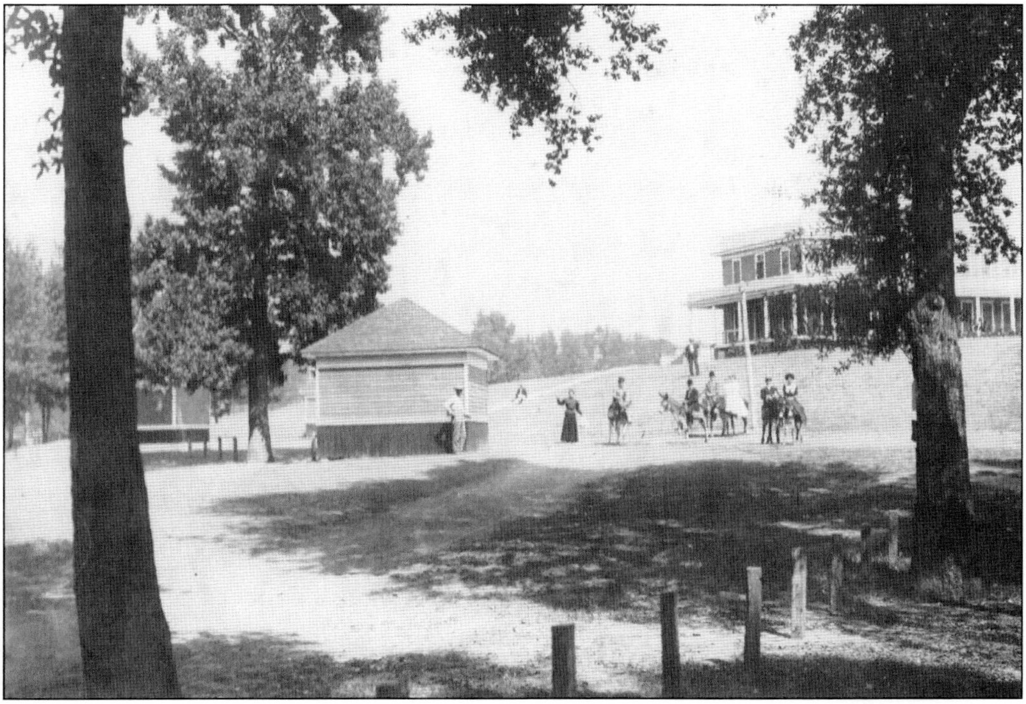

"Come to Dellwood Park, and have a good time, drink the wonderful red water, and get rested and well," proclaimed the resort literature. In this photograph capturing the opening-day festivities at the Dellwood, a woman displays a freshly caught fish just below Dellwood Hotel. Several riders pose atop some of the donkeys available for rental. The resort offered a variety of trails throughout the property. (Courtesy of Mount Pleasant Public Library and Historical Museum.)

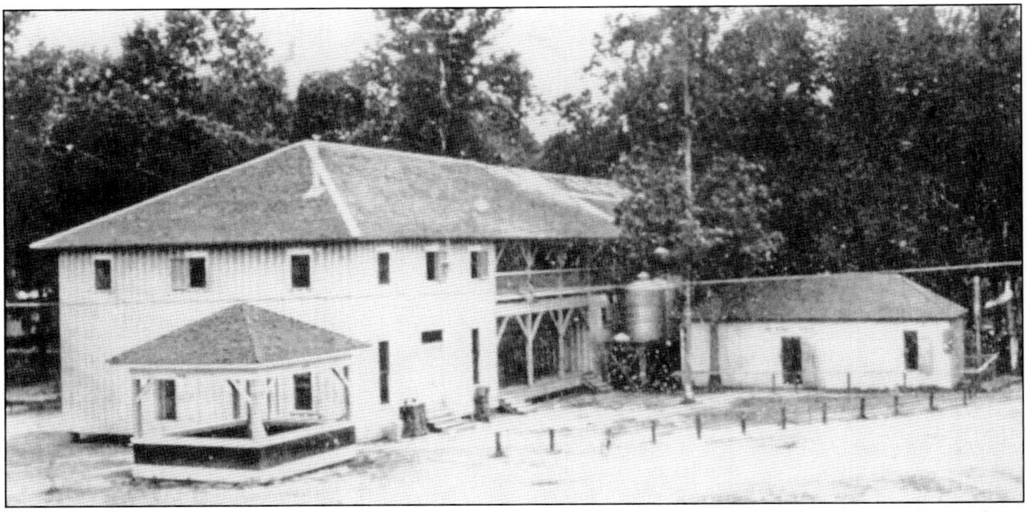

This postcard shows the completed dance pavilion. The resort offered a band that featured Woodson Gaines on piccolo, Zeph William on guitar, Tom Lewis on bass fiddle, and Will Rutherford playing mandolin. The band performed in the pavilion for the dances as well as at public gatherings and conventions. (Courtesy of Mount Pleasant Public Library and Historical Museum.)

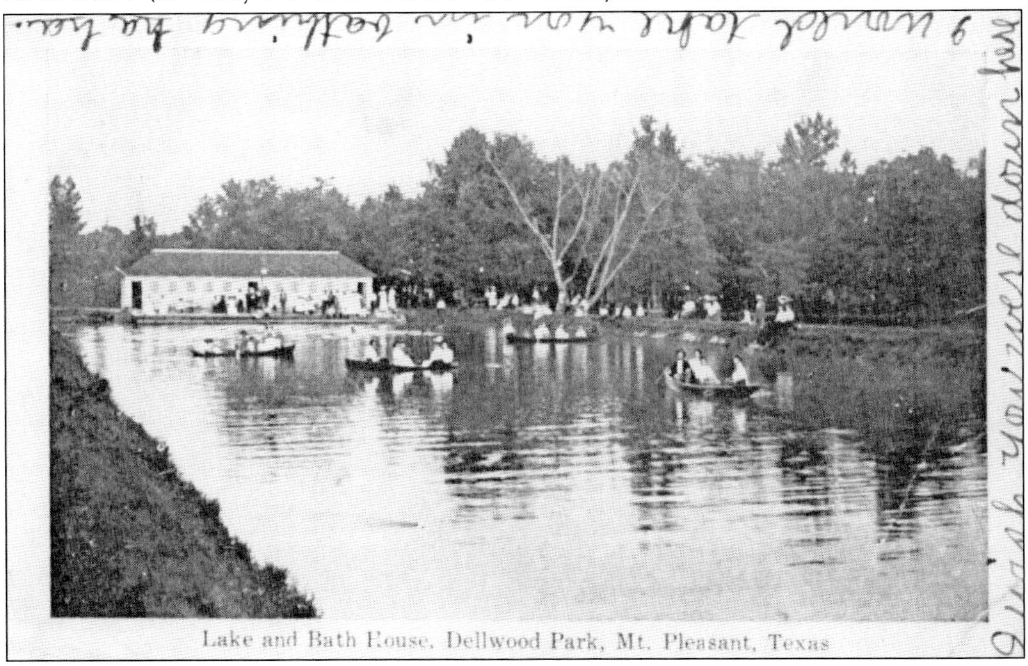


"I wish you were down here. I would take you in bathing. Haha." The writer of this postcard would certainly agree with the developers' description of the Dellwood as a place for cultivating friendships and romance. The resort literature stated that "seats and swings are provided throughout the park, and the tired man or woman, or the fellow with his best girl, may find a place to unload his troubles in fresh, pure air; and if the 'dear girl' faints, she may fall on the grassy lawn under a beautiful shelter provided by nature, and be cared for until the shock is over. Conventions of every kind are invited, and it will be the pleasure of the management to cater to the notions and whims of the fellow who was born on the 'dark of the moon.' " (Courtesy of Mount Pleasant Public Library and Historical Museum.)

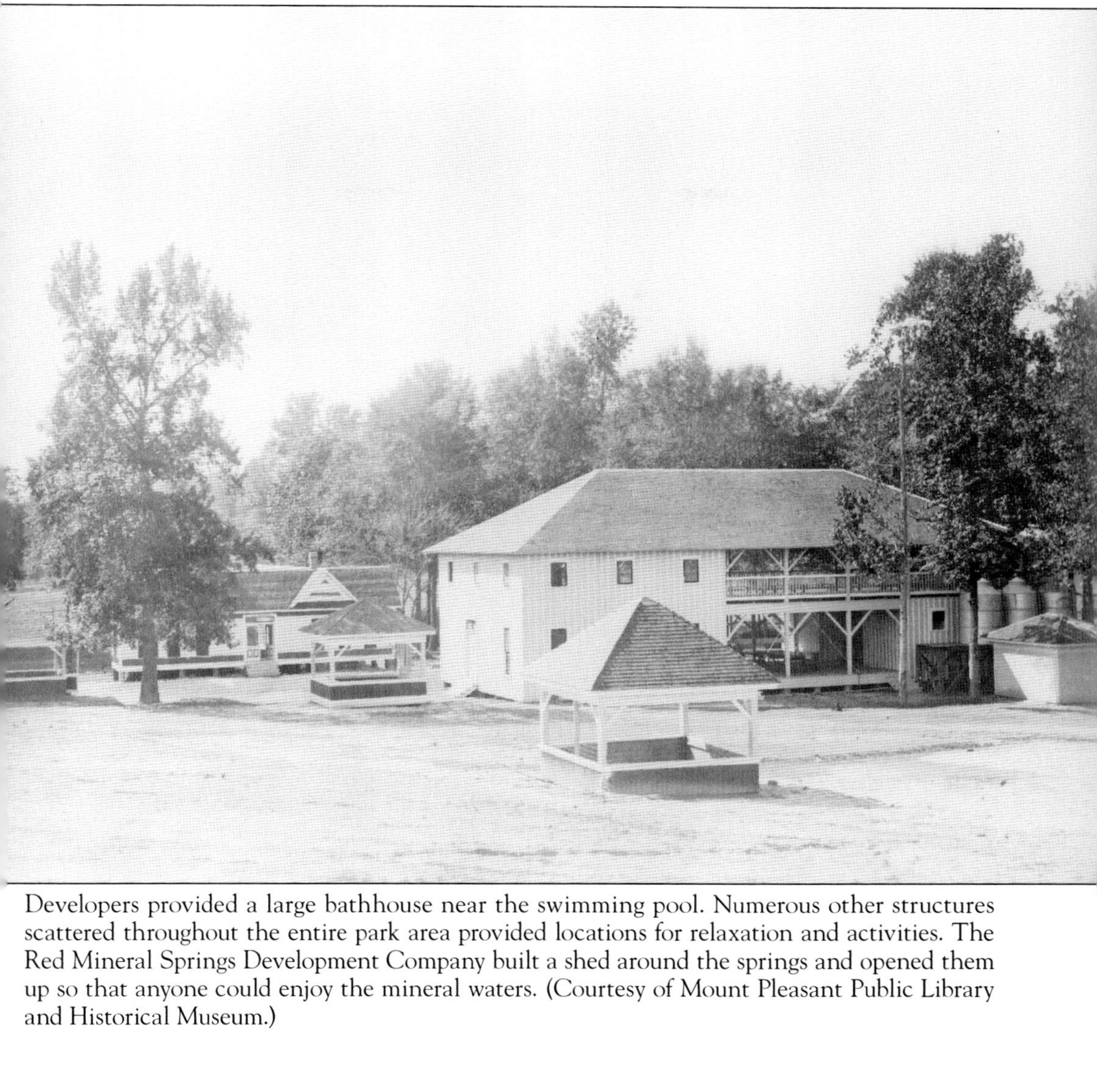

Developers provided a large bathhouse near the swimming pool. Numerous other structures scattered throughout the entire park area provided locations for relaxation and activities. The Red Mineral Springs Development Company built a shed around the springs and opened them up so that anyone could enjoy the mineral waters. (Courtesy of Mount Pleasant Public Library and Historical Museum.)

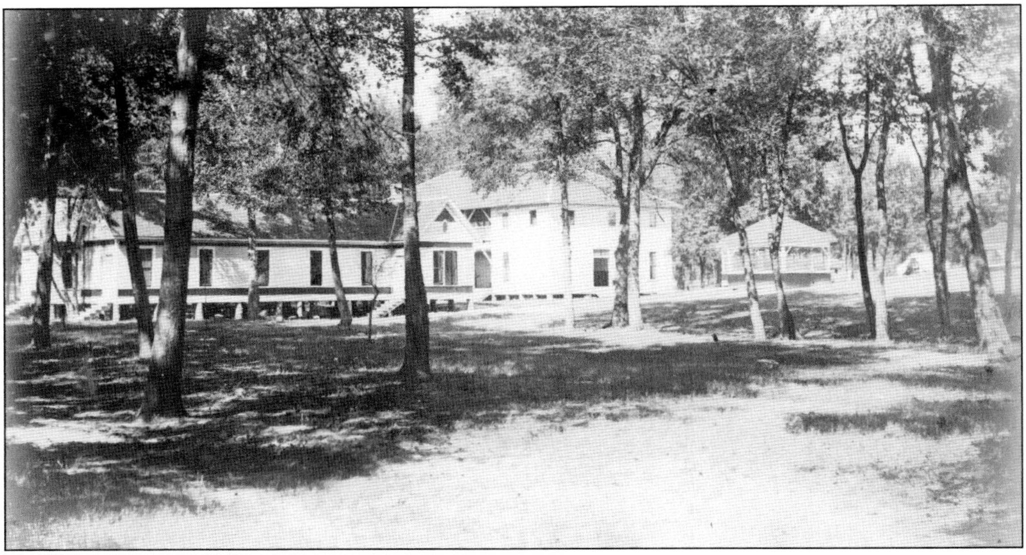

Leisure activities at the Dellwood included dancing, boating, bowling, tennis, and croquet. As advertised, the park provided "All kinds of Amusements to add Health, Strength, and Innocent Pleasure for the Young and Old." (Courtesy of Mount Pleasant Public Library and Historical Museum.)

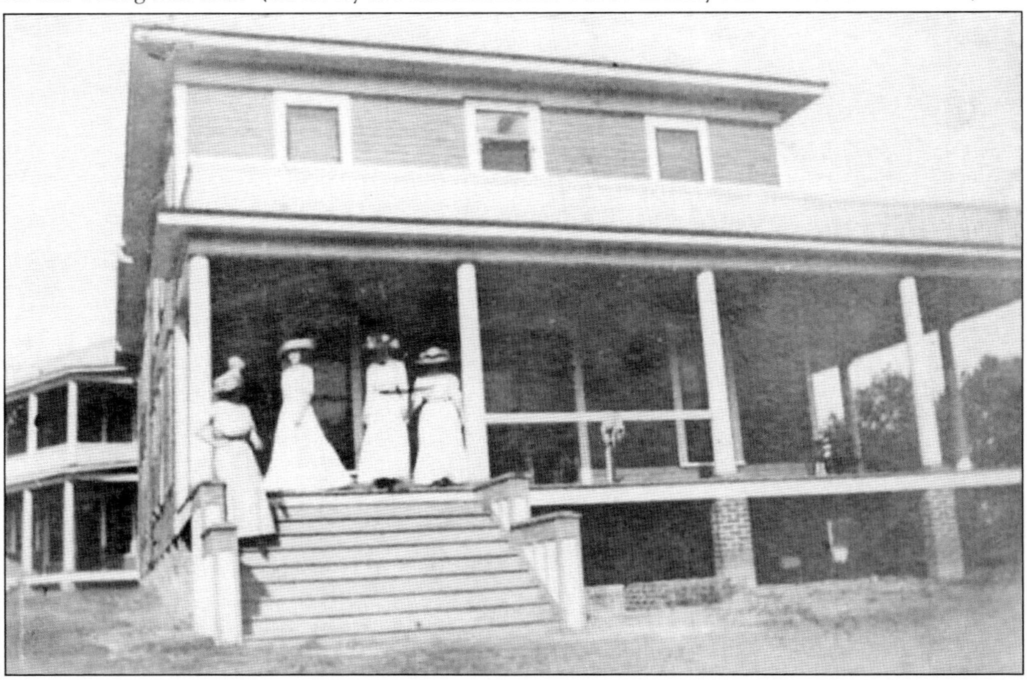

The two-story, 70-room hotel, built in the shape of a Y, stood atop a hill overlooking the man-made lake. The ground floor housed a dining room and lobby. Spring-fed fountains adorned the hotel lobby: one with red water, another with white (or clear), and a third with blue. On the second floor, a large parlor offered a meeting place for balls or receptions. The hotel also boasted a barbershop and steam baths, as well as its own light, water, and sewage systems. A street railway and motorcar ran from the hotel to nearby downtown Mount Pleasant. Several ladies dressed in their finest stand on the steps of one of the wings of the Dellwood hotel. (Courtesy of Mount Pleasant Public Library and Historical Museum.)

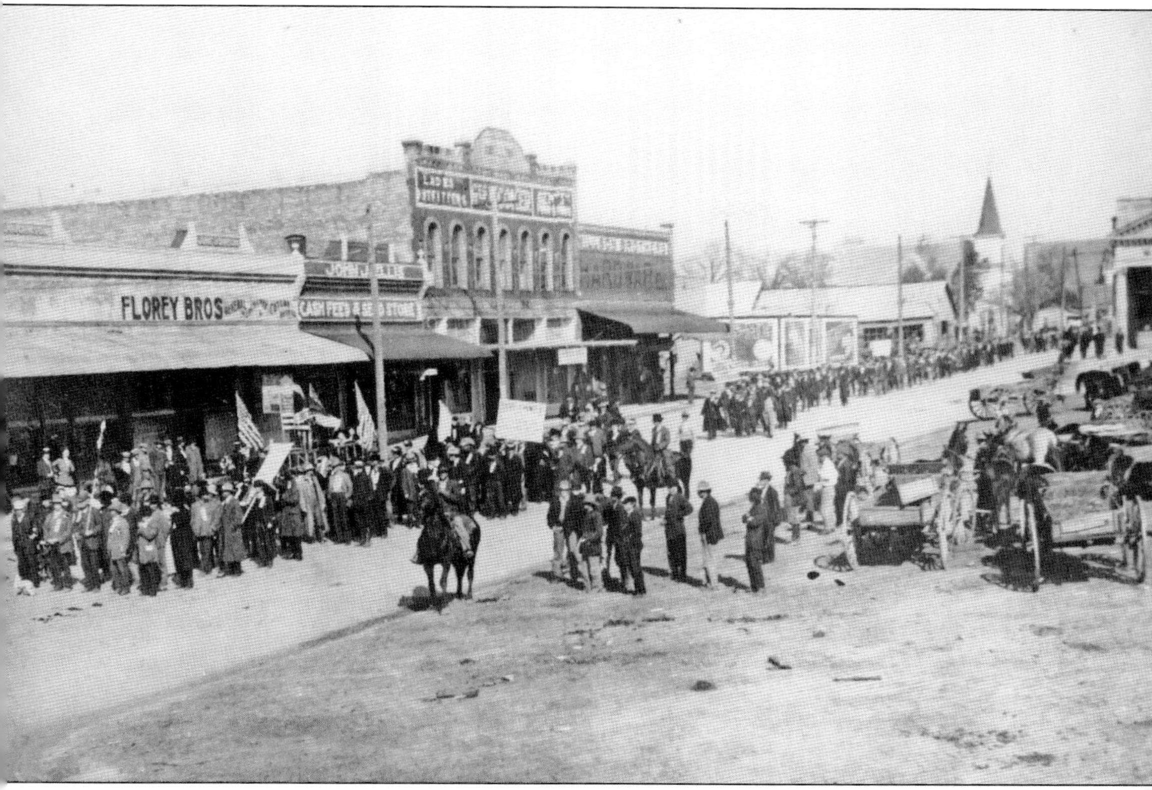


In 1910, Dellwood resort promoters advertised all over Northeast Texas that there would be a Confederate veterans' reunion at the Dellwood resort. It was to be a three-day affair. The parade, pictured here as the men are lining up, began downtown on Madison Street. The 70 rooms at the Dellwood resort proved inadequate for the large crowds that descended upon the location. Several thousand people came and camped in the area surrounding the resort. Fifty men climbed onto the motorized trolley car to ride it out to the resort, but the extra weight ruined the overtaxed motor. After that, a horse or mule pulled the trolley car. Mount Pleasant found itself unprepared to deal with such large crowds, and by the third day, all supplies in the town had been used up. (Courtesy of the *East Texas Journal.*)

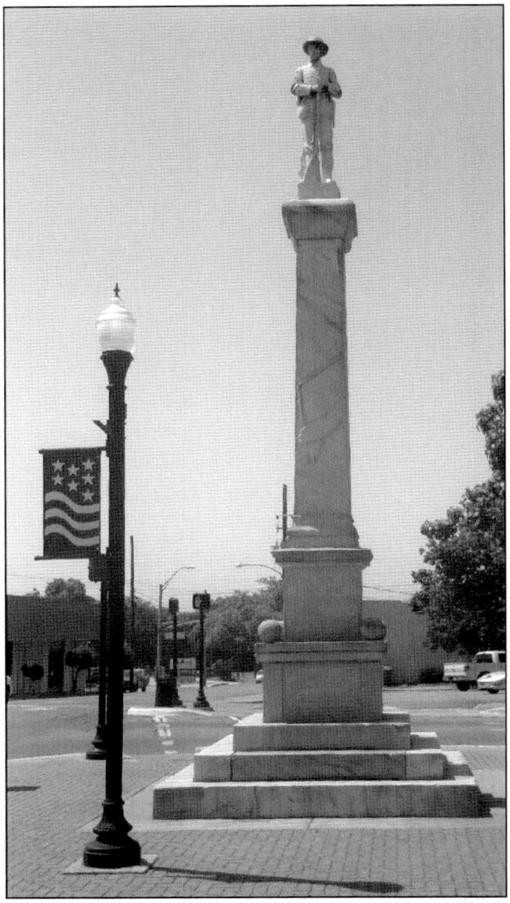

A few months after the large gathering of Confederate veterans, the Dudley Jones Camp and the United Daughters of the Confederacy began funding to erect the Titus County Confederate Veterans Monument. Within two years, they raised approximately $25,000. The monument was unveiled outside the Titus County Courthouse in November 1912. (Authors.)

After the school he operated in Lancaster, Texas, burned in 1912, A.C. Speer rented the vacant facilities at Dellwood and opened Speer's School for Boys. During its brief existence, the school fielded a football team that played some of the smaller colleges in the area, such as Burleson and Wesley. Speer School also fielded track and baseball teams and had a school band, pictured here. Although Speer was apparently considered an excellent teacher (as attested by the number of students who came from Dallas to attend school in Mount Pleasant), the school was never a financial success and closed in 1914. (Courtesy of Mount Pleasant Public Library and Historical Museum.)

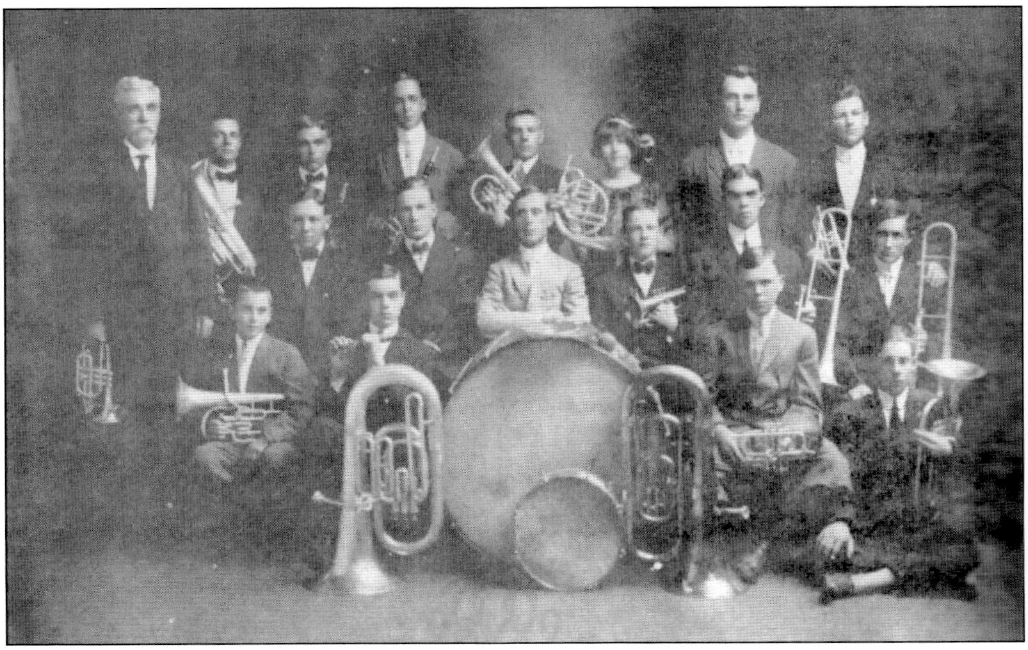

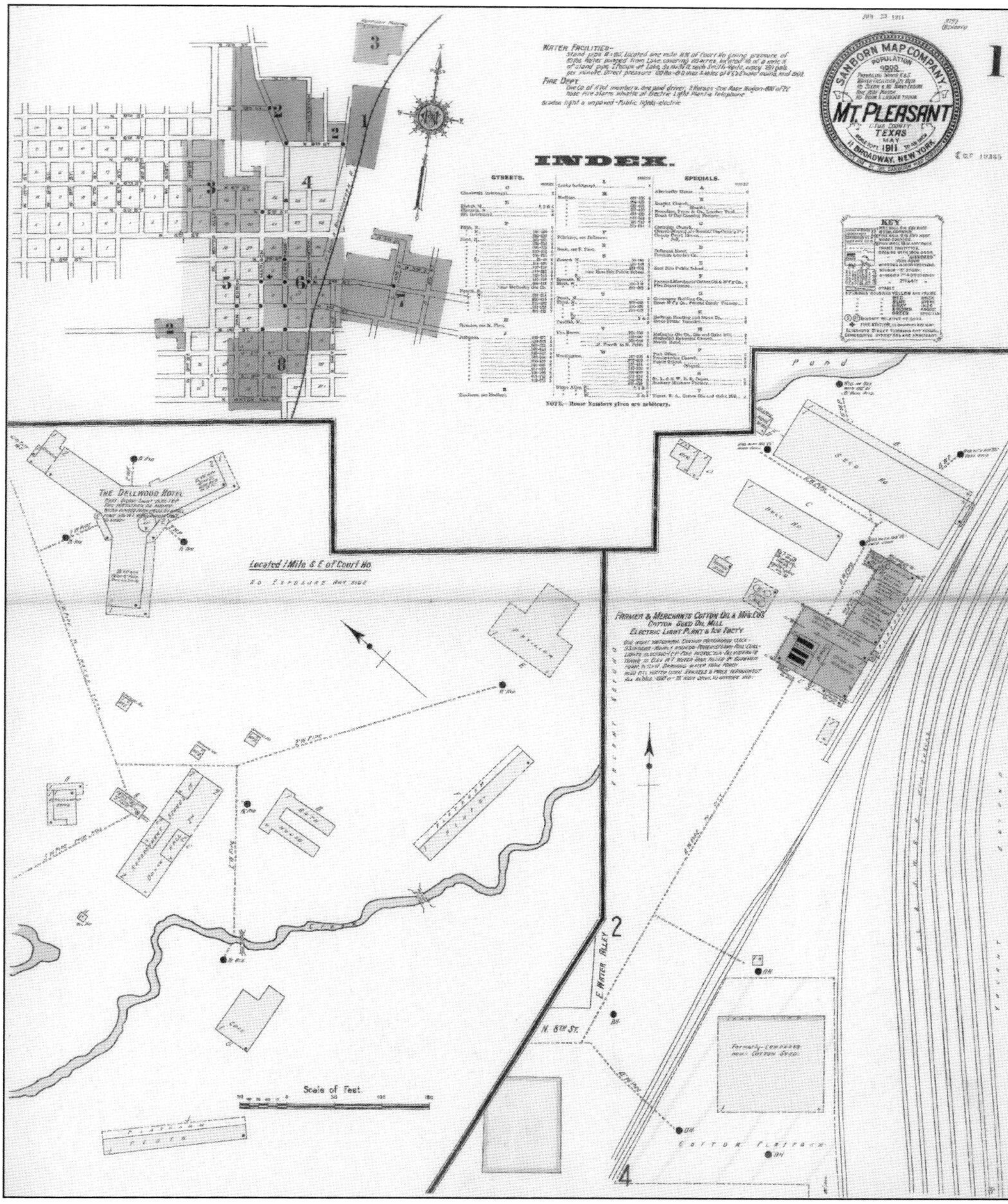


The colored mineral springs that originally made the area a popular campground and gathering spot for Caddo natives went through several manifestations. First came Jessie Reed's Iridescent Springs, then the Red Mineral Springs Development Company's Dellwood, and finally the Speer School for Boys, until it was abandoned altogether. In 1925 the former hotel burned, leaving behind only the stone steps as a reminder of the resort's former glory. The City of Mount Pleasant acquired 45 acres of the property in 1951 and created Dellwood Park. Although the mineral springs are no longer available and the earlier facilities are destroyed, some of the same activities available at the resort can still be enjoyed at the location, including a swimming pool, a jogging and nature trail, tennis courts, picnic tables, picnic pavilions, a playground, and sports fields. This 1911 map shows the city during the height of the Dellwood as a resort and tourist attraction. (Courtesy of Dolph Briscoe Center for American History, University of Texas in Austin.)

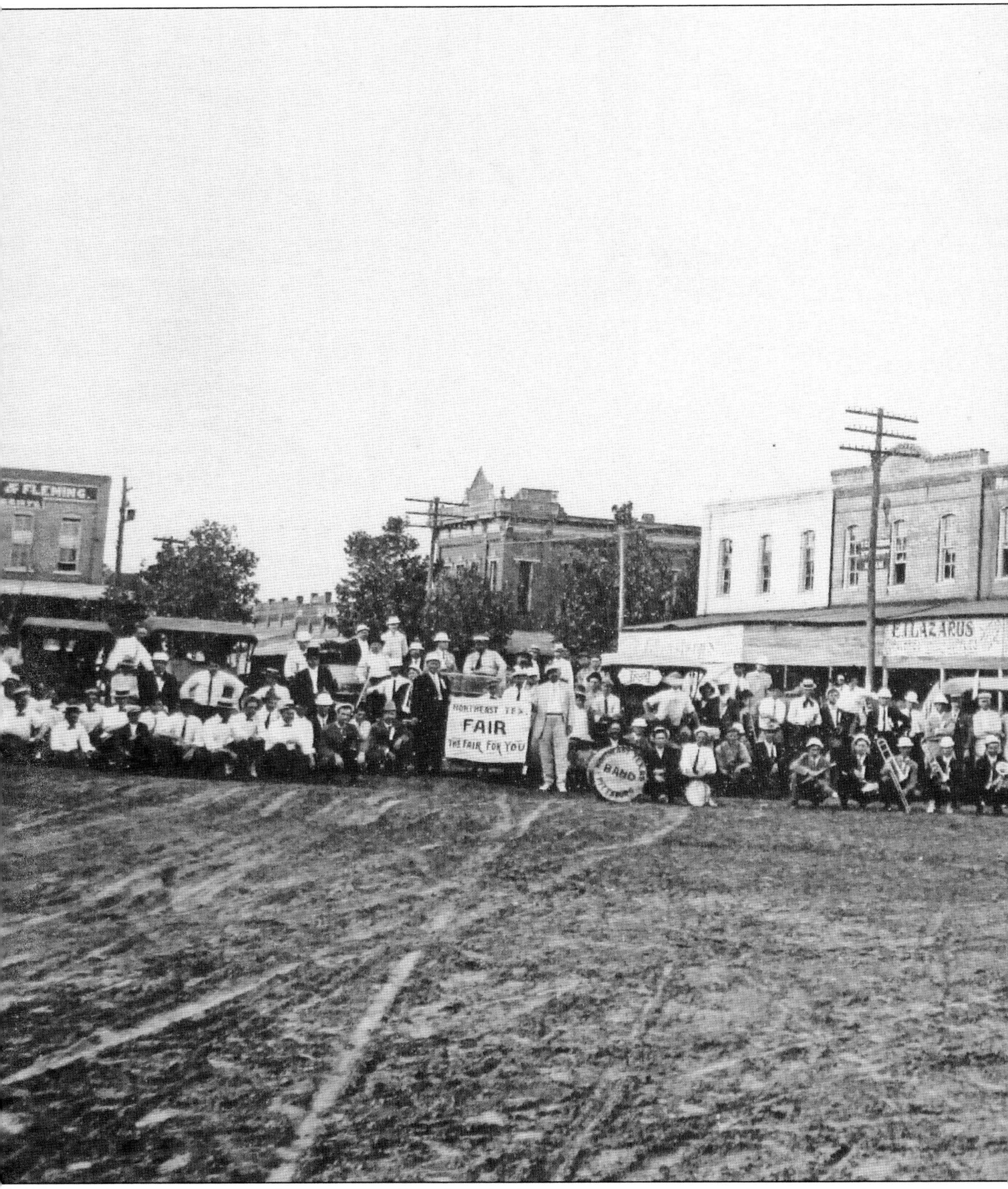


A precursor to the Titus County Fair, the Northeast Texas Fair attracted visitors to Mount Pleasant from around the area during the early 1900s. The Northeast Texas Band is pictured here in downtown looking north up Jefferson Avenue. A number of local business are visible, including

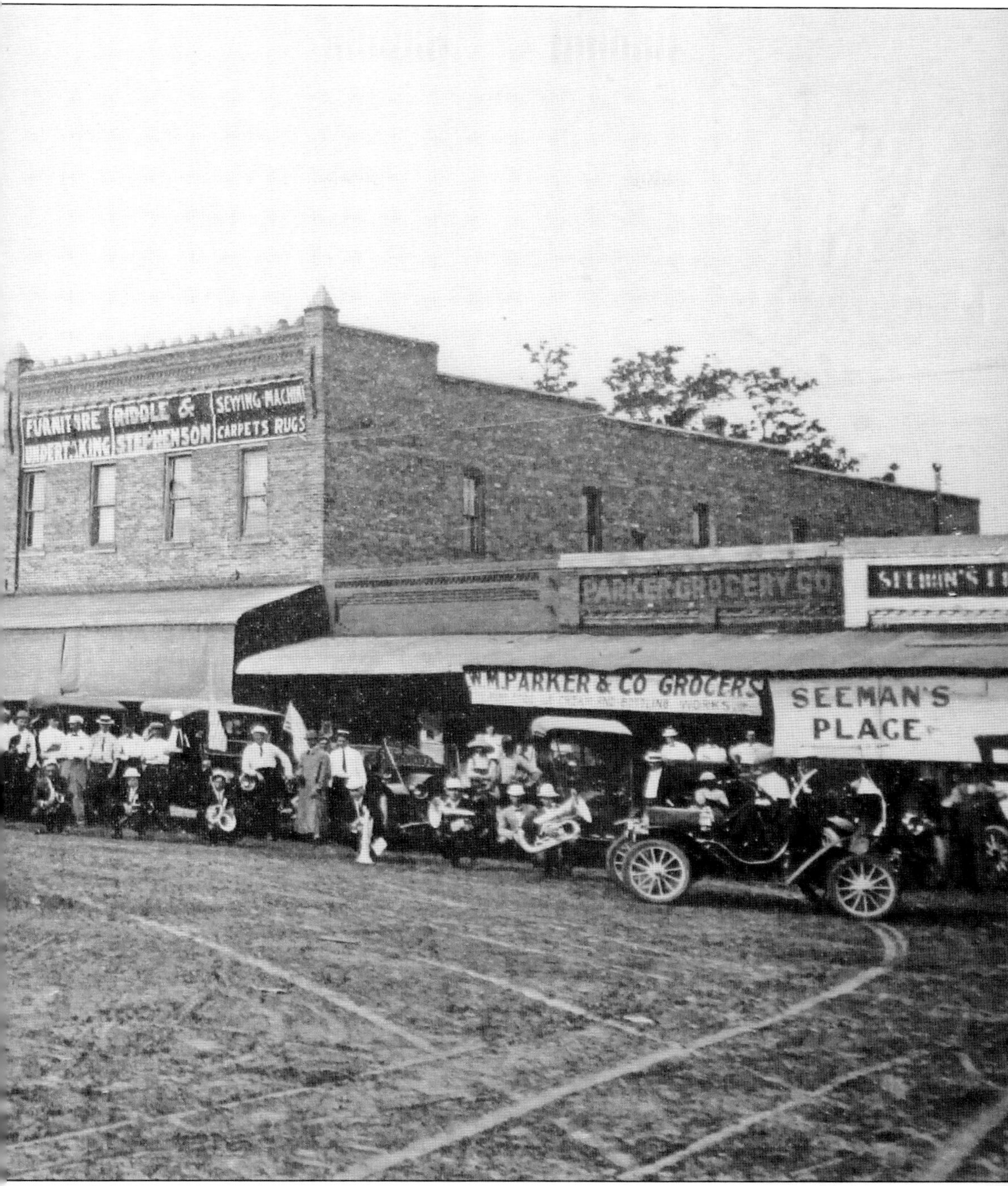


the Riddle furniture and undertaking company, the Parker Grocery Company, Lilienstern's department store, and the First National Bank. (Courtesy of John Williams.)

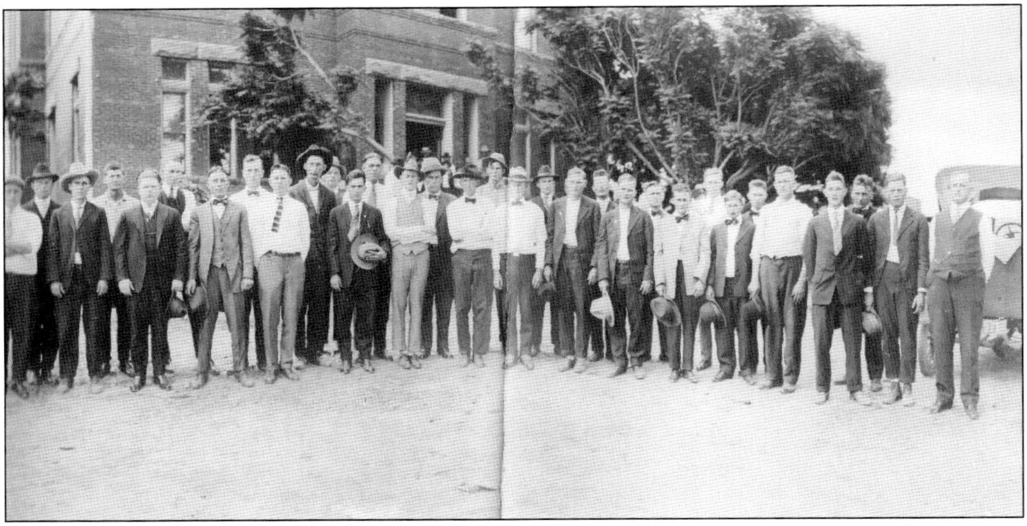

When the United States joined the "Great War" that was already underway overseas, the patriotic men of Mount Pleasant did what they would do for every conflict—fight bravely. These residents who volunteered for service in World War I pose in front of the Titus County Courthouse. (Courtesy of Mount Pleasant Public Library and Historical Museum.)

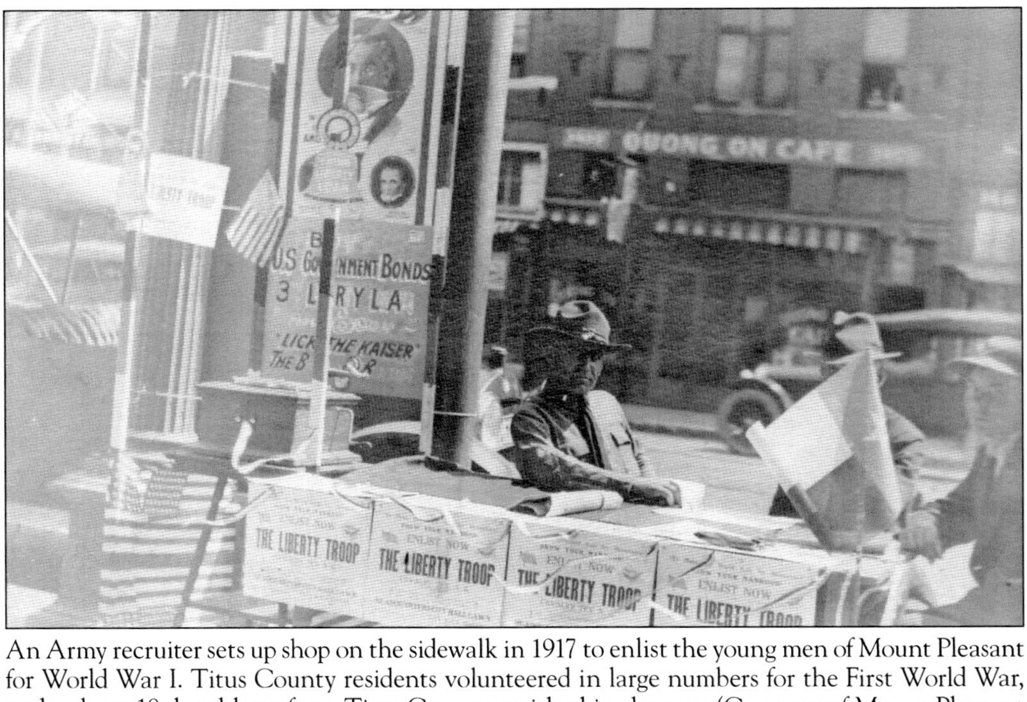


An Army recruiter sets up shop on the sidewalk in 1917 to enlist the young men of Mount Pleasant for World War I. Titus County residents volunteered in large numbers for the First World War, and at least 18 doughboys from Titus County perished in the war. (Courtesy of Mount Pleasant Public Library and Historical Museum.)

A Mount Pleasant resident displays his new uniform before leaving to serve in World War I. (Courtesy of Mount Pleasant Public Library and Historical Museum.)

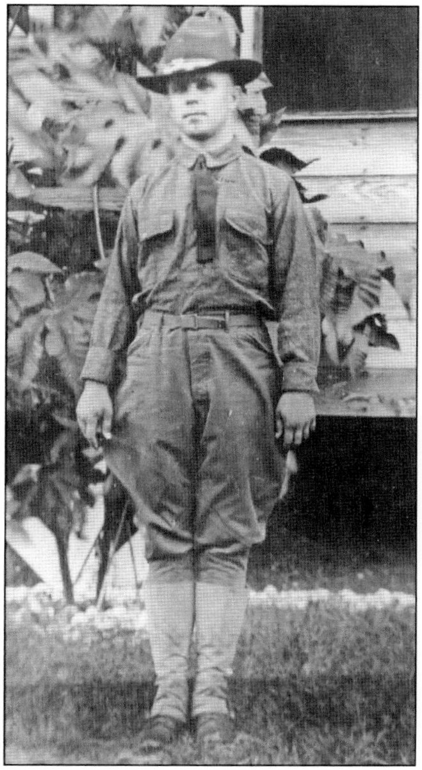

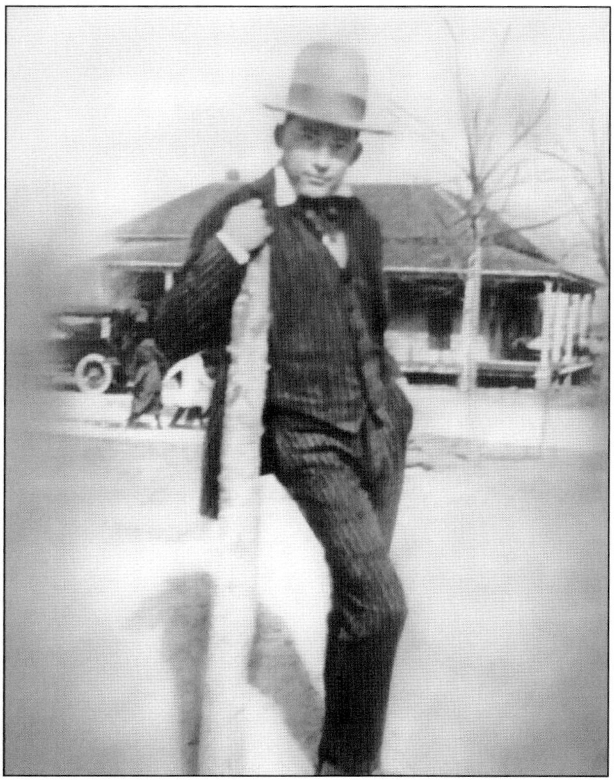

A.B. "Jack" Jessup was the first Titus County resident to die during World War I. He enlisted in the US Navy in April 1917 and died in June of the same year aboard the USS *Texas*. (Courtesy of Mount Pleasant Public Library and Historical Museum.)

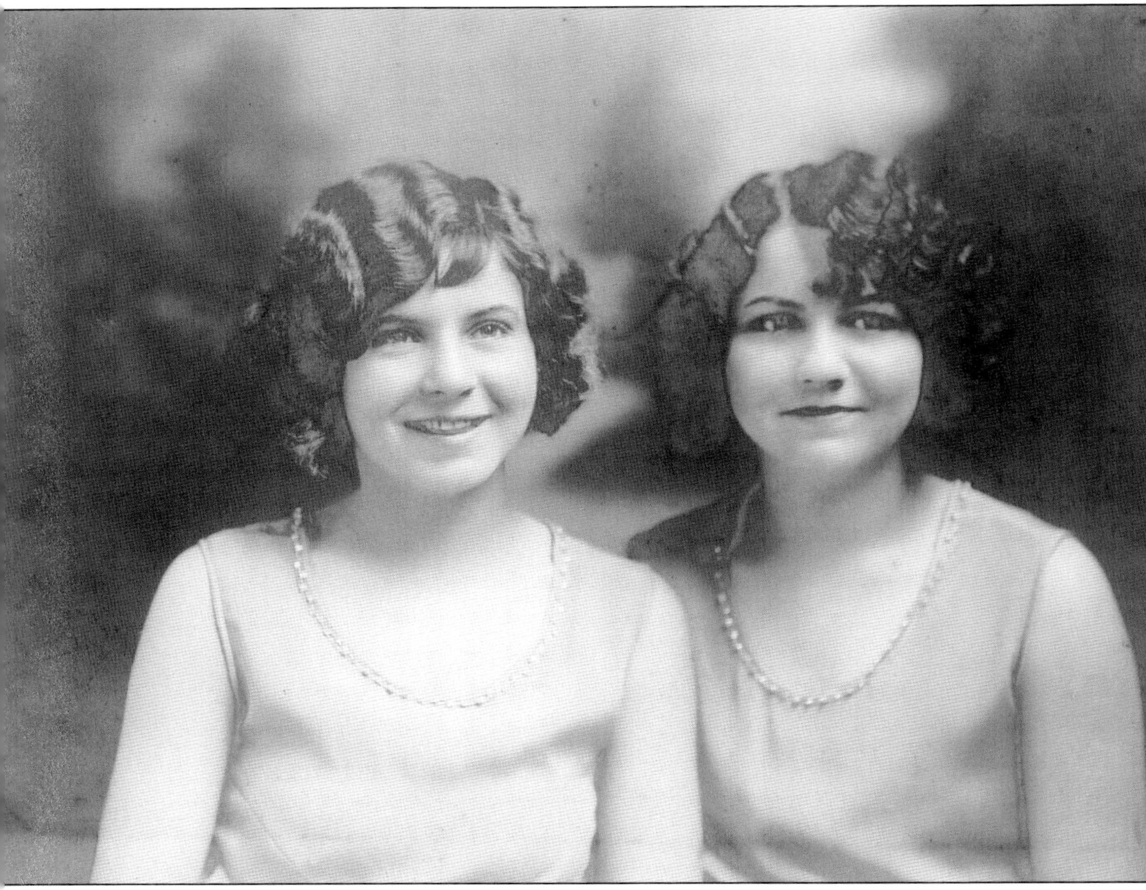

These two Mount Pleasant girls are representative of the flapper style of the 1920s. After World War I, Victorian sensibilities about style changed as liberated women began wearing more cosmetics, shorter skirts, and bobbed hair. (Courtesy of Mount Pleasant Public Library and Historical Museum.)

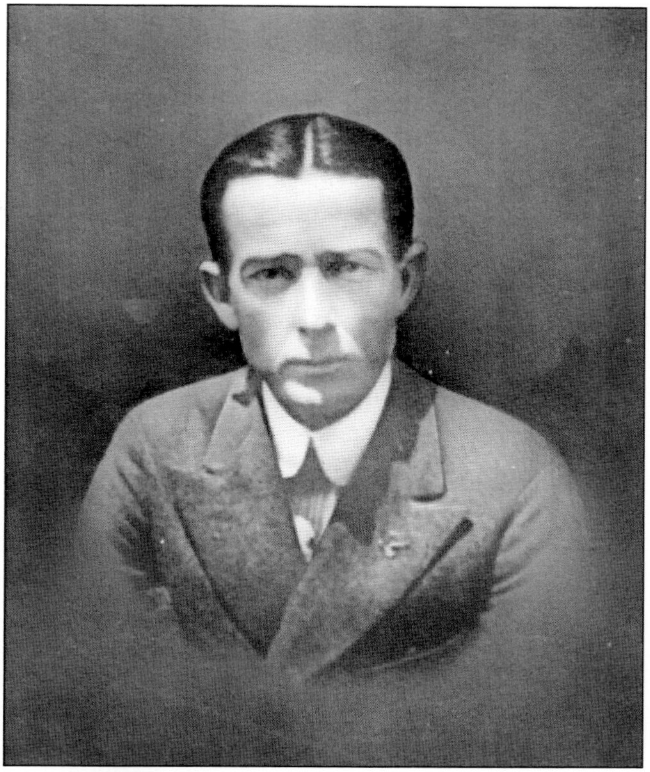

Johnny Martin owned and operated the Martin Theatre in downtown Mount Pleasant. He married Norma Fuller, daughter of local merchant Henry Fuller, and they operated the theater together. (Both, courtesy of Mount Pleasant Public Library and Historical Museum.)

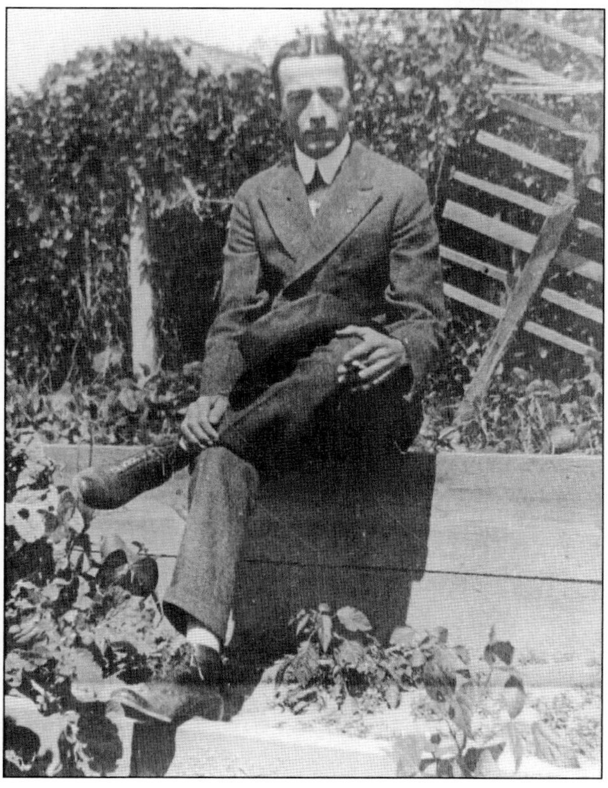

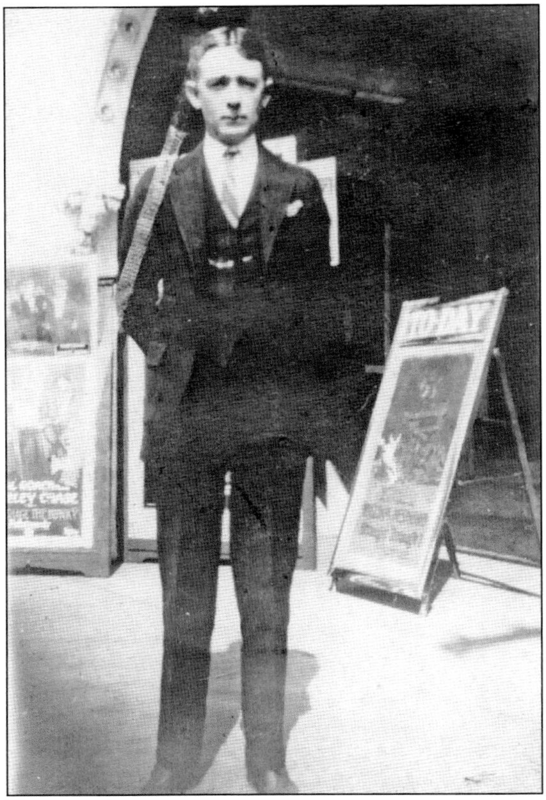

Johnny Martin stands in front of his theater, which opened in 1913. Martin and his wife operated the theater in Mount Pleasant for several decades. Movies were a major source of entertainment in rural Titus County. In the early 20th century movies were silent, but in 1929, the first "talking movie," *The Jazz Singer*, premiered. Movies continued to be popular even during the Great Depression, when money was difficult to come by. They provided a relatively cheap source of entertainment that allowed moviegoers to temporarily escape the difficulties they faced during the Depression. (Courtesy of Mount Pleasant Public Library and Historical Museum.)

The architectural design of the Martin Theatre was copied from a theater in Chicago. The Martin Theater had a "Grand Re-Opening" in 1937. The renovations cost a total of $20,000. Even after other theaters came to Mount Pleasant, the Martin was considered the preeminent theater in town. (Courtesy of Mount Pleasant Public Library and Historical Museum.)

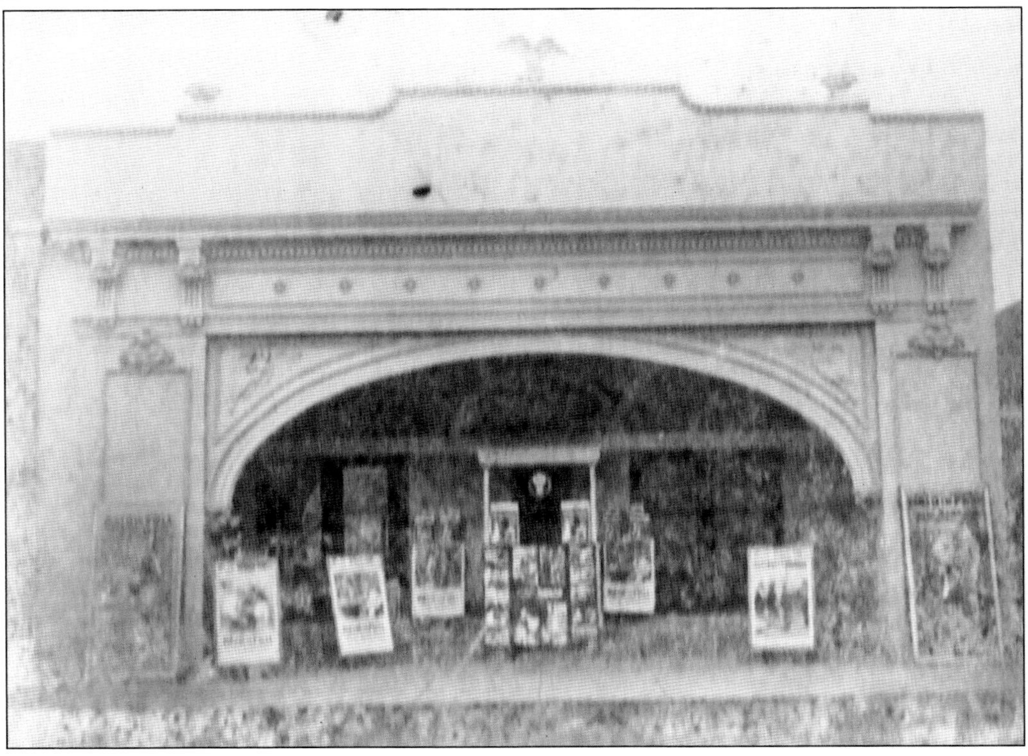

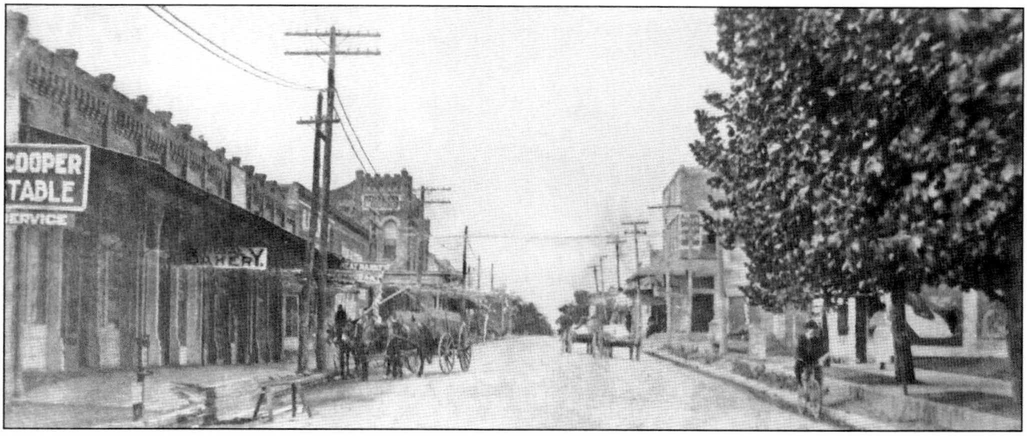


Pictured here in 1910, Third Street between Washington and Jefferson Streets was home to a number of Mount Pleasant businesses, including a stable, a bakery, and the Morris Hotel. The nearby railroad provided merchants with access to consumer goods to sell in their retail outlets and local farmers with access to markets for their agricultural products such as cotton and corn. (Courtesy of the *East Texas Journal.*)

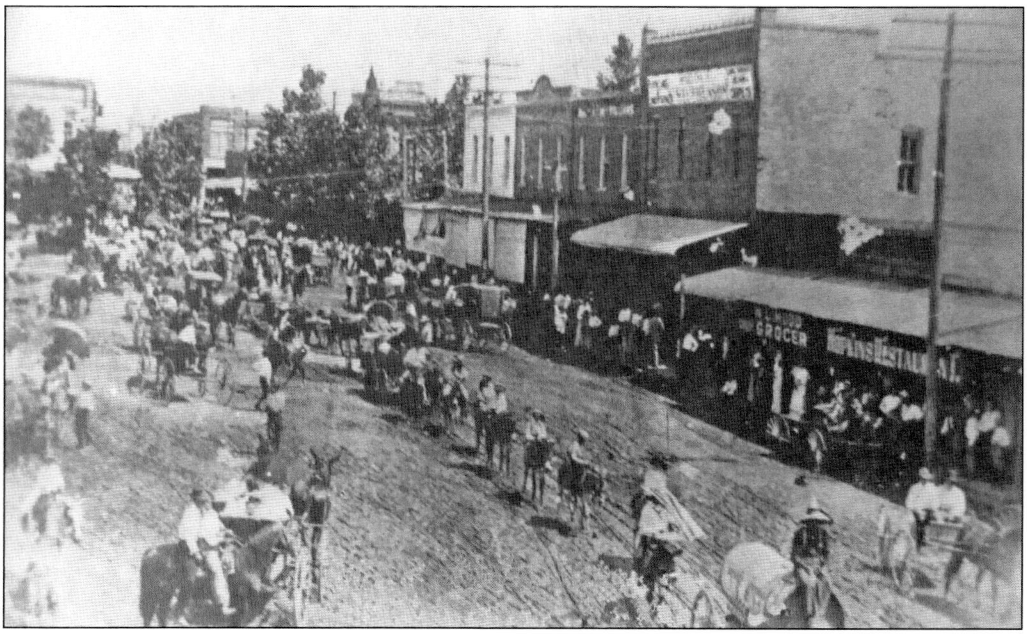


As this photograph of downtown in 1909 attests, Mount Pleasant was rapidly becoming a busy commercial hub for Northeast Texas. (Courtesy of *East Texas Journal.*)

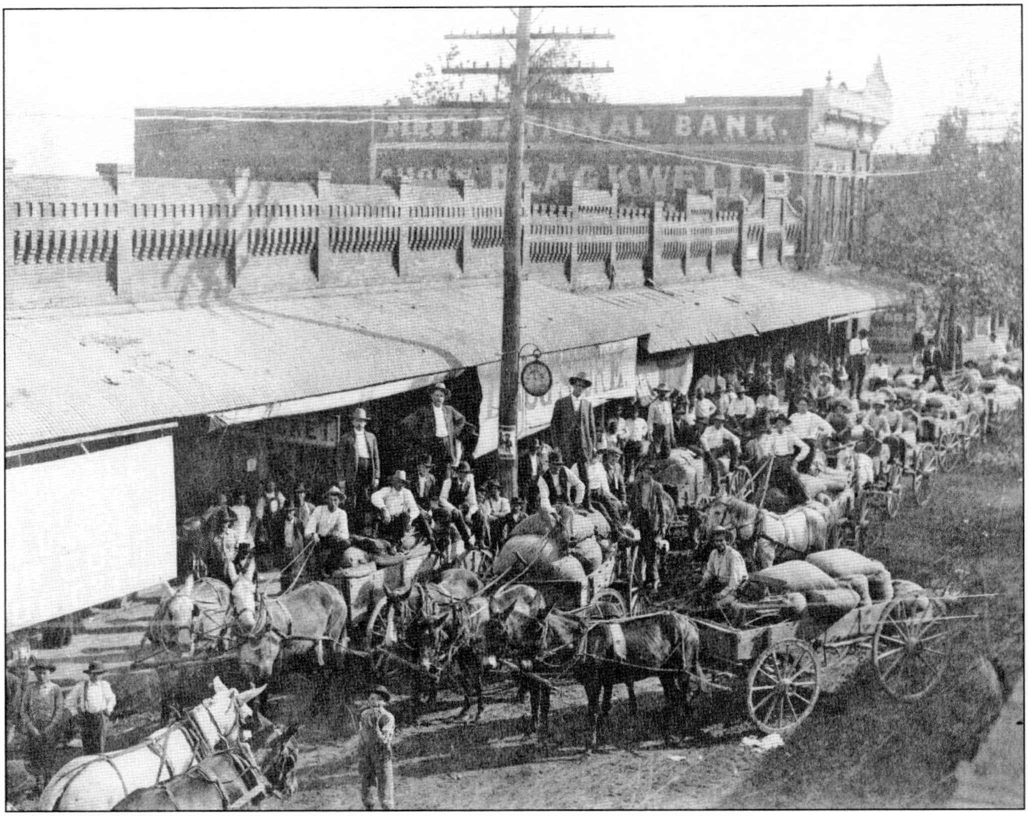

A variety of businesses, including a drugstore, a grocery store, and the First National Bank, line Jefferson Avenue looking back towards Second Street. The streets of Mount Pleasant were still unpaved in the early 20th century, and the primary means of transportation was still horse and wagon. Here, townspeople gather for a sale. (Courtesy of John Williams.)

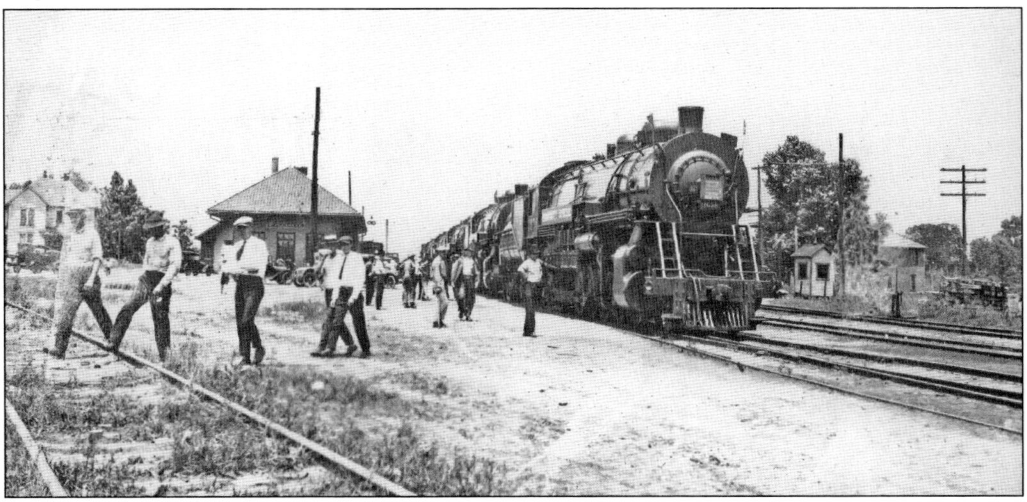

The Cotton Belt Depot, part of the Texas & St. Louis Railway, helped make Mount Pleasant a hub of transportation in the late 19th and early 20th centuries. The Texas & St. Louis was originally the Tyler Tap Railroad, which connected Mount Pleasant to Tyler in 1878. (Courtesy of the *East Texas Journal.*)

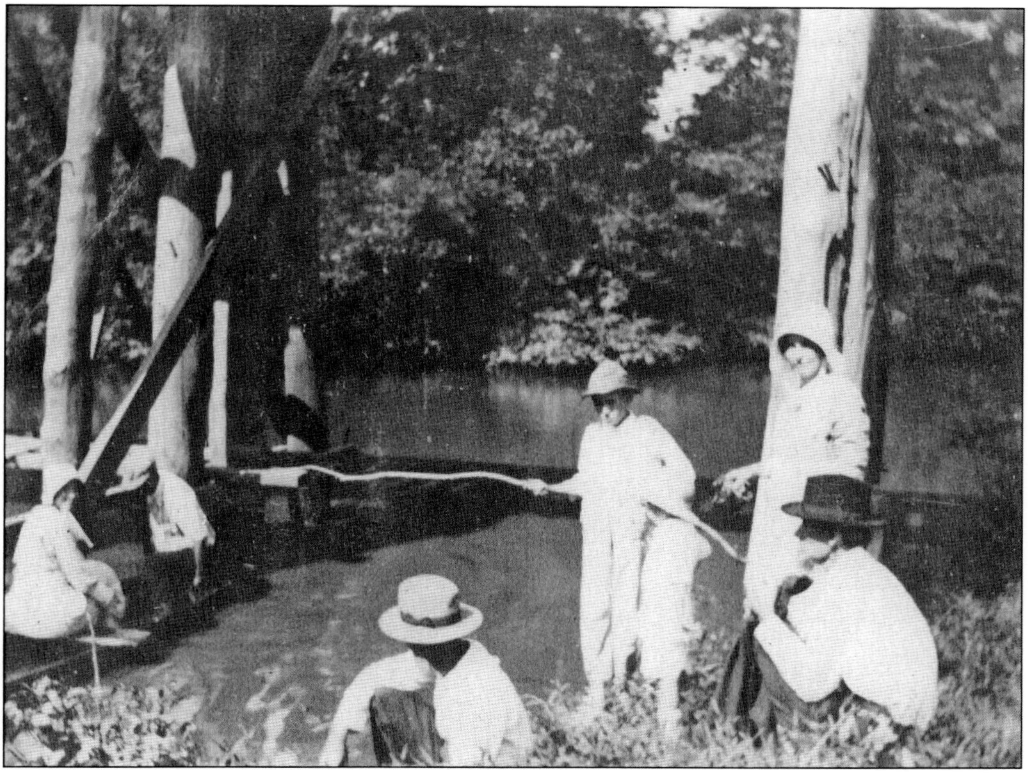

Children play under a railroad switch on the Mount Pleasant & Paris Railroad. The "Ma & Pa" was completed in 1913 and connected its two namesake towns. The railroad helped make Mount Pleasant a hub of local commerce and transportation. (Courtesy of Mount Pleasant Public Library and Historical Museum.)

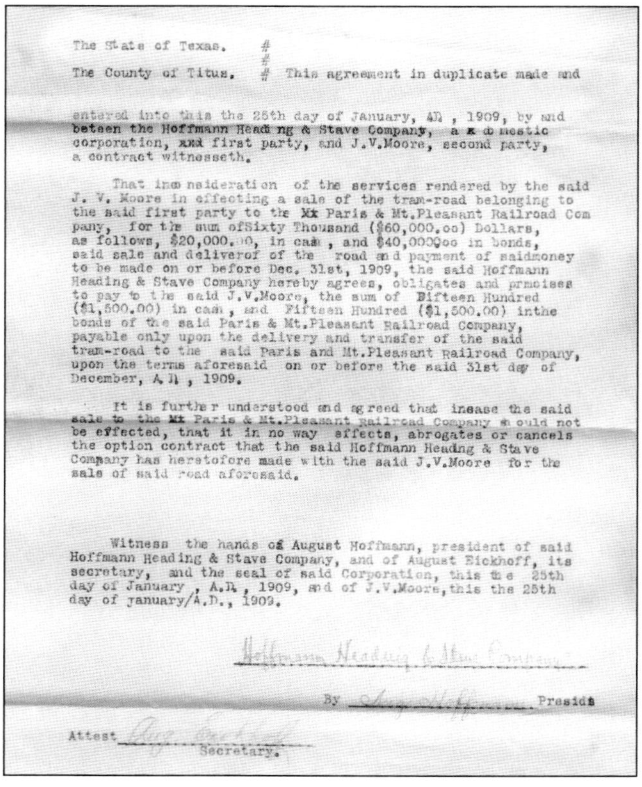

The State of Texas. #
#
The County of Titus. # This agreement in duplicate made and

entered into this the 25th day of January, AD , 1909, by and beteen the Hoffmann Heading & Stave Company, a domestic corporation, and first party, and J.V.Moore, second party, a contract witnesseth.

That in consideration of the services rendered by the said J. V. Moore in effecting a sale of the tram-road belonging to the said first party to the Paris & Mt.Pleasant Railroad Company, for the sum of Sixty Thousand ($60,000.oo) Dollars, as follows, $20,000.00, in cash , and $40,000.oo in bonds, said sale and deliverof of the road and payment of saidmoney to be made on or before Dec. 31st, 1909, the said Hoffmann Heading & Stave Company hereby agrees, obligates and prmoises to pay to the said J.V.Moore, the sum of Fifteen Hundred ($1,500.00) in cash , and Fifteen Hundred ($1,500.00) inthe bonds of the said Paris & Mt.Pleasant Railroad Company, payable only upon the delivery and transfer of the said tram-road to the said Paris and Mt.Pleasant Railroad Company, upon the terms aforesaid on or before the said 31st day of December, A.D , 1909.

It is further understood and agreed that incase the said sale to the Paris & Mt.Pleasant Railroad Company should not be effected, that it in no way effects, abrogates or cancels the option contract that the said Hoffmann Heading & Stave Company has heretofore made with the said J.V.Moore for the sale of said road aforesaid.

Witness the hands of August Hoffmann, president of said Hoffmann Heading & Stave Company, and of August Eickhoff, its secretary, and the seal of said Corporation, this the 25th day of January , A.D , 1909, and of J.V.Moore, this the 25th day of January/A.D., 1909.

Hoffmann Heading & Stave Company

By Aug. Hoffmann Presidt

Attest Aug. Eickhoff
Secretary.

This contract, signed in 1909, facilitated the completion of the Mount Pleasant & Paris Railroad a few years later in 1913. The tram railway built by the Hoffman Heading and Stave Company to move timber from the White Oak Creek Bottom to its factory in downtown Mount Pleasant was sold to the "Ma & Pa" for $60,000. (Courtesy of Mount Pleasant Public Library and Historical Museum.)

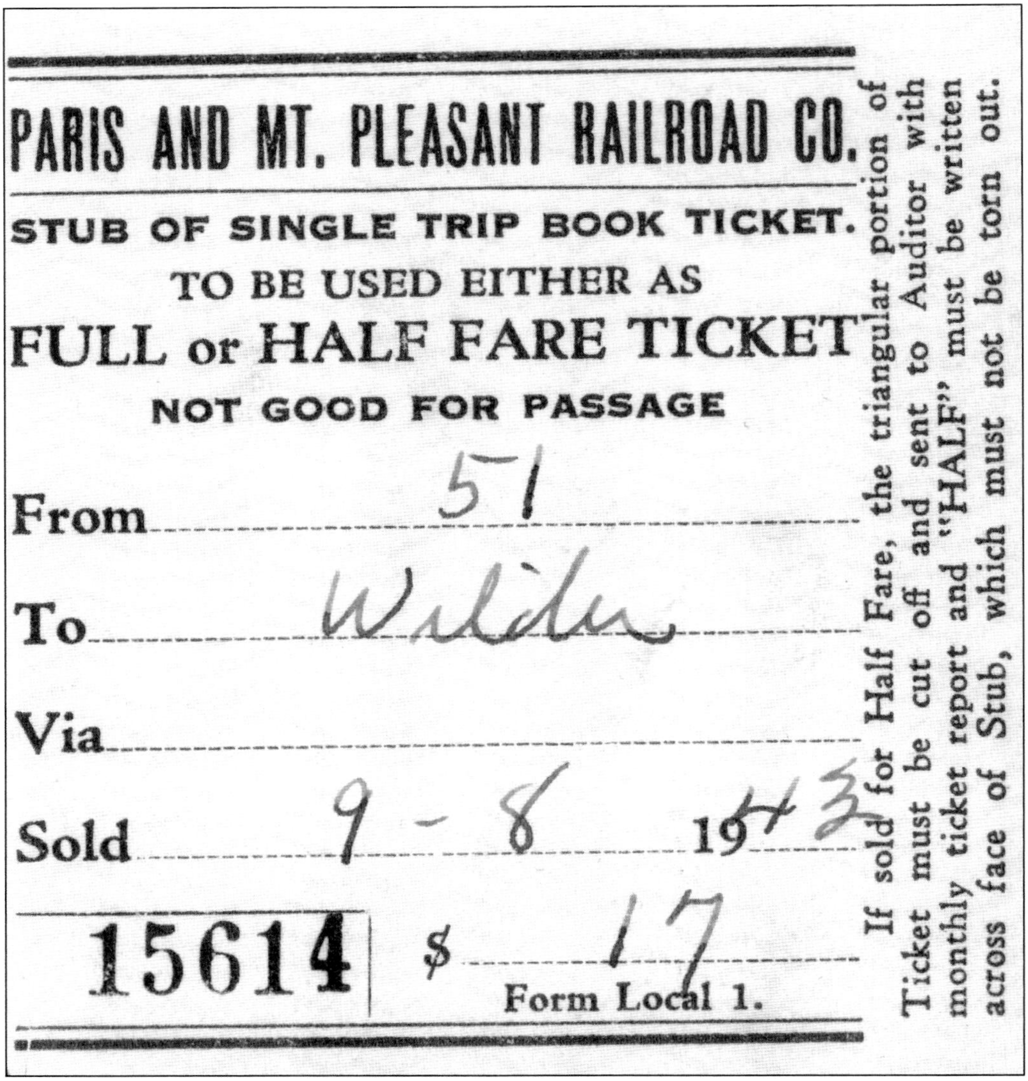

PARIS AND MT. PLEASANT RAILROAD CO.

STUB OF SINGLE TRIP BOOK TICKET.

TO BE USED EITHER AS

FULL or HALF FARE TICKET

NOT GOOD FOR PASSAGE

From 51

To Wilder

Via

Sold 9 - 8 1943

15614 $ 17

Form Local 1.

If sold for Half Fare, the triangular portion of Ticket must be cut off and sent to Auditor with monthly ticket report and "HALF" must be written across face of Stub, which must not be torn out.

Pictured here is a ticket stub from the Mount Pleasant & Paris Railroad from 1943. When it was completed in 1913, fifty miles of track connected Paris to the St. Louis Southwestern in Mount Pleasant, greatly benefiting the economies of both cities. The "Ma & Pa" operated on and off until 1956, when the St. Louis Southwestern abandoned it. (Courtesy of Mount Pleasant Public Library and Historical Museum.)

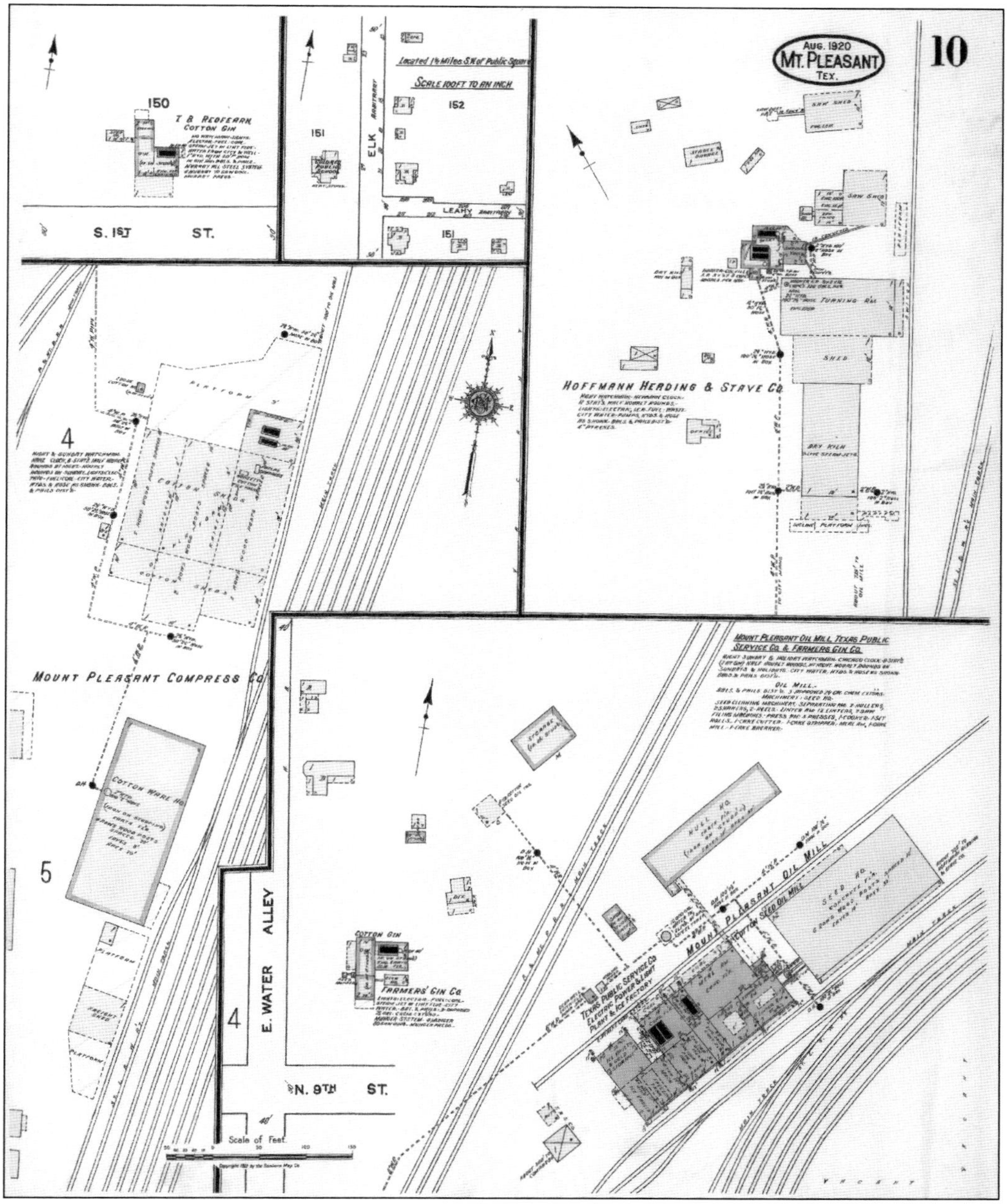


This 1920 Sanborn map demonstrates the rapid growth of industry in Mount Pleasant. A number of industries were located in the downtown area near the St. Louis Southwestern Railroad, including a cottonseed oil mill, a heading and stave factory, an ice manufacturer, a power company, and several cotton gins. (Courtesy of Dolph Briscoe Center for American History, University of Texas in Austin.)

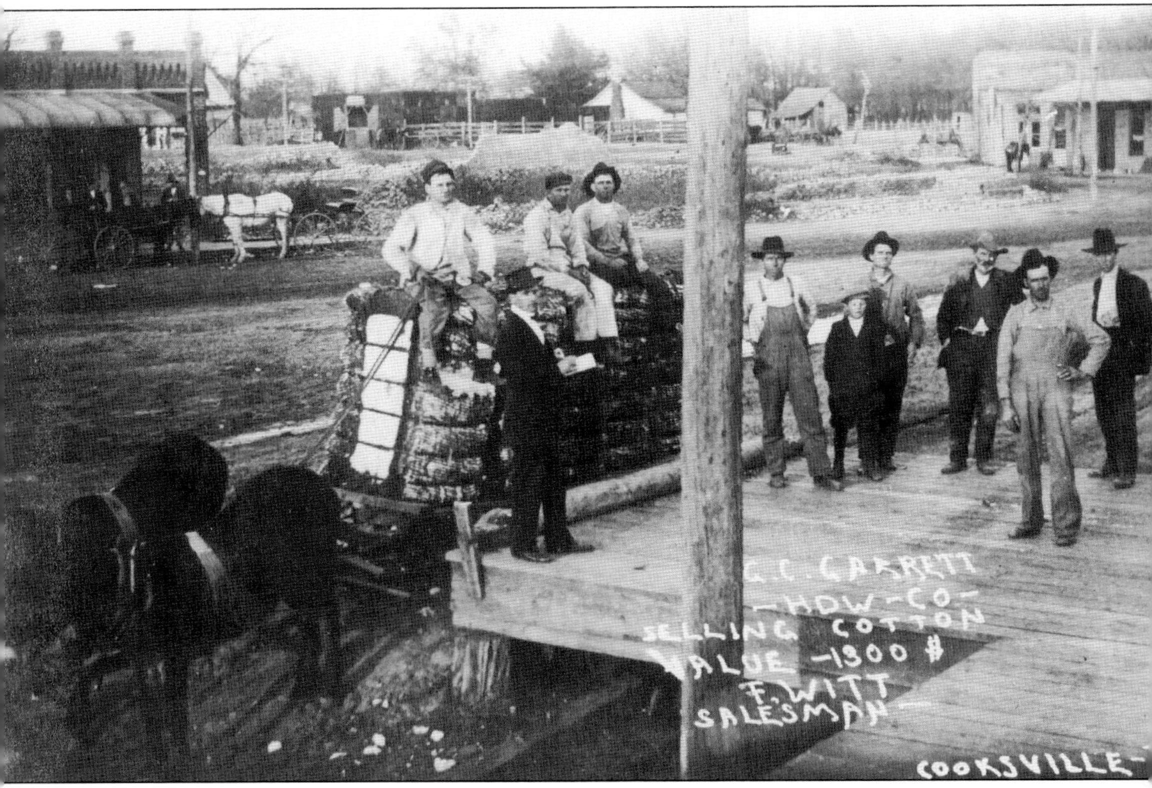


Local farmers sell cotton in Cookville just east of Mount Pleasant. Cotton remained an important staple for area farmers until the 1950s, when they largely abandoned cotton and corn agriculture for livestock. Local cotton could be processed in one of the city's many cotton gins and shipped via rail anywhere in the country. (Courtesy of Mount Pleasant Public Library and Historical Museum.)

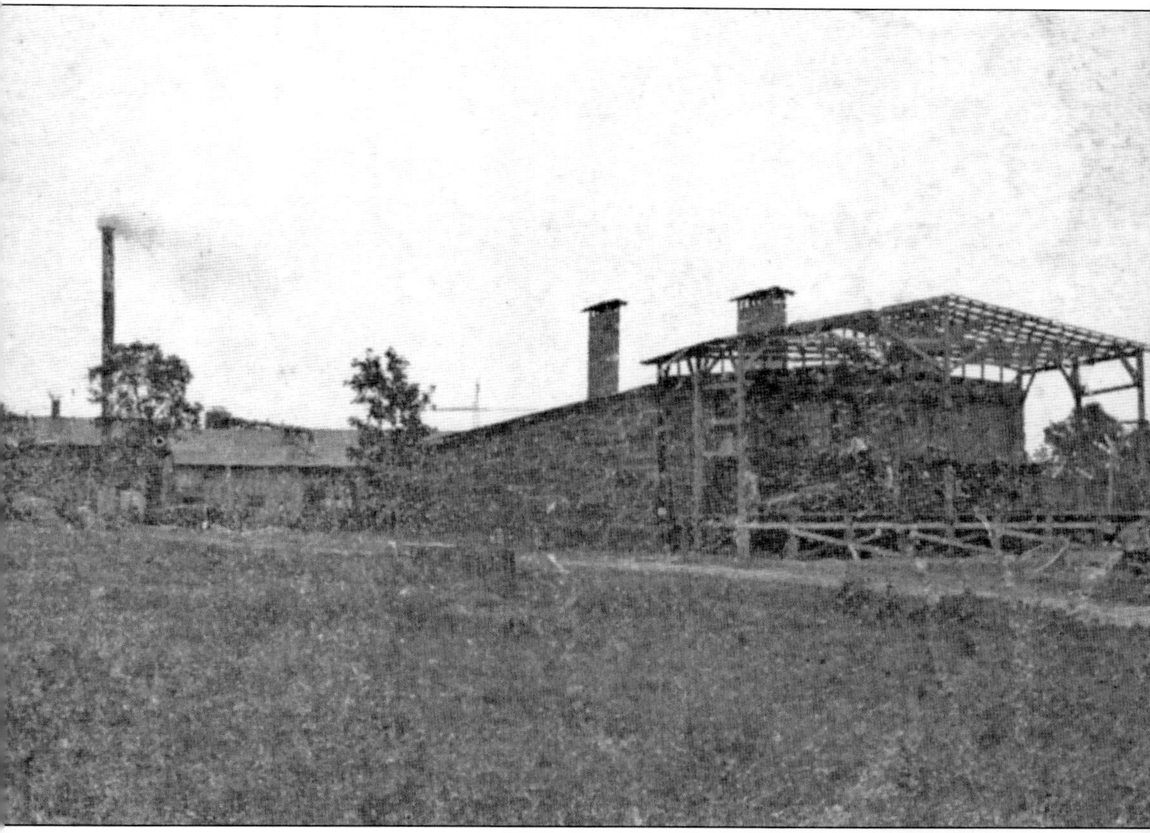

The Hoffman Heading and Stave Company was constructed in Mount Pleasant around 1906. The company manufactured headings and staves from timber in nearby White Oak Creek. Hoffman Heading and Stave was a major employer in the city during the early 20th century. (Courtesy of Mount Pleasant Public Library and Historical Museum.)

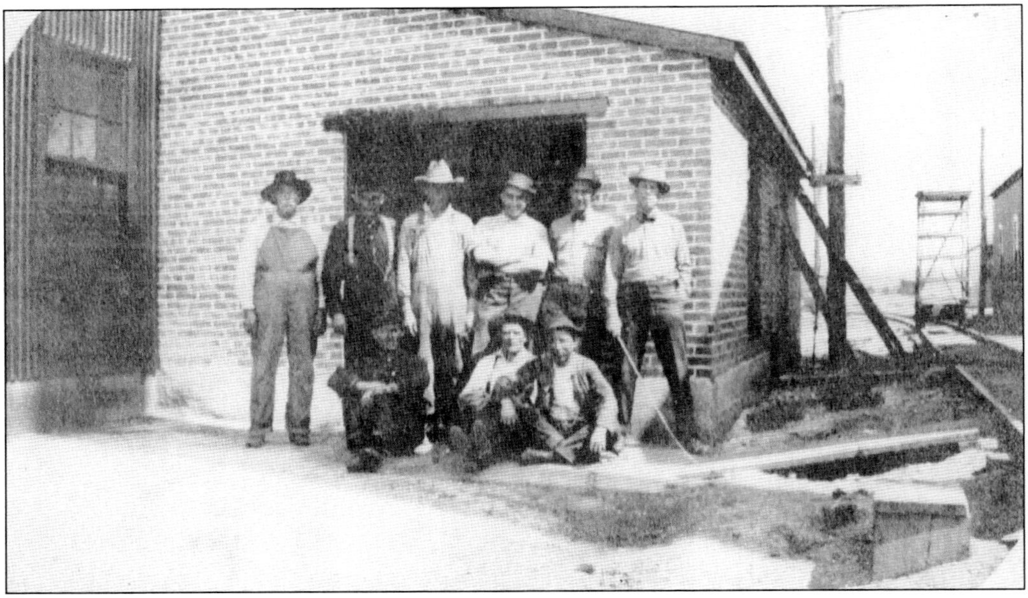

Employees of the Hoffman Heading and Stave Company are pictured here in 1911 at its location just east of the Titus County Courthouse on the St. Louis Southwestern Railroad. (Courtesy of Mount Pleasant Public Library and Historical Museum.)

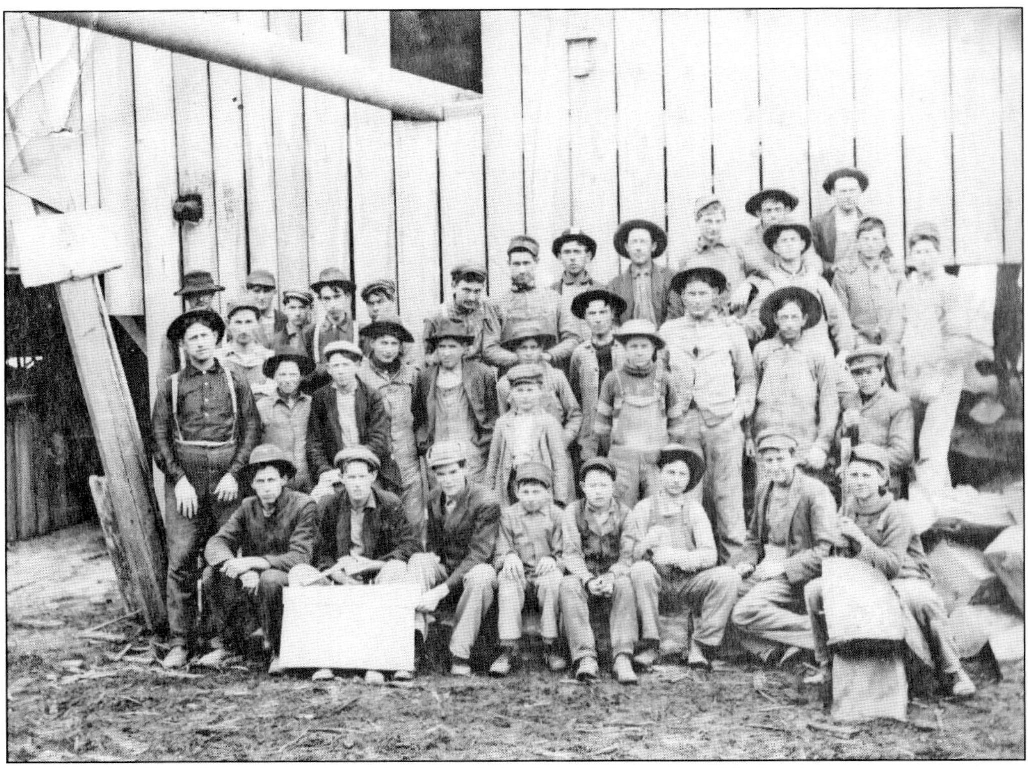

The crew of the Hoffman Heading and Stave Company in 1911 included a number of young boys. It was common for children to work in industrial jobs well into the 20th century. (Courtesy of Mount Pleasant Public Library and Historical Museum.)

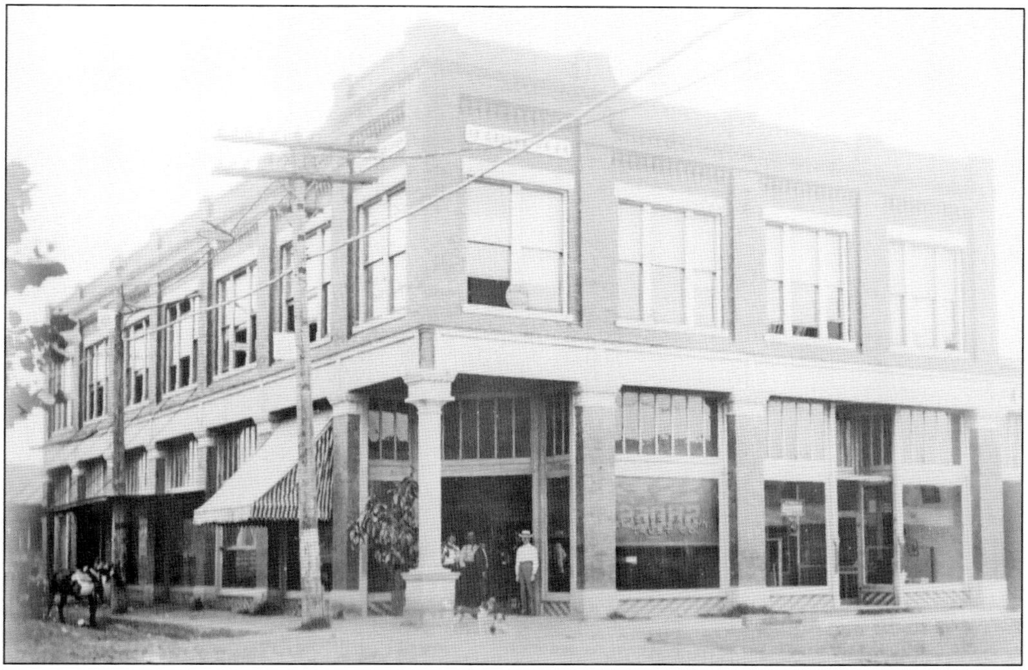

The Greenspun Building, located at Jefferson Avenue and Third Street, housed a laundry, the Citizens Trust Company, and Southwestern Bell. (Courtesy of John Williams)

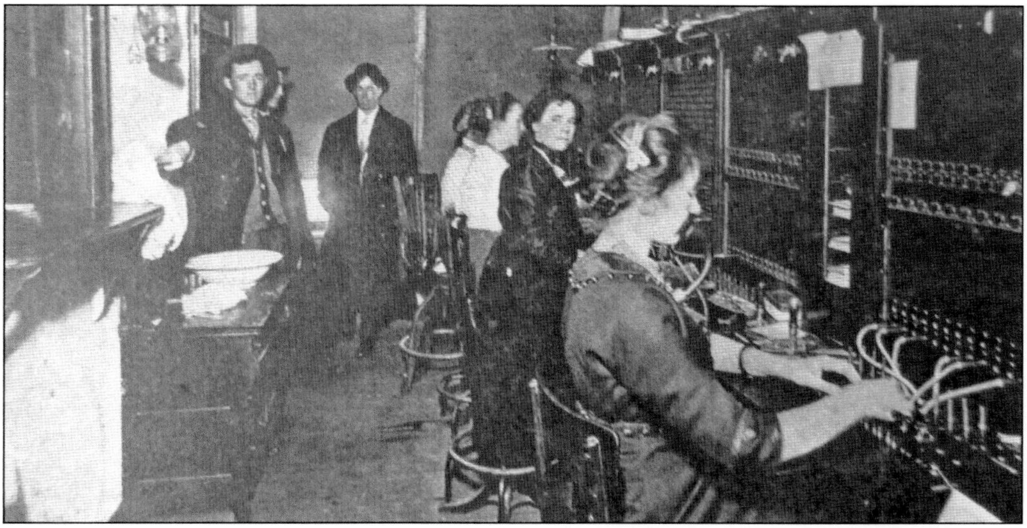

Alexander Graham Bell received the first US patent for the telephone in 1876, and switchboards were soon constructed in many of the urban centers in the Northeast. Although telephones were initially uncommon in rural areas, by 1904 there were over three million phones in the United States. Telephones quickly replaced the telegraph as the primary means of personal and business communication in the country. I.M. Greenspun owned the Mount Pleasant Telephone Company and installed the first exchange in 1902. It was housed in the Greenspun Building at Jefferson Avenue and Third Street. Joseph "Booker" Tennison, a Mount Pleasant hardware merchant, operated the exchange for a time with his two sons before going back into the hardware business. Southwestern Bell eventually purchased the Mount Pleasant Telephone Company. (Courtesy of the *East Texas Journal*.)

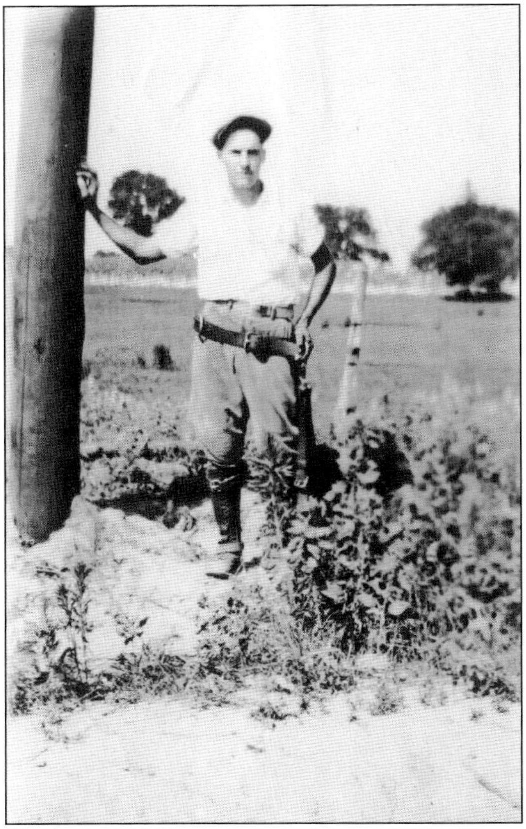

Mount Pleasant linesman Jack Pope is pictured here in the 1920s. (Courtesy of Mount Pleasant Public Library and Historical Museum.)

Frank Delgado's open-air hamburger restaurant, pictured here in 1911, served hungry customers in downtown Mount Pleasant on Washington Street between the train station and the First National Bank. (Courtesy of the *East Texas Journal*.)

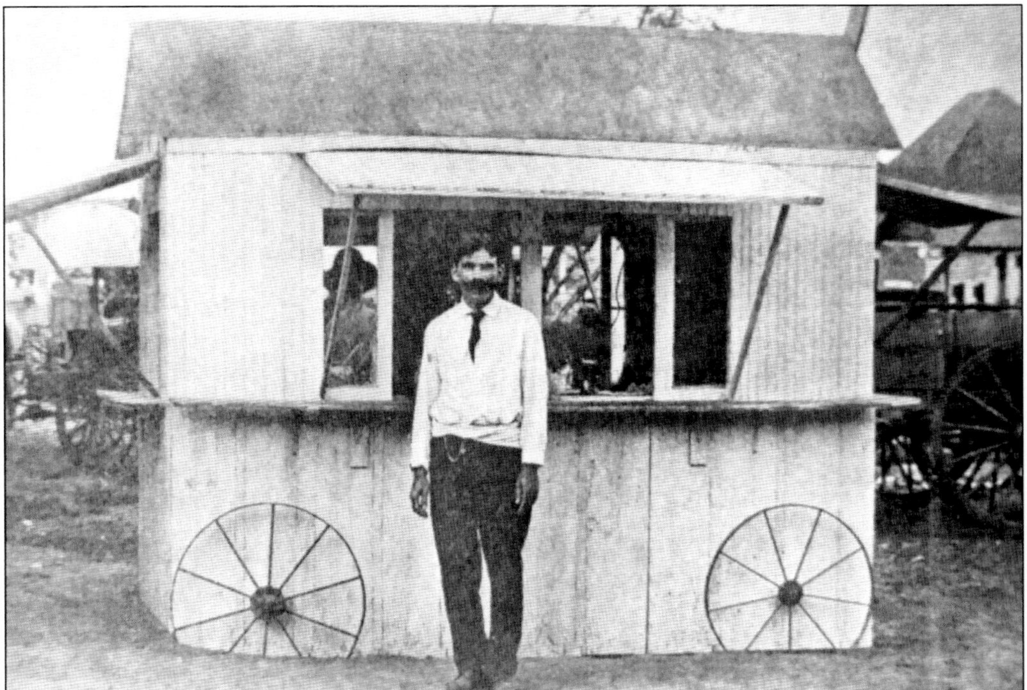

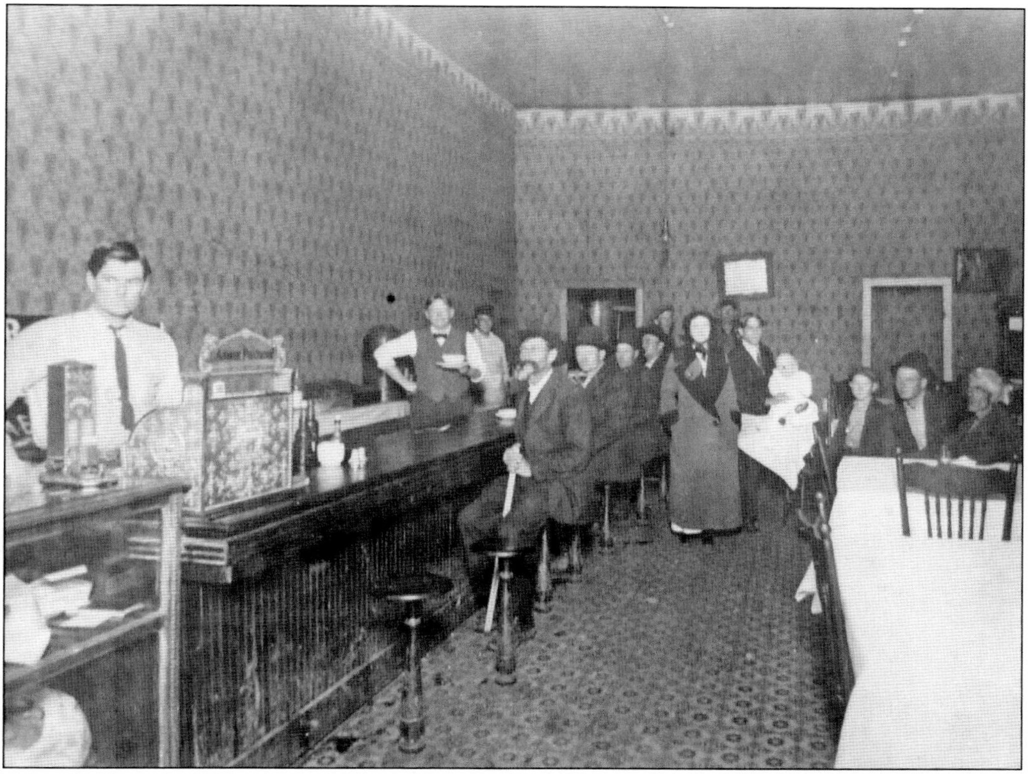

The Third Street Diner, pictured here in 1906, was one of many restaurants in early-20th-century Mount Pleasant. (Courtesy of the *East Texas Journal.*)

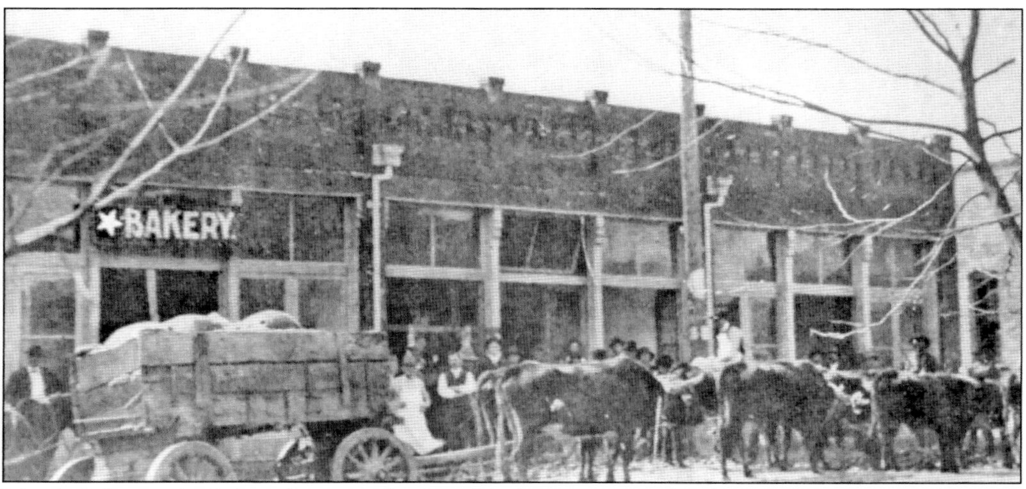


Myer's Bakery, which later became the Royal Bakery, was on Third Street between Washington and Jefferson Avenues. (Courtesy of the *East Texas Journal.*)

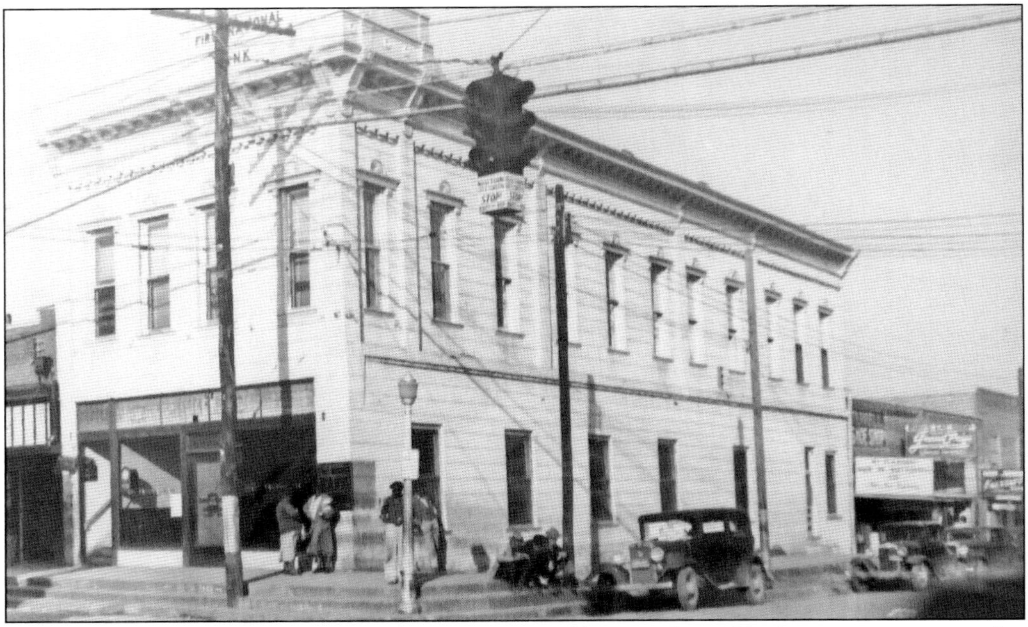

The First National Bank of Mount Pleasant, pictured here in the 1930s, began operation at this location on the corner of Jefferson Avenue and Second Street in the 1890s. Although First National is no longer in business, the building is now home to Country Cottage Florist. The Falstaff Beer sign to the right of the bank dates this photograph to the 1930s, since national Prohibition was repealed in 1933. (Courtesy of Rex Allen.)

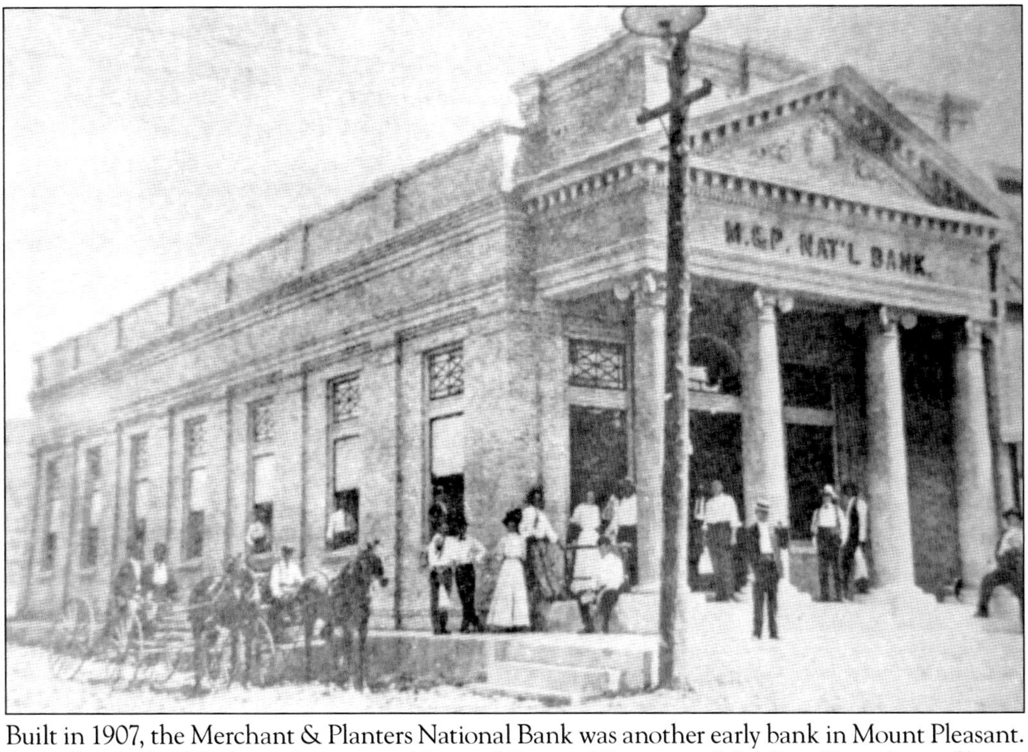


Built in 1907, the Merchant & Planters National Bank was another early bank in Mount Pleasant. It was located at Madison Avenue and Second Street. (Courtesy of the *East Texas Journal*.)

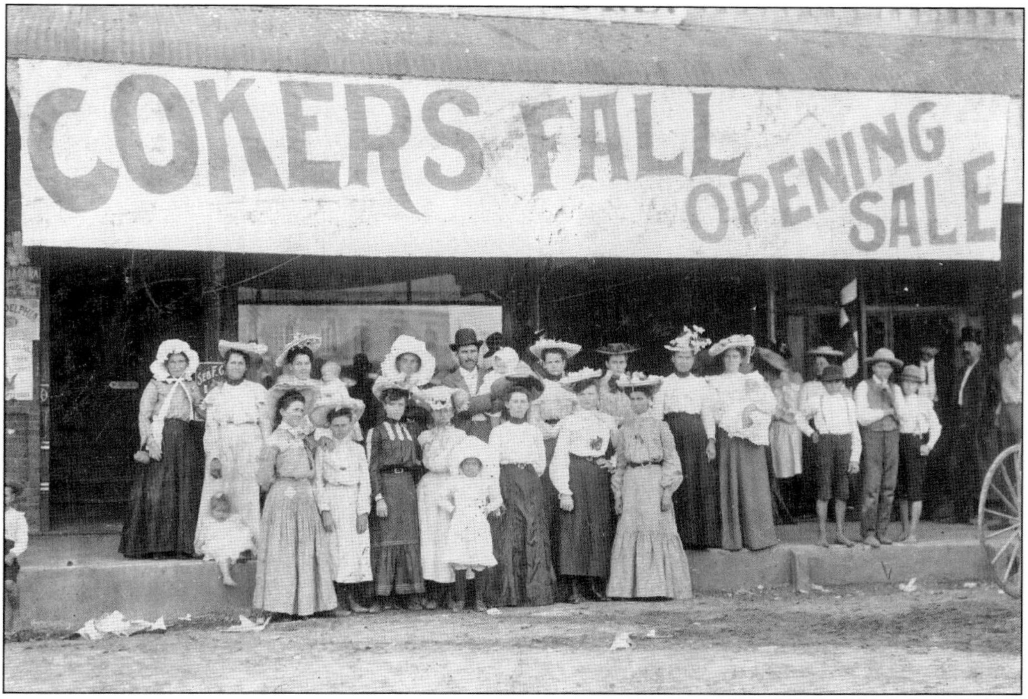


Coker's Department Store, located on the corner of Second Street and Madison Avenue, was one of many businesses built in downtown Mount Pleasant as the city grew in the early 20th century. To encourage customers to come to its fall opening sale in 1904, Coker's gave a free pair of shoes to the customer who brought the largest group to the store. The winner, H.M. Combs, brought the group pictured here in front of the store. (Courtesy of the *East Texas Journal.*)

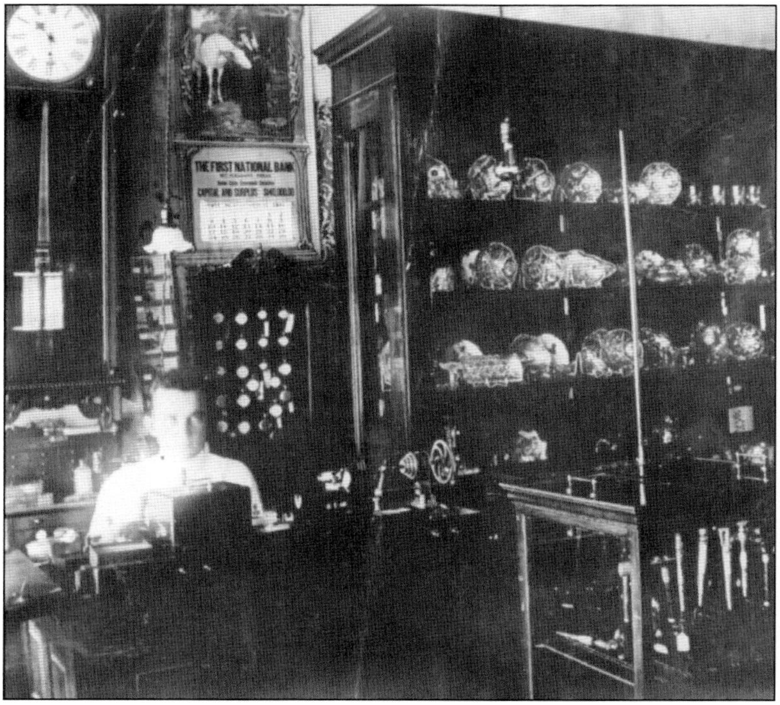


Hamilton's Jewelry first opened in 1904 on Jefferson Avenue between Second and Third Streets. The original store shared space with the Wallace Drug Store. Joseph Benjamin Hamilton, pictured here in 1911, operated the business until 1938. (Courtesy of Barry Hamilton.)

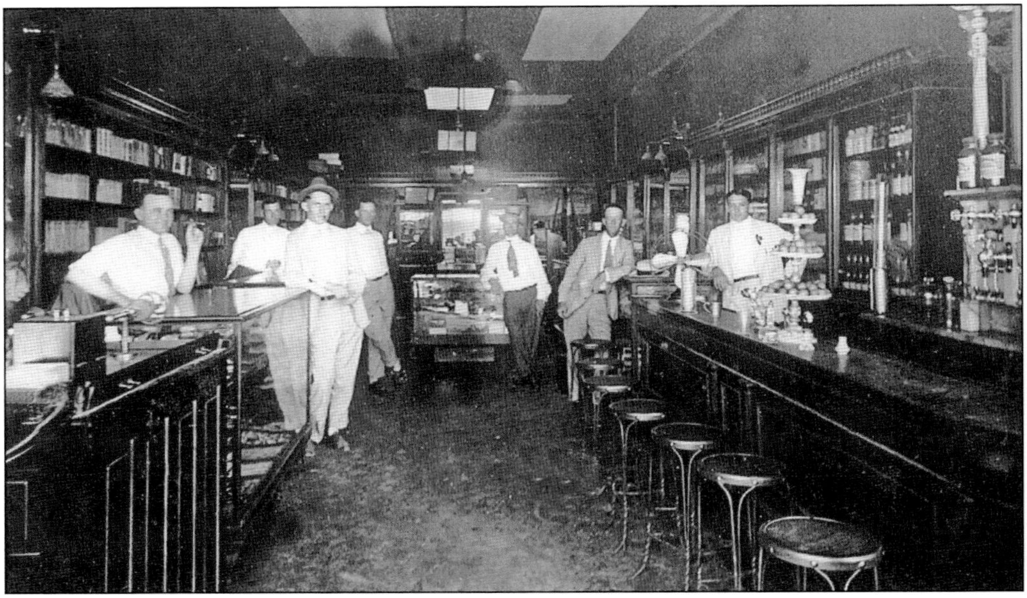

Wallace Drug and Hamilton Jewelry shared space in a building on Jefferson Avenue between Second and Third Streets. Pictured here in 1908 are, from left to right, Joseph Hamilton, Percy E. Wallace, Lee Wallace, and Addie Wallace. (Courtesy of Barry Hamilton.)

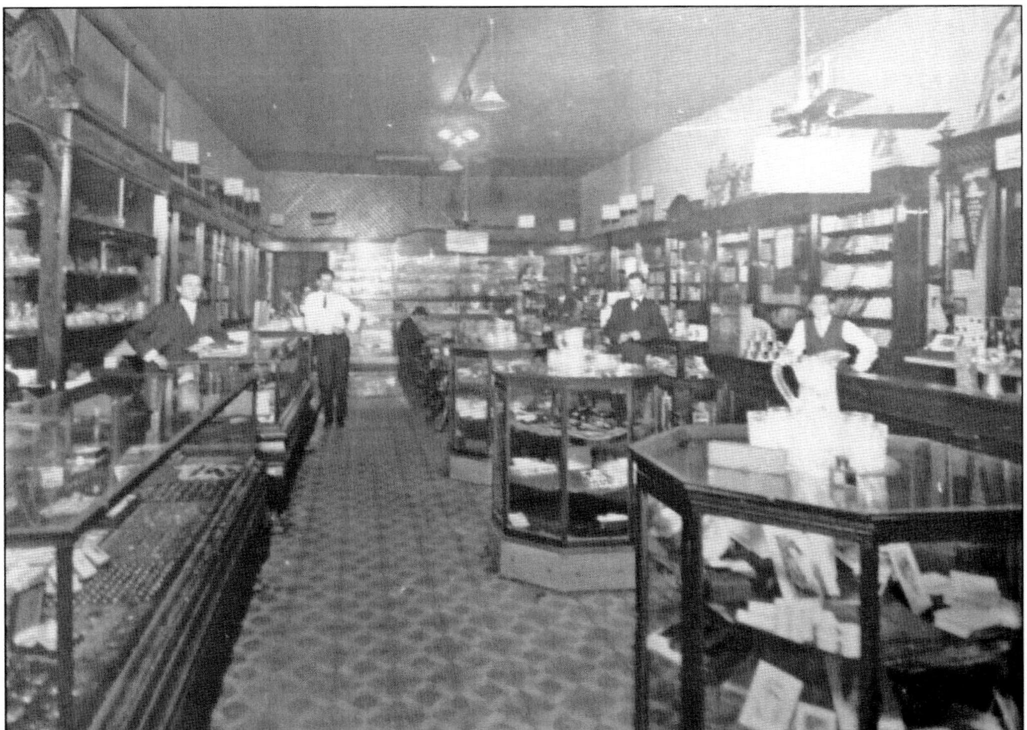

Hamilton Jewelry remained on Jefferson Avenue until 1945, but by the 1920s, the business had relocated a few doors down to the Stevens Drug Store. Pictured here are Joseph Hamilton (far left) and John B. Stevens (second from left). Stevens owned a number of other businesses, including the Stevens Hotel, and was the first city marshal. (Courtesy of Barry Hamilton.)

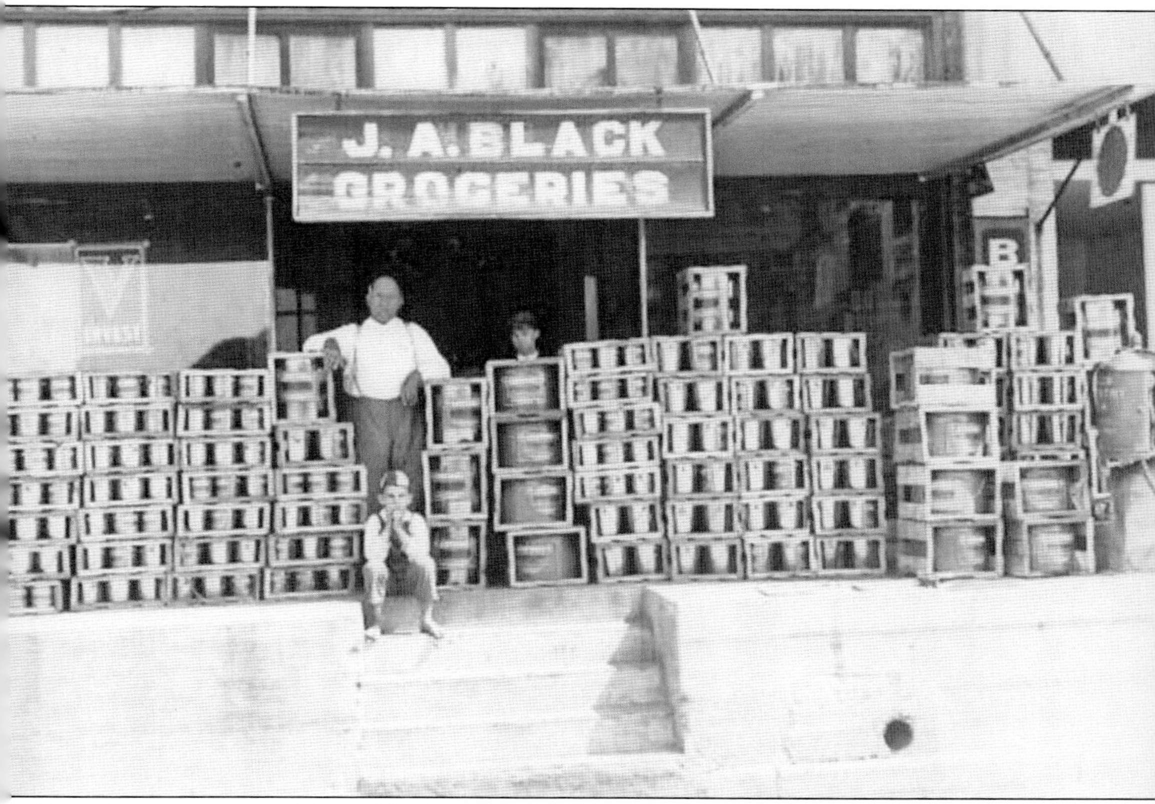


One of many grocers in Mount Pleasant, J.A. Black, pictured here in front of his store in 1917, owned a grocery store in Indiana before moving to Texas in the early 1900s. (Courtesy of Mount Pleasant Public Library and Historical Museum.)

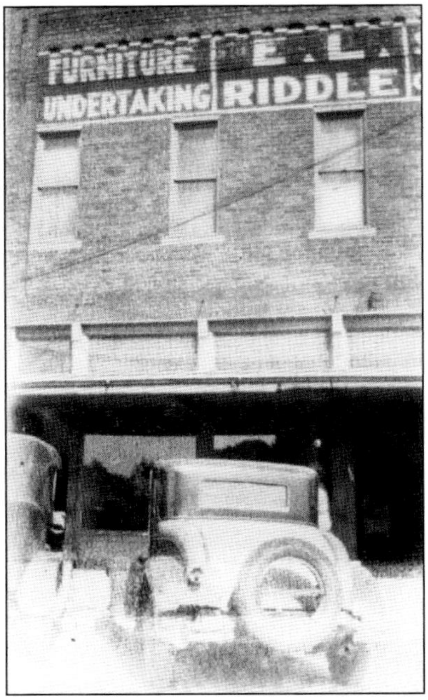


As indicated in this photograph of Riddle Furniture in the 1920s, undertaking was a common side line for furniture businesses of the era. At one time, American families took care of their dead on their own, holding a vigil or visiting in the home and hiring a carpenter to make a coffin to be used for burial in a family graveyard. Starting in the mid-19th century, furniture dealers, who had sold coffins, began to offer to "undertake" all the after-death responsibilities, relieving the family of those arrangements. The concept of a separate business offering only those after-death responsibilities, a funeral home, would not become common until later in the 20th century. (Courtesy of the *East Texas Journal.*)

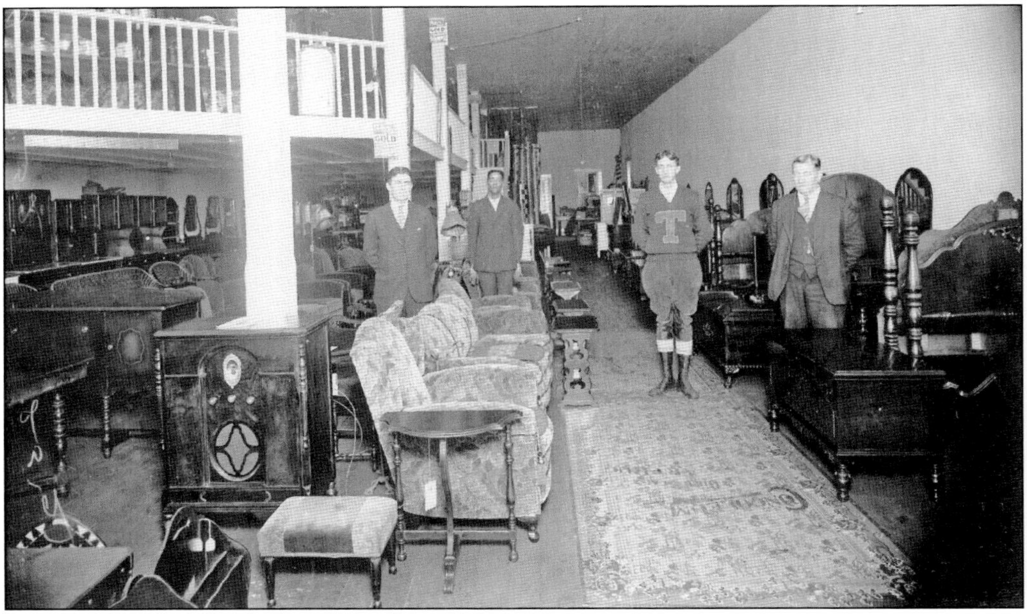

Riddle operated a thriving business in the downtown area with a wide array of products, such as furniture, sewing machines, and carpets, as well as undertaking. Riddle's success was the result of a local boy's hard work. Elam L. Riddle, born in 1871, lived his whole life in Mount Pleasant. As a youngster, he worked in the furniture and hardware store of H.W. Cheney. When Cheney sold the store to Fuller & Swint, Riddle continued working as a clerk in the same store. In 1906, Riddle had the experience and the means to go from clerk to owner and partnered with John Stephenson to buy Oscar Lilienstern's furniture store. Riddle continued to climb up the entrepreneurial ladder by buying Stephenson out and becoming sole owner in 1920. He operated the store as the E.L. Riddle Furniture Company until his death in 1948. Riddle's sons ran the business until they sold it in 1973. (Courtesy of the *East Texas Journal.*)

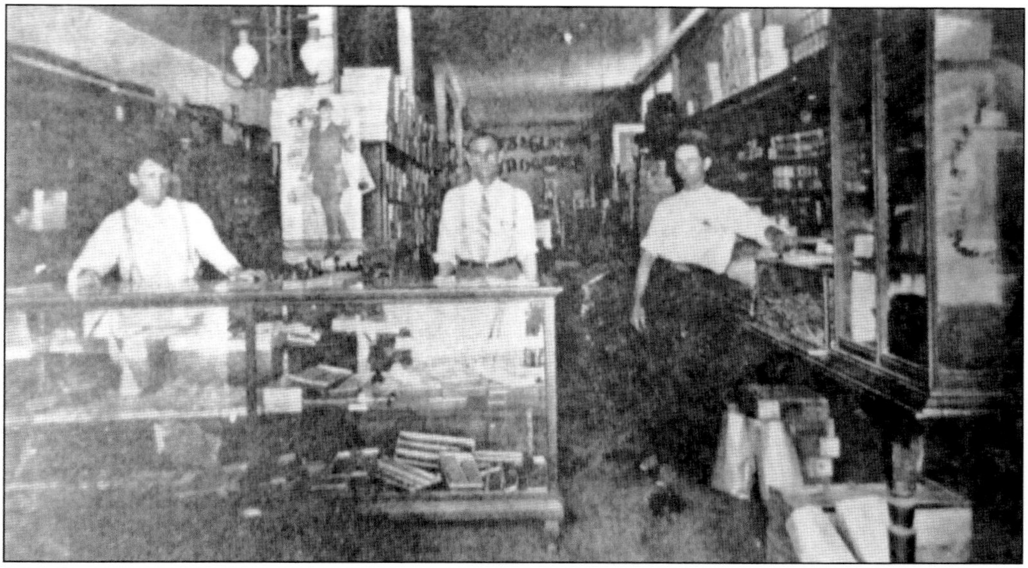

Charles Oscar Lide also took advantage of the economic opportunities in Mount Pleasant for hard-working individuals to become independent businessmen. Lide moved to Mount Pleasant in 1887 and worked as a clerk for T.C. Morris for several years. Then he, Jeff Tingle, and T.W. Vaughan started a dry goods store known as Lide-Tingle-Vaughan. In 1893, Lide bought out his partners. In 1920, the C.W. Webber dry goods store, which faced North Jefferson Avenue, burned. Lide bought this store and connected the two buildings. The resultant new store had fronts on the second block of North Jefferson and the first block of West Second Street. This made it the largest dry goods store in Mount Pleasant at the time. (Courtesy of the *East Texas Journal*.)

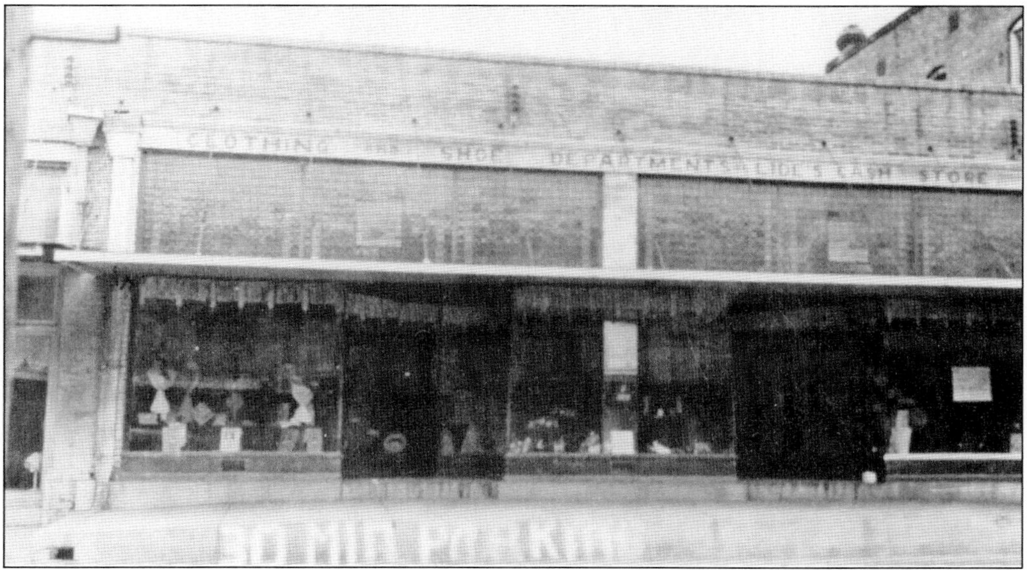

Lide's, a typical small-town department store of the 1920s, offered urban residents consumer goods that had previously only been available in mail-order catalogs. Dean and Charles Lide, sons of Charles Oscar Lide, sold the business to J.C. Penney in 1927. This photograph, taken in 1929, shows J.C. Penney on Jefferson Avenue between Second and Third Streets, across the street from what is currently Glyn's Western Wear. (Courtesy of Mount Pleasant Public Library and Historical Museum.)

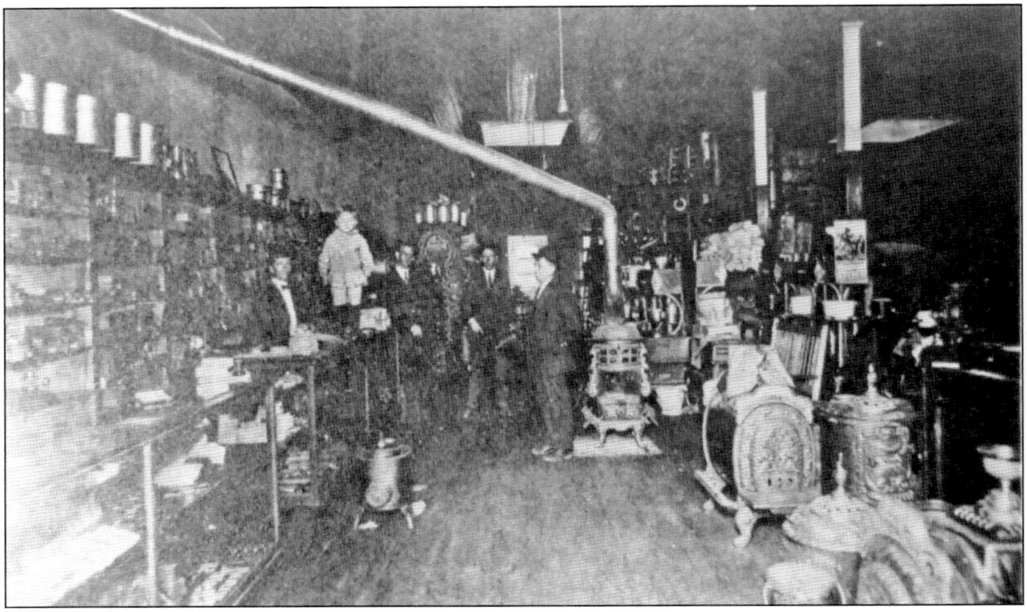

In addition to several furniture and dry goods stores, Mount Pleasant boasted several hardware stores. R.H. Meadows Hardware Store was originally located on Madison Avenue between First and Second Streets but had relocated to Jefferson Avenue by 1917. (Courtesy of the *East Texas Journal.*)

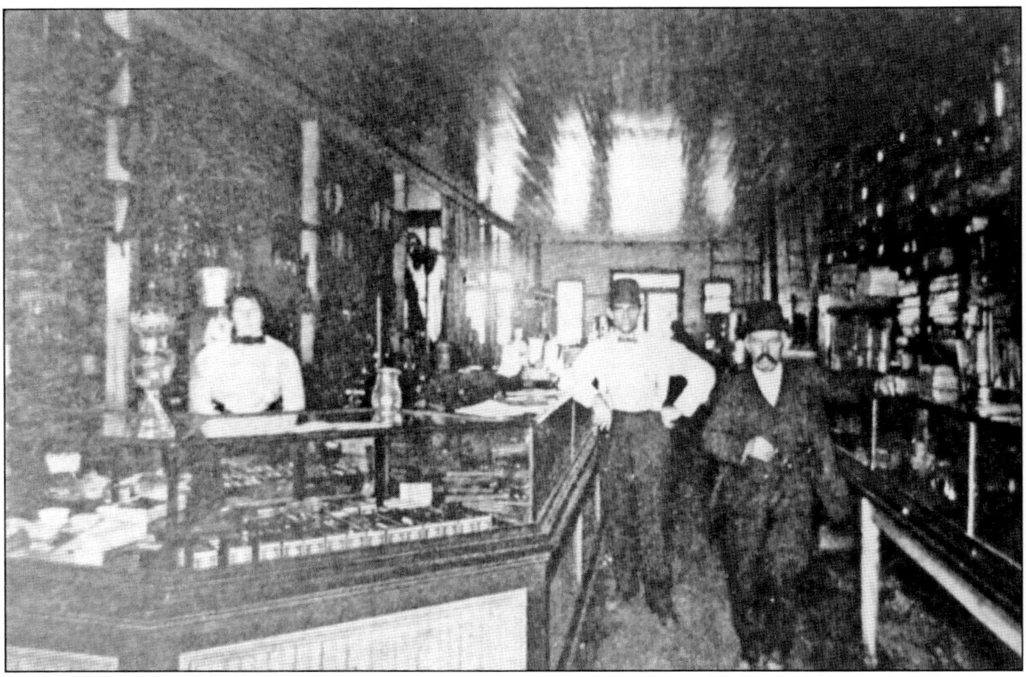

Established in 1906, Roger's Hardware served the needs of residents from its location on Madison Avenue between First and Second Streets. Pictured here are, from left to right, Mary Rogers Crigler, Mellie Rogers, and the store's owner, M.C. Rogers. (Courtesy of the *East Texas Journal.*)

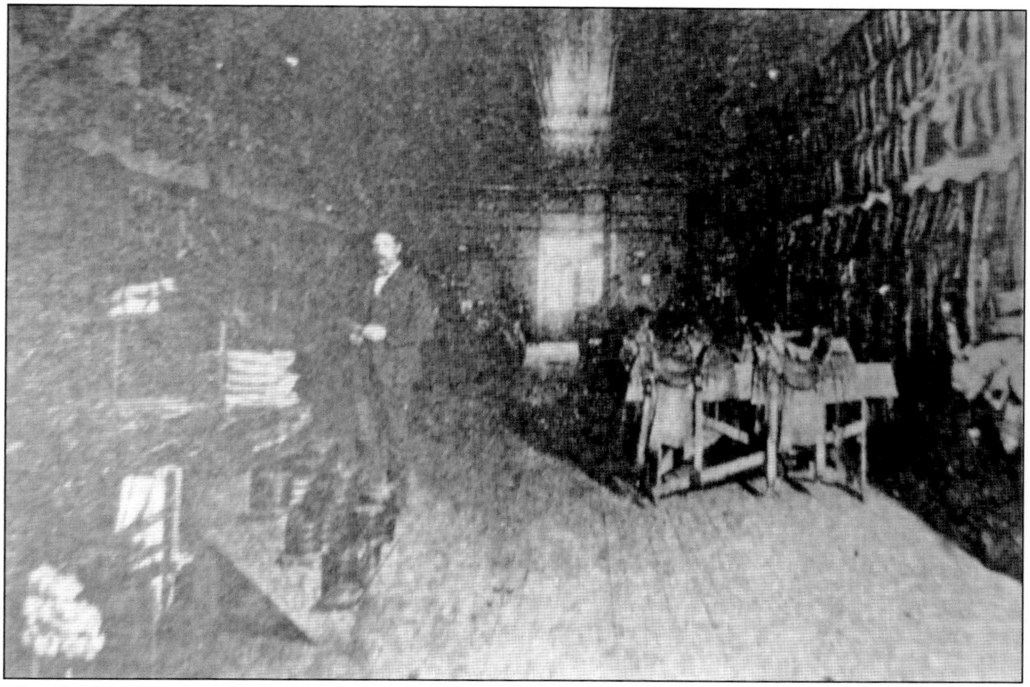

The R.H. Fuller Saddle and Harness Store was located on Second Street between Madison and Jefferson Avenues. Businesses that sold saddles and other horse tack were common in Mount Pleasant before the automobile replaced the horse as the primary means of transportation in the 1920s. (Courtesy of the *East Texas Journal*.)

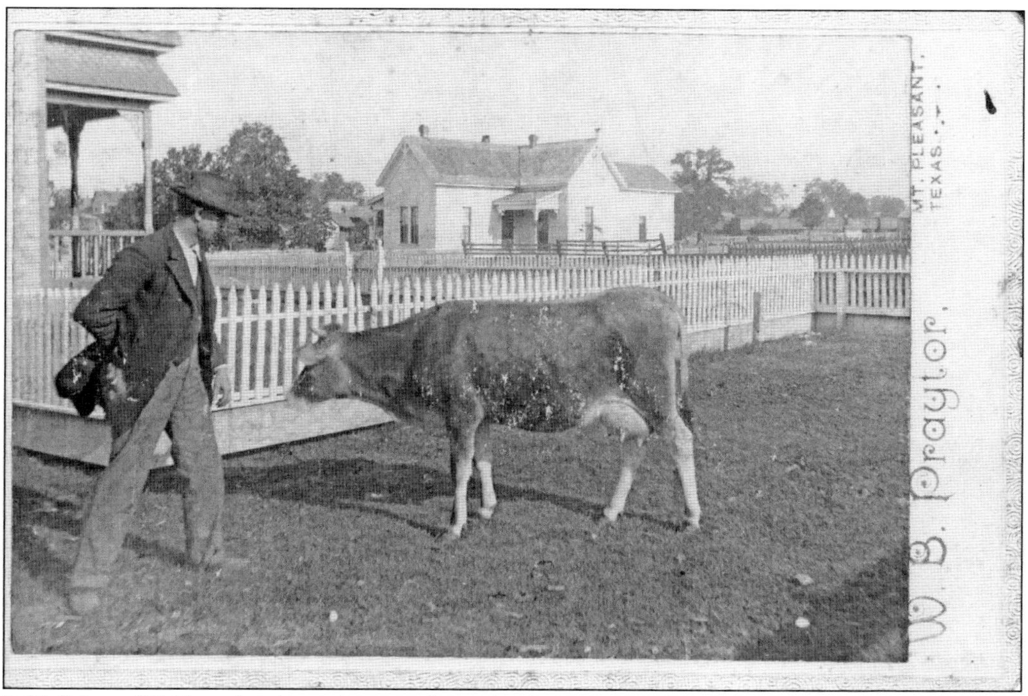


R.H. "Henry" Fuller, a local merchant and civic leader, is pictured here with his milk cow. (Courtesy of Mount Pleasant Public Library and Historical Museum.)

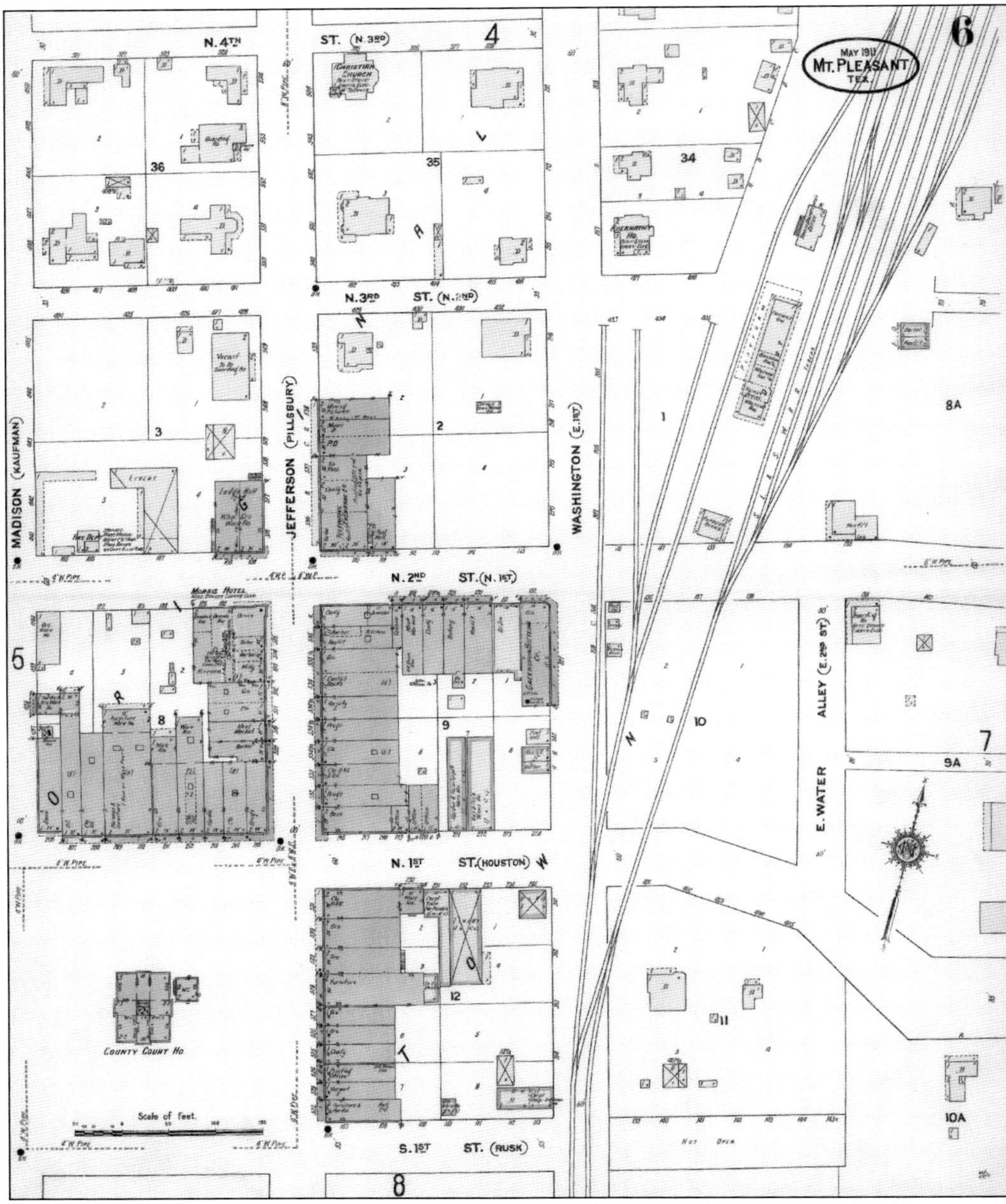


This 1911 Sanborn map of downtown Mount Pleasant illustrates the rapid growth of business in the city during the early 20th century. This map makes evident the wide variety of businesses located on Second and Third Streets between Madison and Jefferson Avenues. Hotels, restaurants, banks, drugstores, bookstores, and grocery stores are all visible, as well as the Titus County Courthouse and the Mount Pleasant Fire Department. (Courtesy of Dolph Briscoe Center for American History, University of Texas in Austin.)

# *Three*

# Expansion

In the aftermath of World War I, national interest in developing a transcontinental highway resulted in the Bankhead Highway. The road, which ran through Mount Pleasant, linked Washington, DC, with San Diego, California, and set the stage for further expansion of the city. Mount Pleasant dealt successfully with chronic flooding problems by building better roads and improved bridges, eliminating the need for cumbersome ferry transport over portions of the local waterways and allowing for continued expansion of the city.

But the decade that followed brought painful economic contraction. The agricultural economy, which had always been the mainstay of Mount Pleasant, suffered significantly. The town's population decreased between 1920 and 1930 as people sought opportunity elsewhere. But Mount Pleasant entered the Depression as resilient as always. In 1936, the Talco Oil Fields temporarily brought in oil. The citizens of Mount Pleasant benefited from New Deal initiatives by refurbishing their schools and building a golf course and lake.

When World War II came, the men and women of Mount Pleasant continued their long-standing tradition of patriotically supporting their country.

After the war, the Eisenhower Interstate System began building a modern transportation system to replace the overloaded existing highway system. Mount Pleasant lies on one of the last sections built on Interstate 30. The city became the site of the first Wal-Mart in the state of Texas. With more than 17,000 acres of lakes, it is also the "Bass Capital of Texas." The first map of Mount Pleasant shows a candy store as one of its first establishments. Many decades and candy stores later, Mount Pleasant garnered the nickname "Sweetest Town in Texas." Several trailer-manufacturing plants operate in the city, earning it the moniker "Trailer Manufacturing Capital" of the United States. Looking to the future, Mount Pleasant (in conjunction with neighboring Morris and Franklin Counties) established a community college to serve the needs of its citizenry. As suits a city lying atop red, white, and blue mineral springs, Mount Pleasant was declared a "Main Street City" in 1993 by the Texas Historical Commission and has been a nationally recognized program since 2010. The city is also claimed to be one of the 100 best small towns in America.

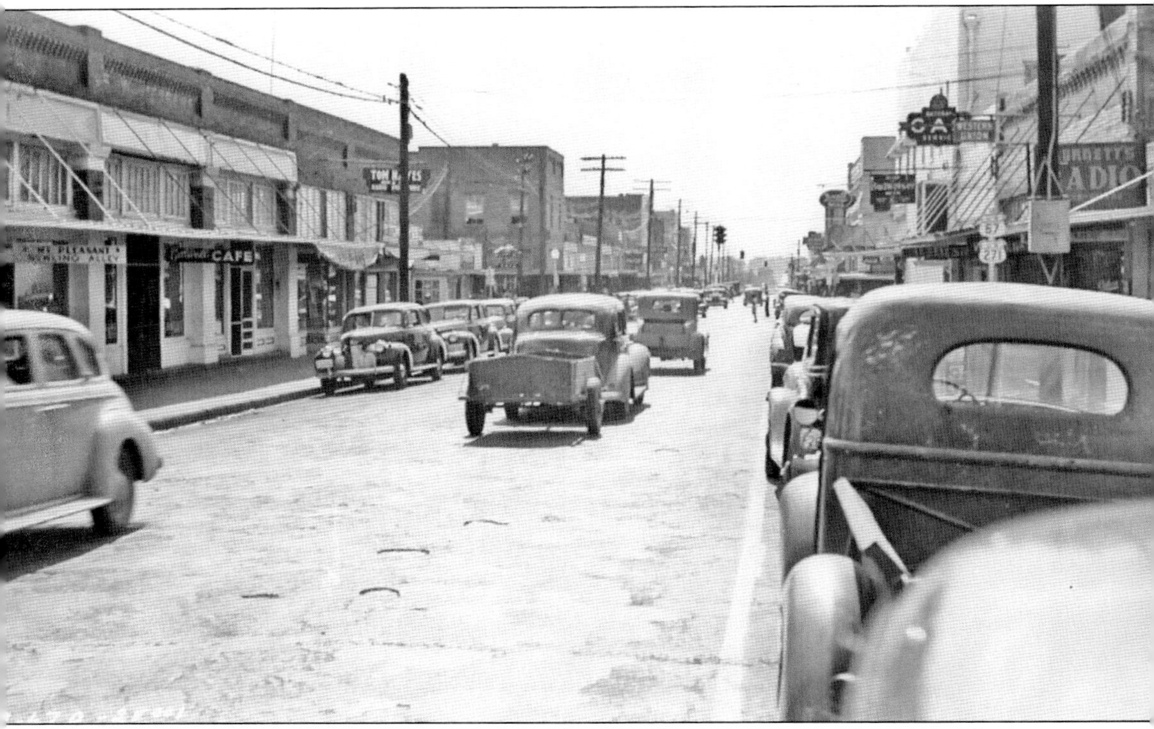


Mount Pleasant from its very beginning owed its growth to its geographic location at the intersection of various transportation options. So it should be no surprise that early-20th-century innovations in transportation once again included Mount Pleasant. In 1916, the Good Roads Movement pushed the idea of creating a truly transcontinental highway. The Bankhead Highway, America's first such came through Mount Pleasant along the way. This photograph shows the Bankhead Highway as it came through town. A bowling alley, a Western Union office, two cafés, and a drugstore are visible alongside the road. (Courtesy of *East Texas Journal*.)

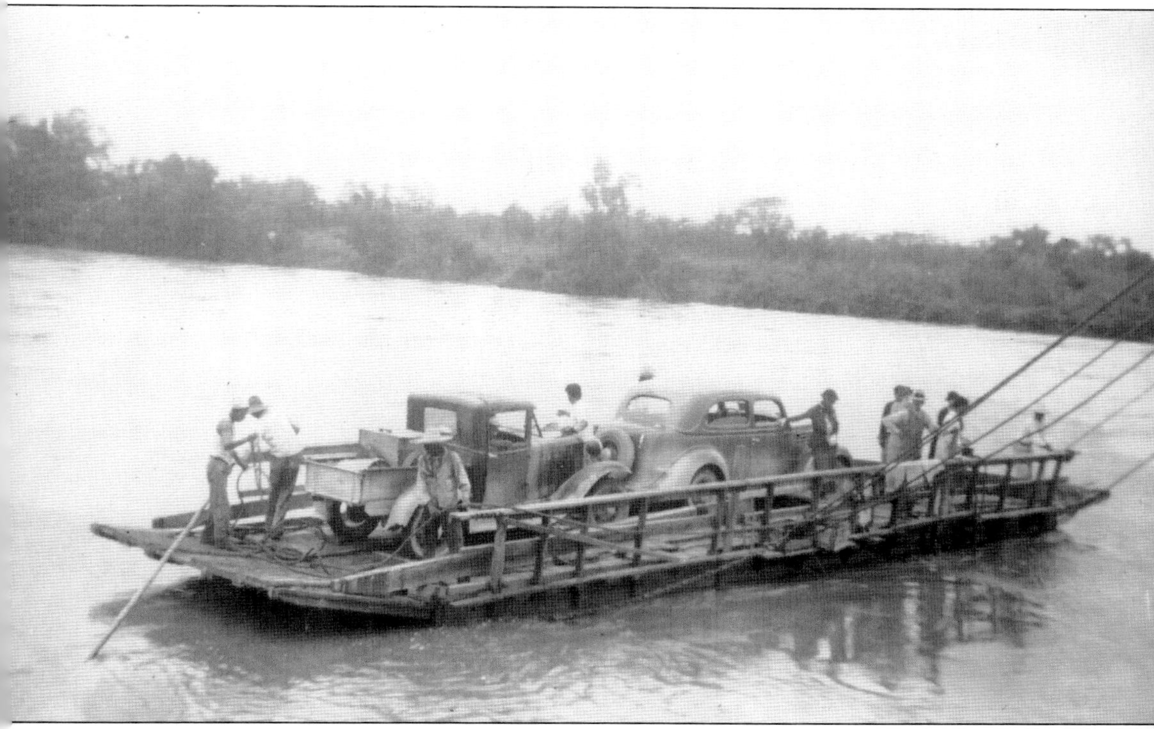

Other transportation options around Mount Pleasant were not always so easy to use. From the very beginning, Mount Pleasant sustained occasional flooding from the numerous rivers and creeks that helped to make it such a pleasant location in the first place. Residents often offered rooms to stranded travelers during the rainy season. Navigating and crossing creeks continued to be an issue until highway bridges provided easy crossings. Here, automobiles are being ferried across the Sulphur River just north of downtown Mount Pleasant. The ferry at Jones Crossing dates back to the mid-19th century, when Mount Pleasant pioneer Henry Jones operated the original ferry at this location. (Courtesy of the *East Texas Journal*.)

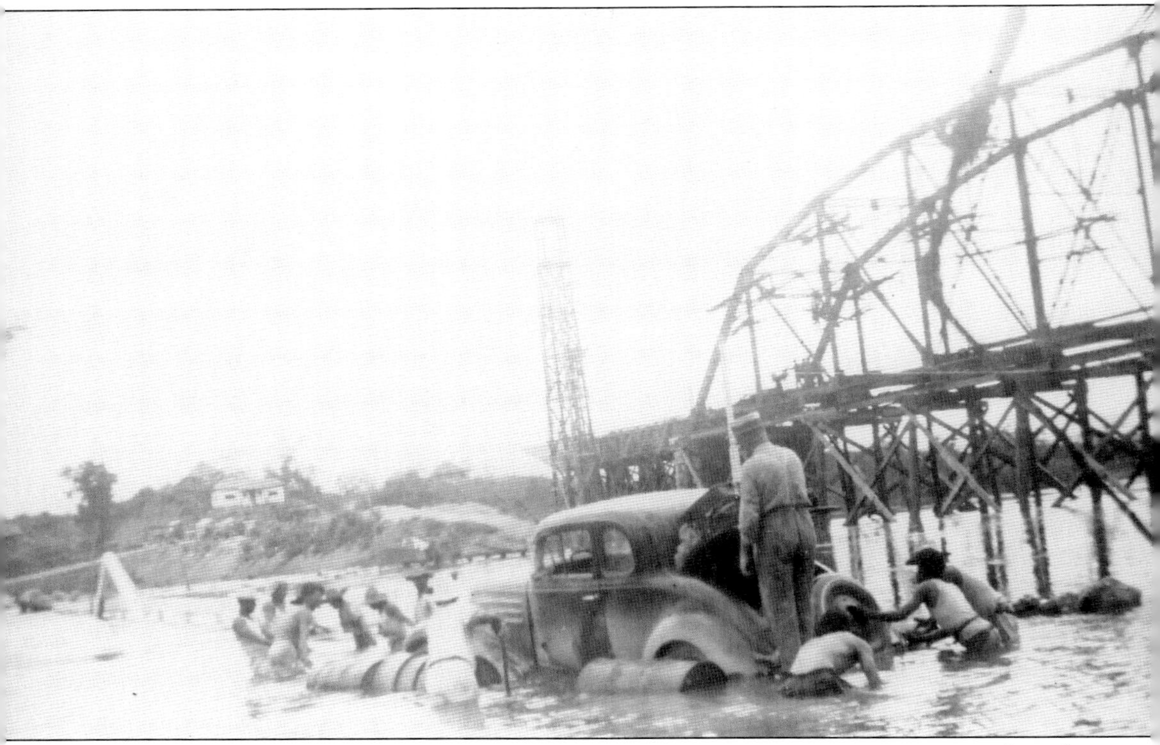

In the background of this c. 1930s photograph of Jones Crossing, construction is currently underway for the bridge across the river. (Courtesy of the *East Texas Journal.*)

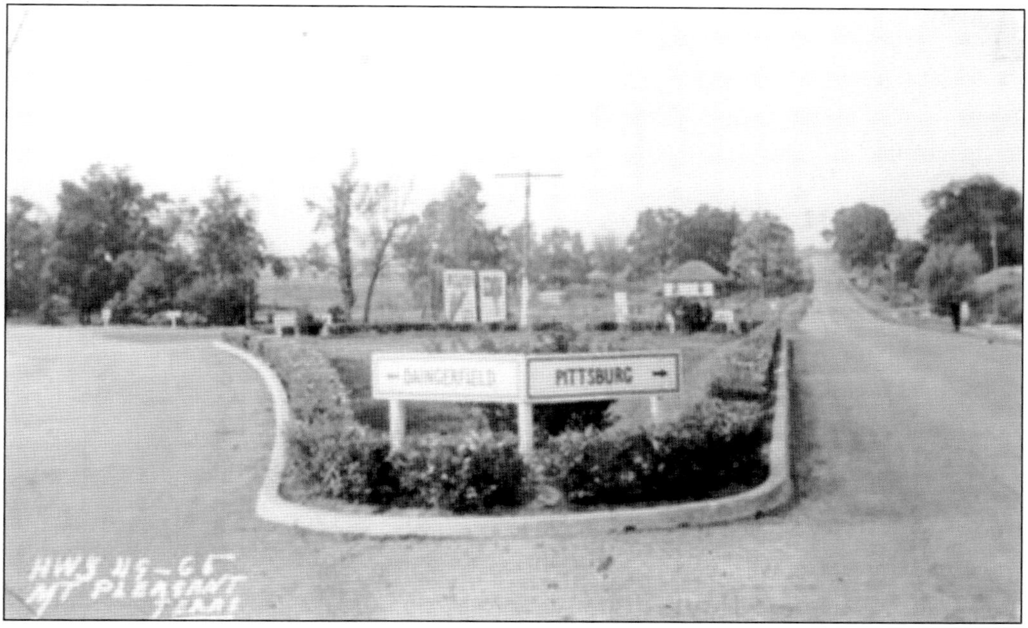


Mount Pleasant served as a conjunction for highways. In this photograph, the routes to Daingerfield and Pittsburg are clearly marked in an earlier style of road signs—lower and less reflective. This intersection today is where State Highway 49 and US Highway 271 meet. (Courtesy of Mount Pleasant Public Library and Historical Museum.)

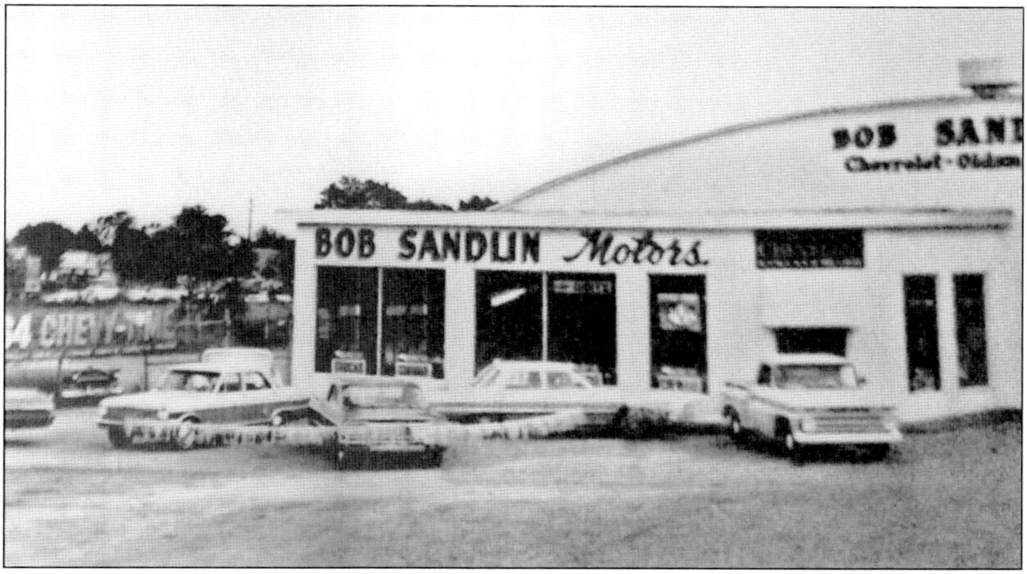


Dealerships seeking to meet the increased demand for automobiles sprang up throughout the country, and Mount Pleasant was no exception. Bob Sandlin realized the potential for profit in the automobile industry that the "Hub of East Texas" offered and left a position in Henderson, Texas, to partner with Irvin Chevrolet Co. in 1937. The company prospered in the aftermath of World War II, building new facilities at the intersection of present day Highways 271 and 67. In 1948, Sandlin purchased the remaining interest and renamed the dealership Bob Sandlin Motors. Sandlin Motors is still a prosperous business in Mount Pleasant. (Courtesy of Mount Pleasant Public Library and Historical Museum.)

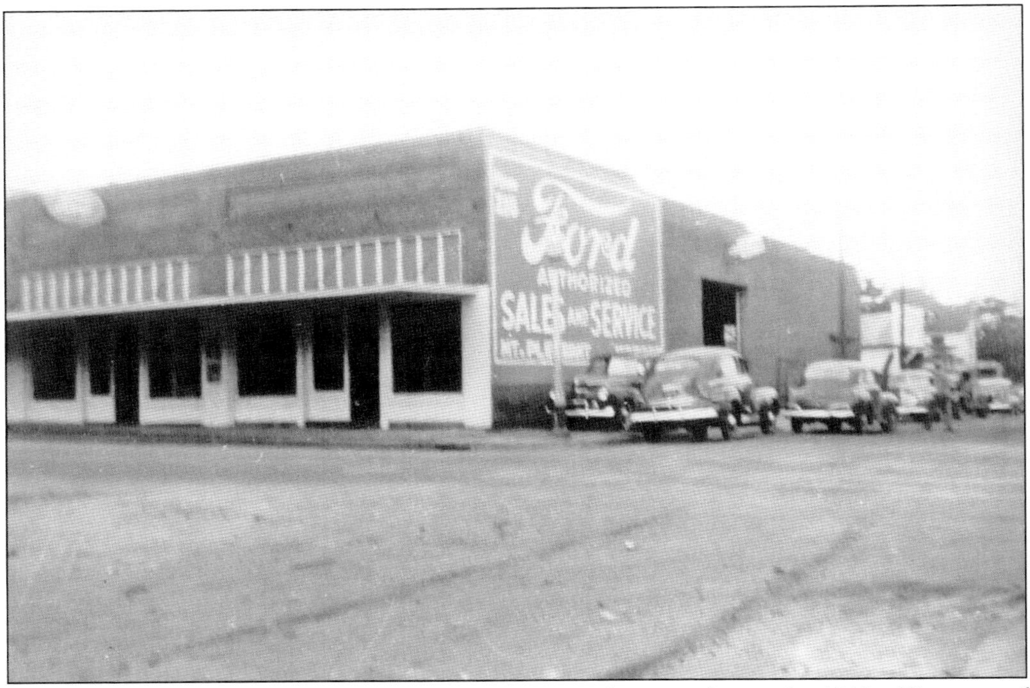

This Ford dealership on North Jefferson Avenue was in business during the 1940s. (Courtesy of the *East Texas Journal.*)

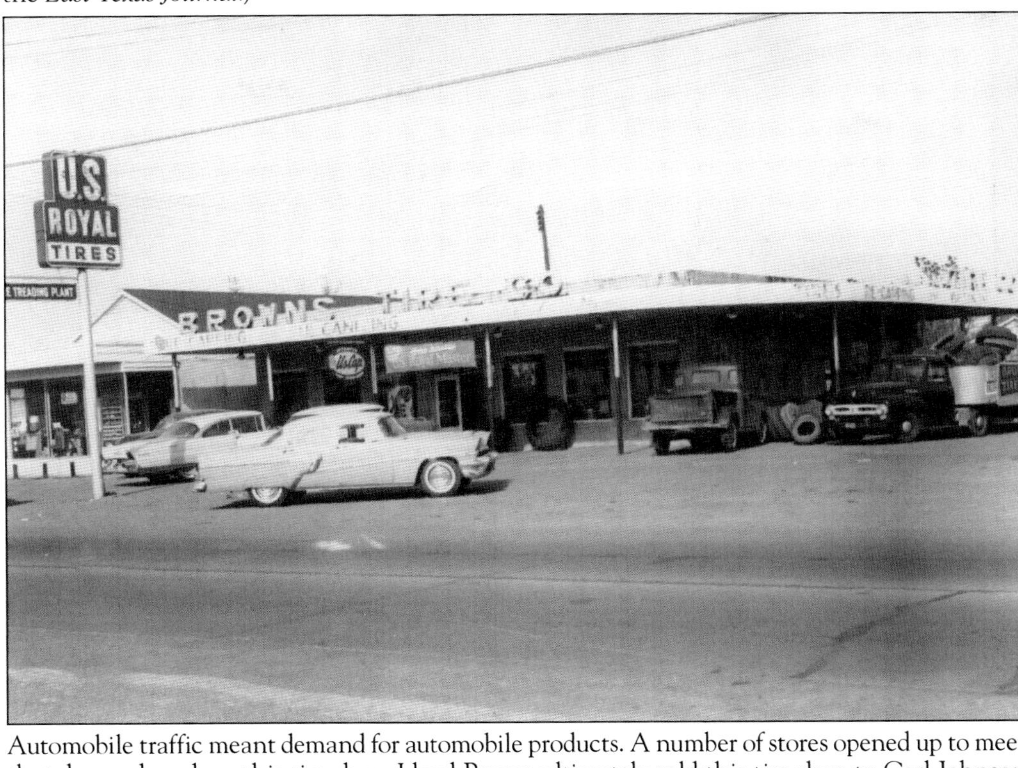

Automobile traffic meant demand for automobile products. A number of stores opened up to meet that demand, such as this tire shop. Lloyd Brown ultimately sold this tire shop to Carl Johnson Sr. (Courtesy of the *East Texas Journal.*)

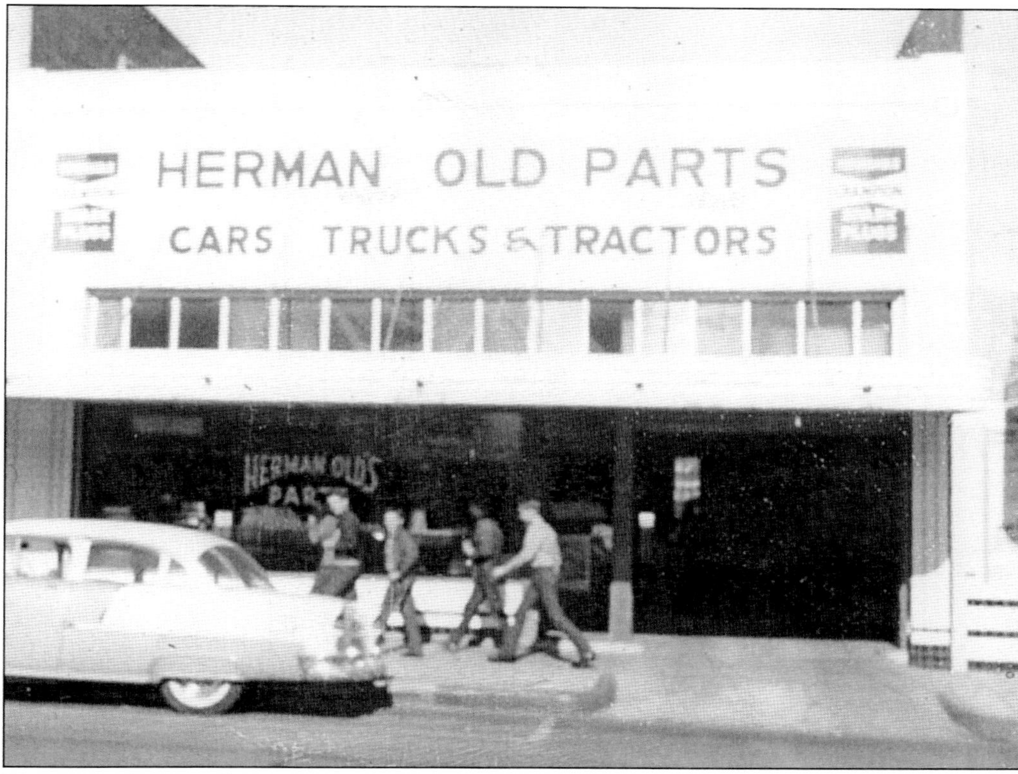


This 1961 photograph shows the Herman Old Parts store, located on Third Street at Jefferson Avenue next to the Martin Theater. (Courtesy of the *East Texas Journal.*)

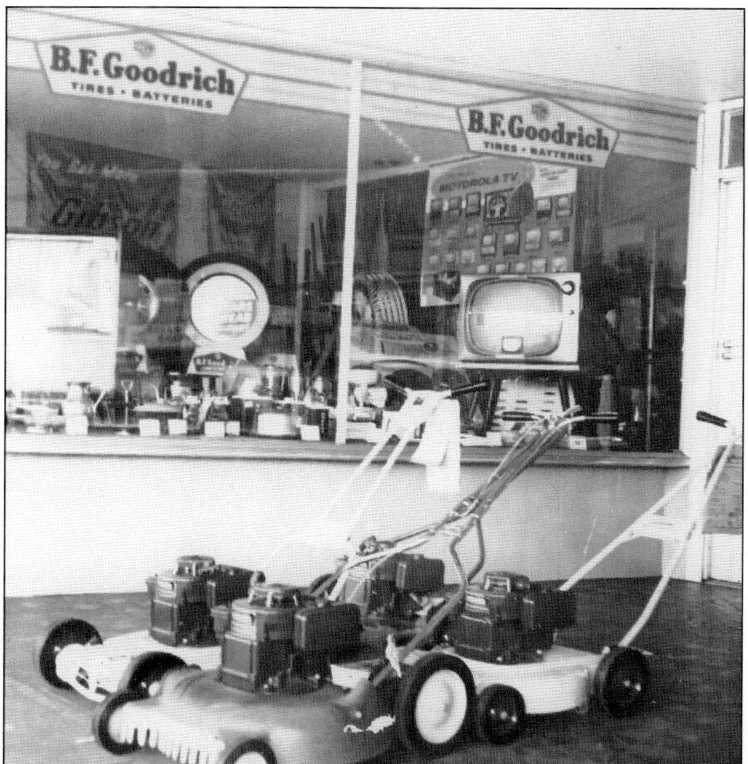


B.F. Goodrich sold tires and other accessories for most types of motorized vehicles. The auto business was located on Jefferson Avenue between First and Second Streets. (Courtesy of the *East Texas Journal.*)

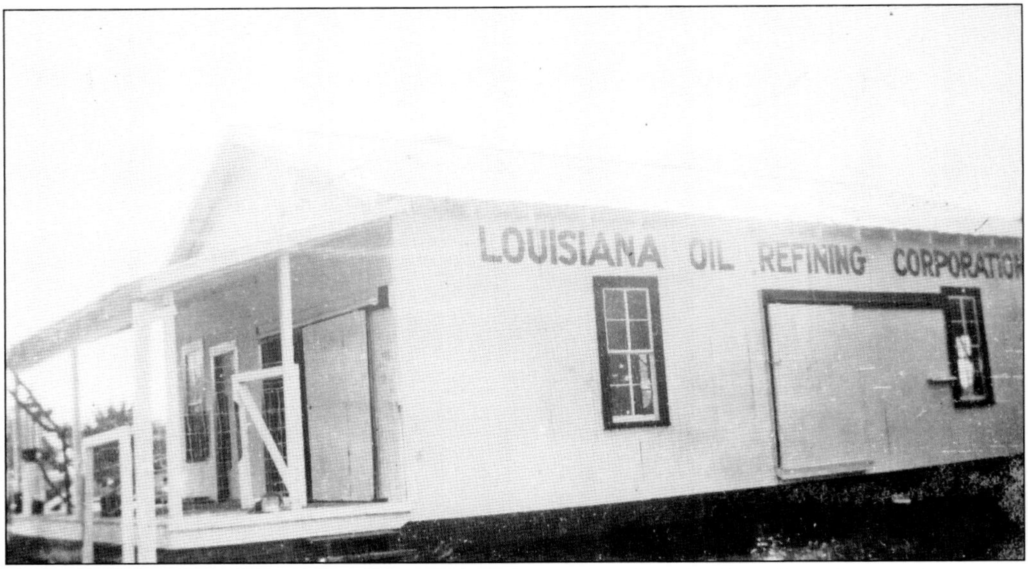


Demand for petroleum products rose dramatically after World War II, and several new gas stations opened in town. This Louisiana Oil Refining Corporation pump served automobiles at the intersection of what is today North Jefferson Avenue and Sixteenth Street. (Courtesy of the *East Texas Journal.*)

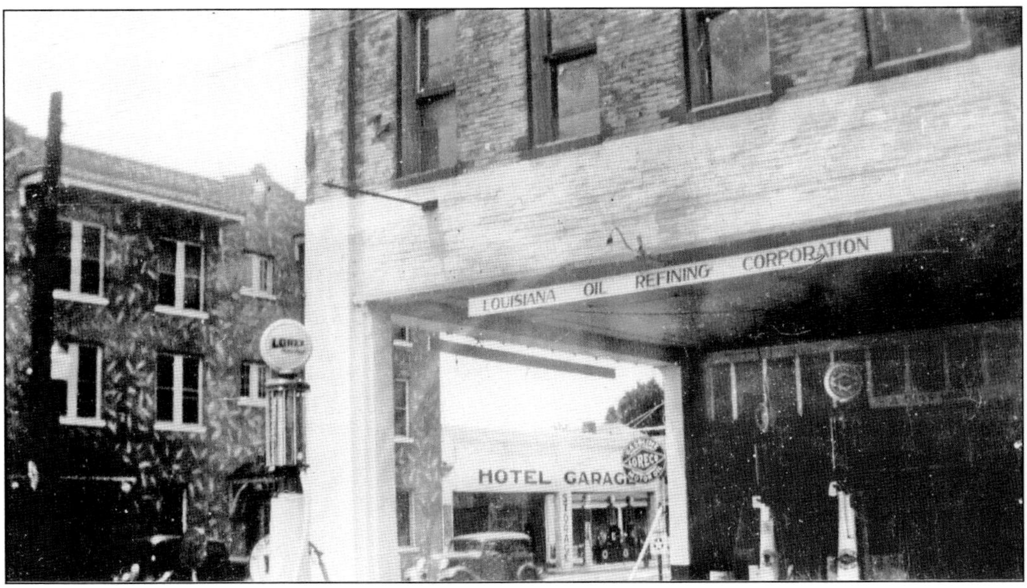


This Louisiana Oil Refining Corporation pump served patrons at the intersection of West Madison Avenue and First Street. It was located across the street from Stephens Hotel. A unique, decorative stucco pattern is visible on the hotel. In 1955, John B. Stephens bought the old Pleasant Hotel, which had previously been the Blythe sanitarium, and remodeled it. It had three stories, an elevator, and a lobby with stone-faced brick and wrought iron planters. The walls of the coffee shop and restaurant featured murals and mirrors. In addition, wall-to-wall carpet throughout the air-conditioned hotel made it a unique destination for travelers. (Courtesy of the *East Texas Journal.*)

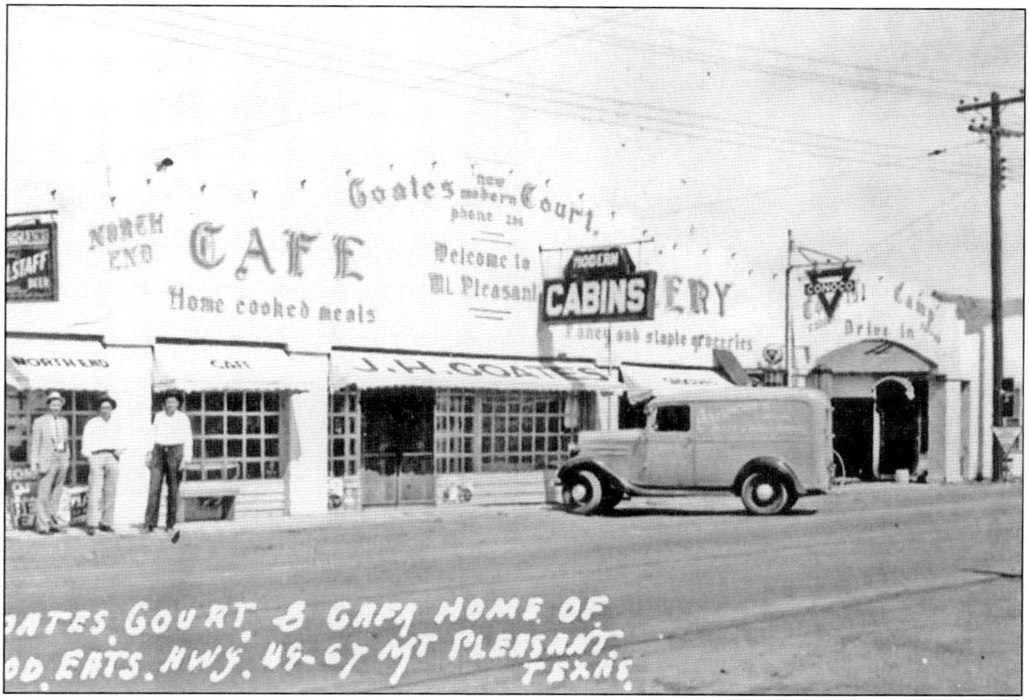


Mount Pleasant's location along the Bankhead Highway and position as a transportation hub for Northeast Texas encouraged the development of facilities for travelers. The Goates Court featured "modern cabins" and "home cooked meals" for travelers. The Falstaff beer sign on the far left is reminiscent of a time when Mount Pleasant, although dry for hard liquor, was still wet for beer. Beer sales in the city would end in the 1940s. (Courtesy of the *East Texas Journal.*)

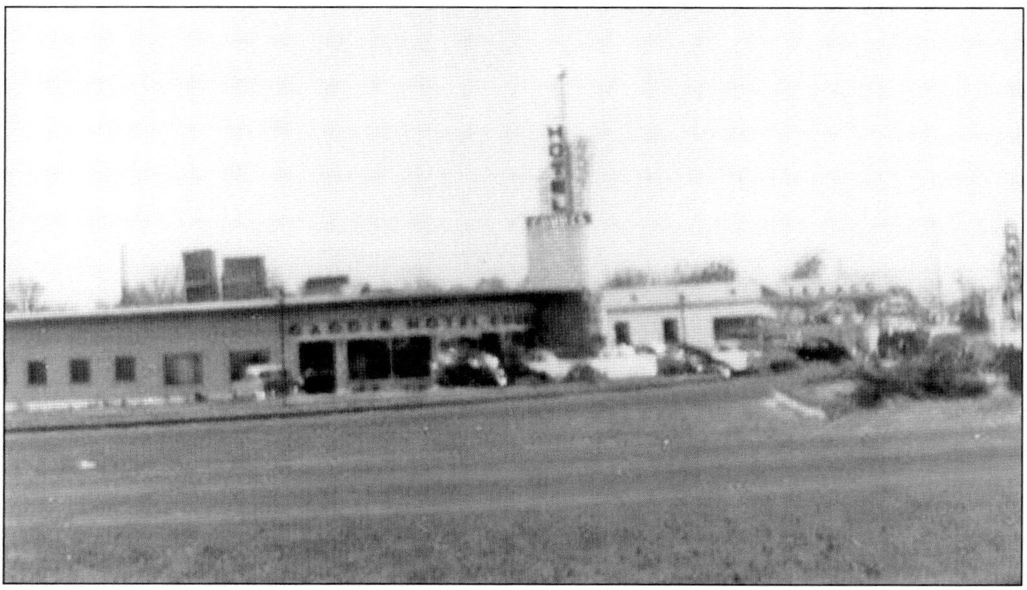


Gaddis Motor Hotel once featured 80 rooms and cabanas, all air-conditioned. It also proudly advertised phones in every room, a television, combination tub and showers, tile baths, and wall-to-wall carpeting. A spacious, nearly 5,000-square-foot pool, surrounded by palm trees and banana plants, offered relaxation and recreation for guests. (Courtesy of the *East Texas Journal.*)

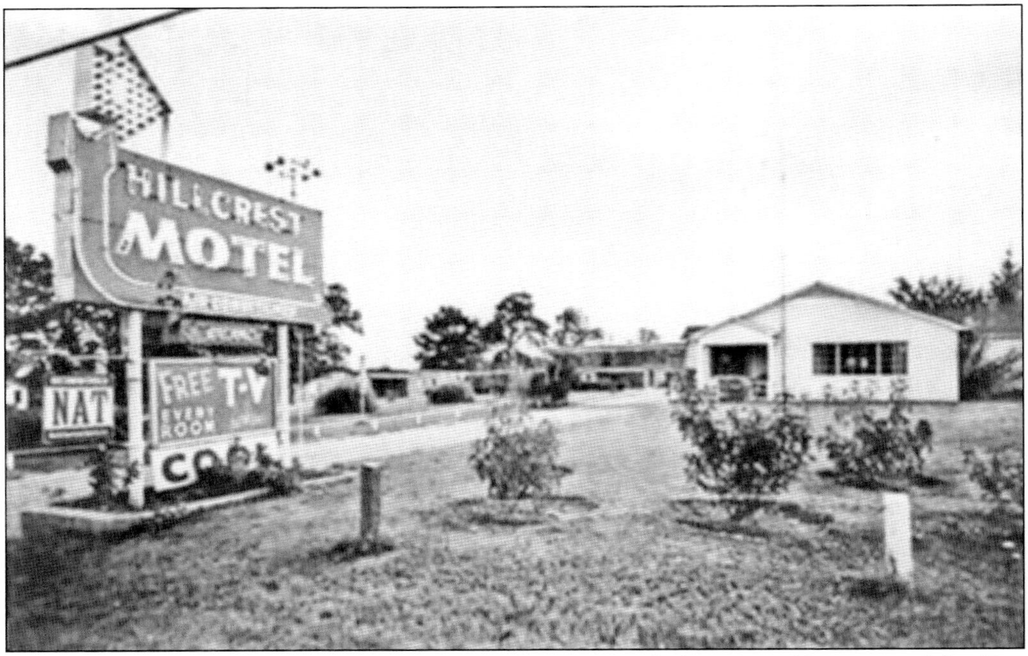


Hillcrest Motel advertised that it had air-conditioning and "free T-V." (Courtesy of the *East Texas Journal.*)

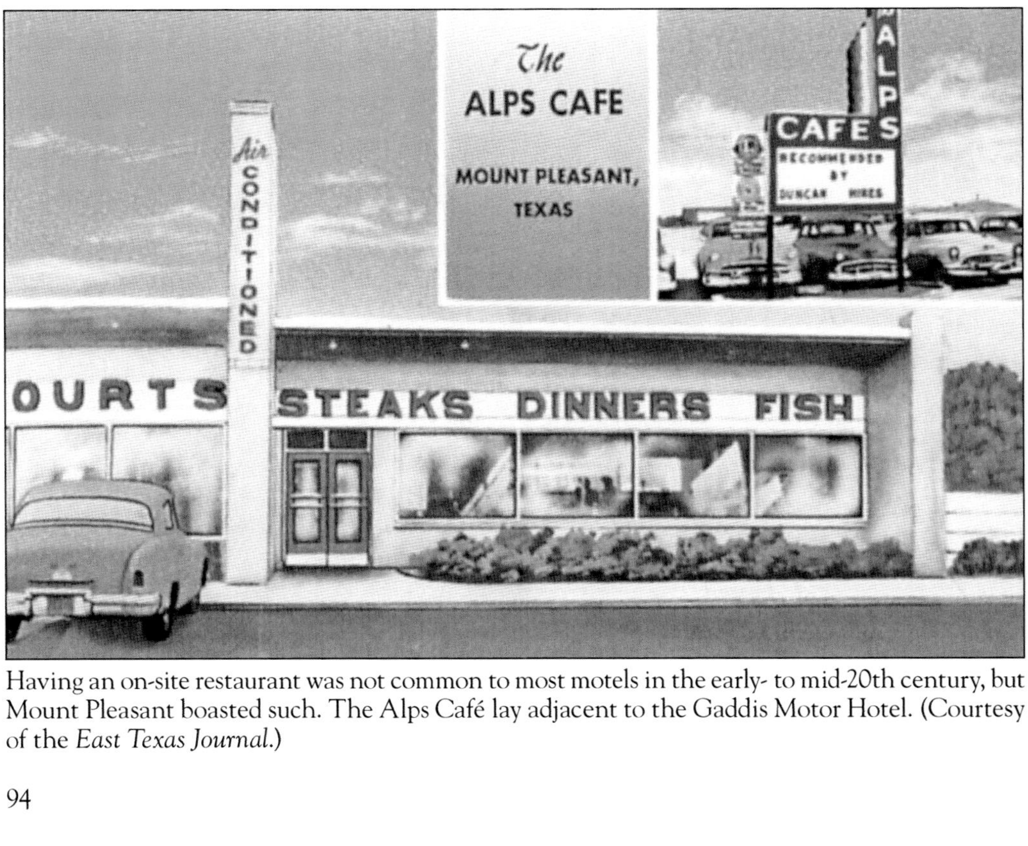


Having an on-site restaurant was not common to most motels in the early- to mid-20th century, but Mount Pleasant boasted such. The Alps Café lay adjacent to the Gaddis Motor Hotel. (Courtesy of the *East Texas Journal.*)

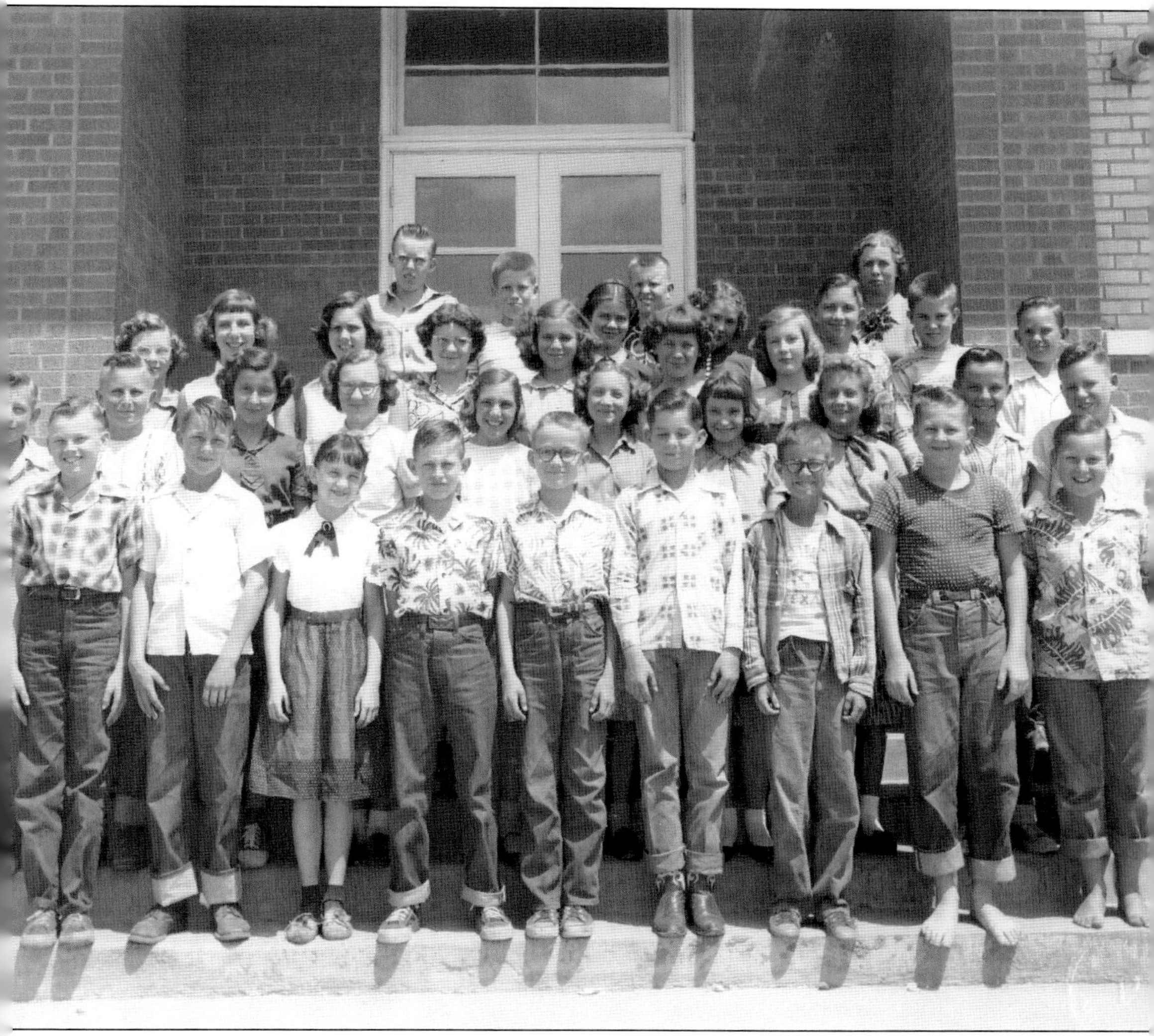

Initially, the names of schools in Mount Pleasant reflected their geographic relationship to the center of town. These smiling children stand atop the steps outside Vivian Fowler Elementary School, initially named the West Ward School. The school changed its name in 1967 to honor a beloved third-grade teacher. This photograph of the sixth grade class of 1952–1953 reflects several of the major fashion trends of the 1950s, including the increasing popularity of bobby pins and jeans. Note the cuffed jeans on several of these young boys and the acceptance of running around barefoot all day. Reflective of the increasing national affluence of the post-war years, children often owned a variety of outfits. From left to right are (first row) Larry Ward, R.C. Huff, Mickey Bailey, Benny Redfearn, Dale Yingling, Glenn McDonald, Dick Fulce, Sammy Spencer, and Rex Allen; (second row) Roger Kidwell, Larry Miller, Linda Gail Riddle, Billy Glover, Buddy Cover, Donna Sue Greeney, Martha Price, Junita Cline, Mary Valintine, and Juadon Thomas; (third row) Glenda Nell Barrett, Ernestine Anders, Mareva Jones, Glenna Sarrett, Peggy Bragg, Gail Perkins, Mat Clark, and Bill Walls; (fourth row) Jesse R., James Copeland, Nancy H., Stuart Florey, Judy C., Edd McElroy, and teacher Mrs. Fitzgerald. (Courtesy of Rex Allen.)

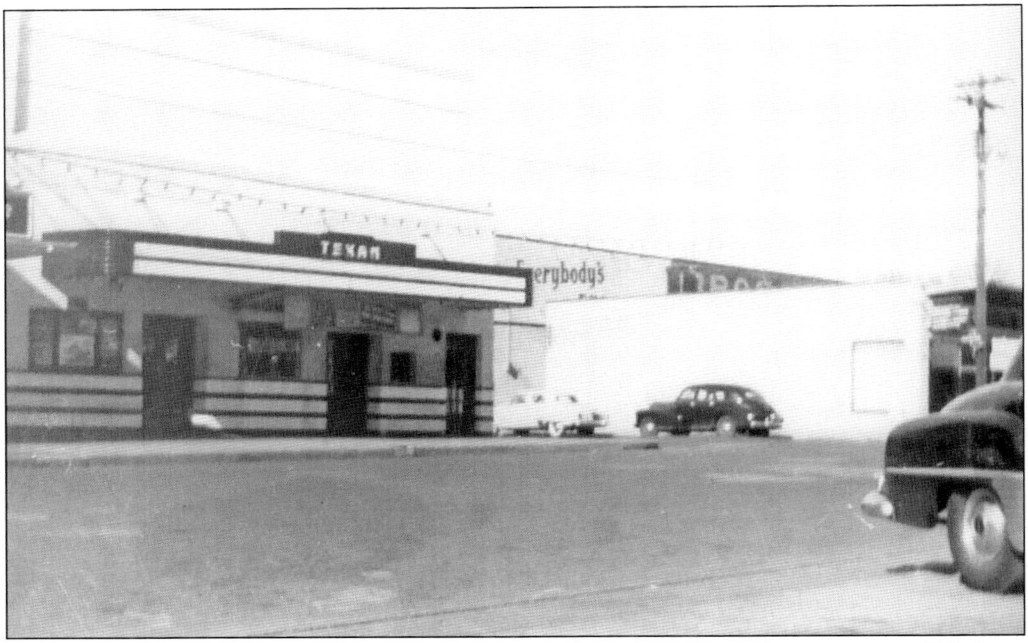


The Texan Theatre, pictured here in the 1940s, was located on the southwest corner of Madison Avenue and Second Street. (Courtesy of Mount Pleasant Public Library and Historical Museum.)

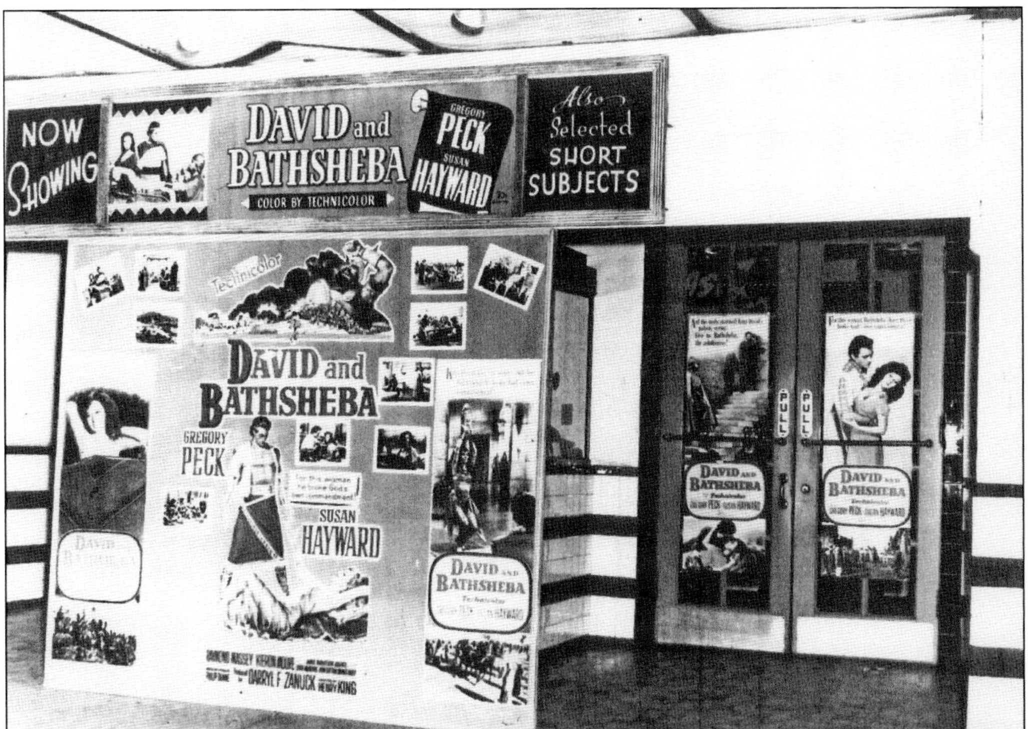


Promotional material outside the Texan Theatre in Mount Pleasant advertises the 1951 opening of *David and Bathsheba* staring Gregory Peck and Susan Heyward. The movie was the top box-office draw of 1951 and was nominated for five academy awards. (Courtesy of Betty Gerhart.)

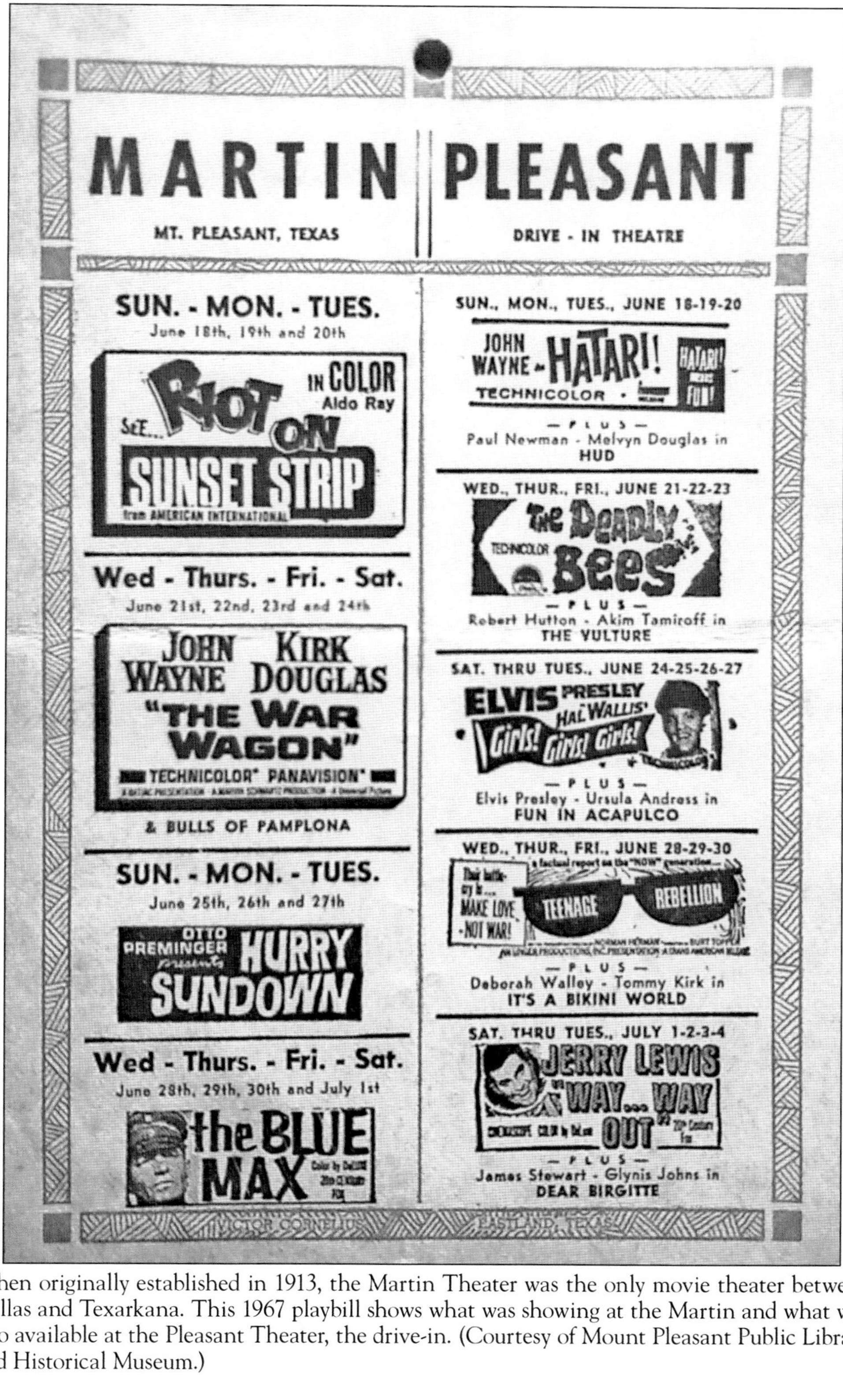


When originally established in 1913, the Martin Theater was the only movie theater between Dallas and Texarkana. This 1967 playbill shows what was showing at the Martin and what was also available at the Pleasant Theater, the drive-in. (Courtesy of Mount Pleasant Public Library and Historical Museum.)

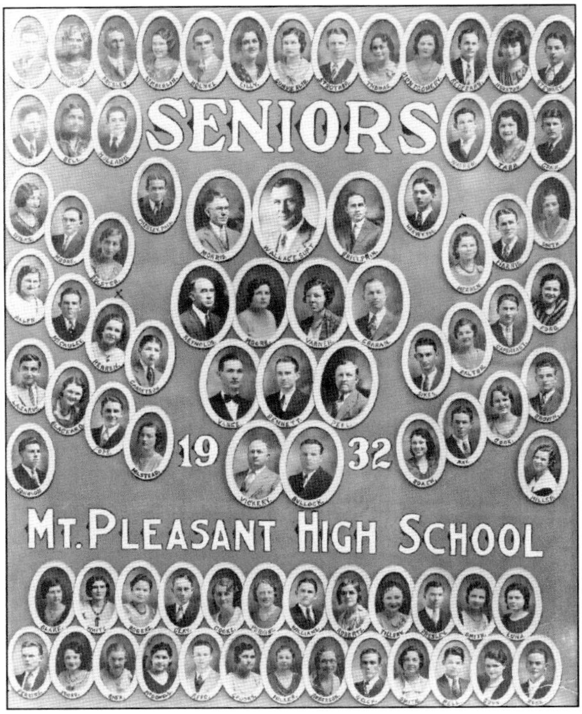


Pictured here is a collage of the 1932 Mount Pleasant High School senior class. The teachers and administrators, including school superintendent P.E. Wallace, are grouped in the center, while students are pictured around the outside. (Courtesy of Mount Pleasant Public Library and Historical Museum.)

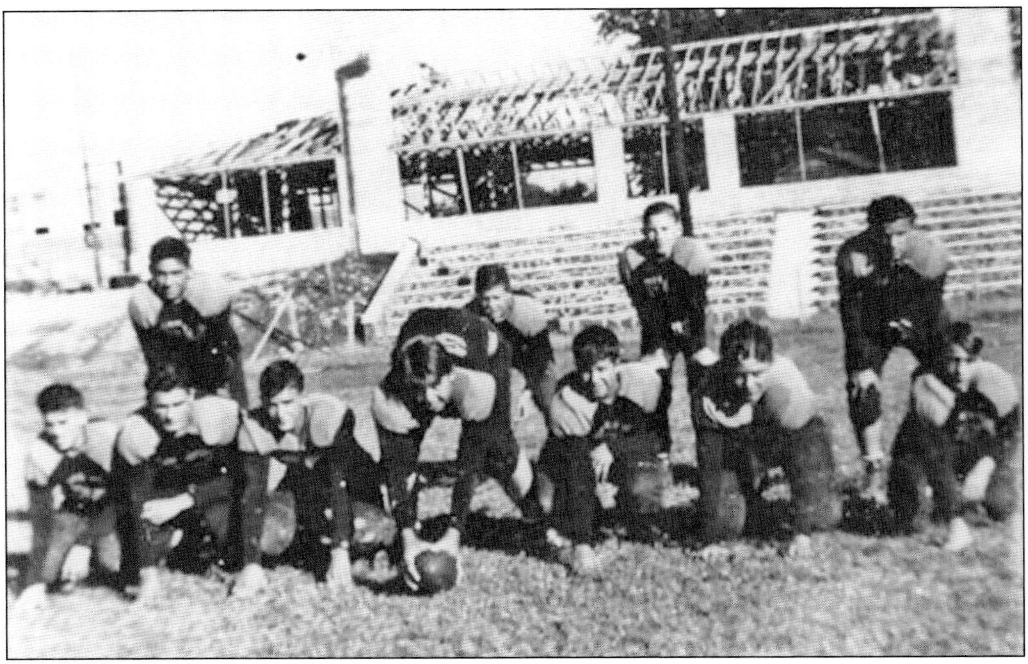

The Mount Pleasant Junior High football team poses in this photograph. From 1938 to 1940, the national Works Projects Administration (WPA) furnished labor for several public works projects. From October 1937 to February 1938, WPA labor was used in extending the football field area, putting in tile drainage and other improvements; constructing wooden bleachers on the west side of the field for a seating capacity of about 400; and building concrete and stone bleachers on the east side of the field. (Courtesy of Mount Pleasant Public Library and Historical Museum.)

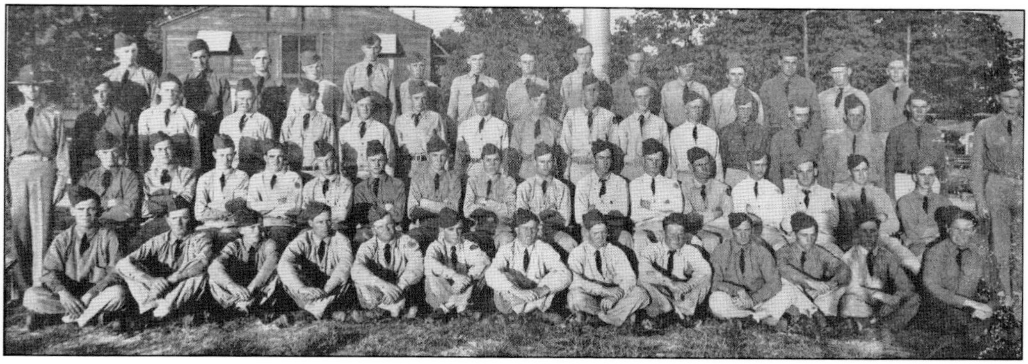

New Deal legislation during the Great Depression also created the Civilian Conservation Corps. As a component of that program, Mount Pleasant created a Soil Conservation Service camp. These images show the men who served in the program. In the background above, the water standpipe that used to be located on North Edwards Avenue is visible. This photograph was taken where Heritage Park is now located on Edwards Avenue. (Both, courtesy of the *East Texas Journal*.)

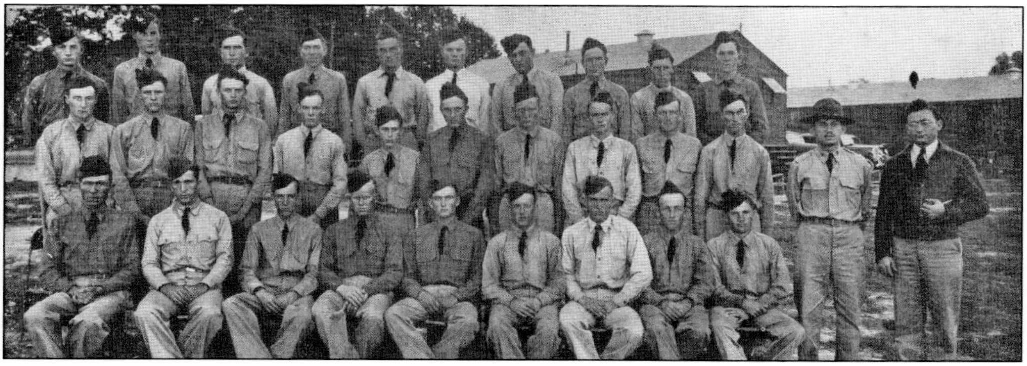

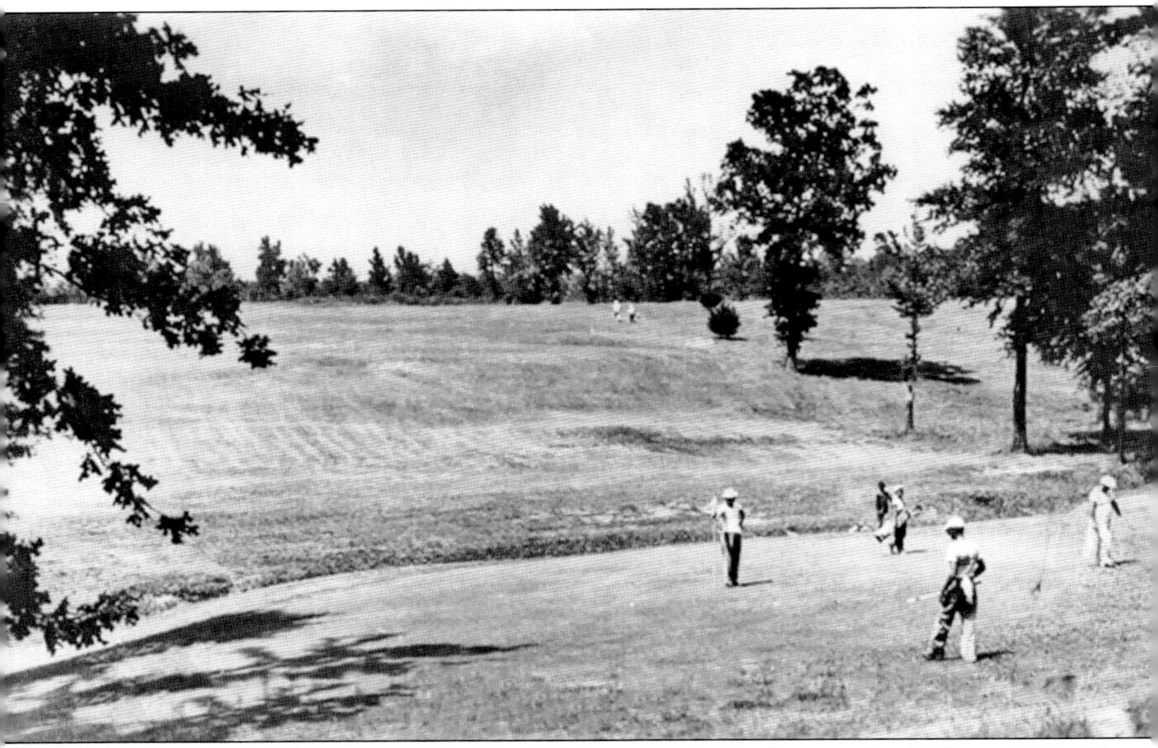

This picture of the Mount Pleasant Golf Course probably dates to the 1940s or 1950s. The course was built in 1939 and designed by Perry Maxwell, who designed a number of well-known courses throughout Texas and Oklahoma. The golf course was designed around Town Lake, constructed in the late 1930s as the main municipal water source for the city of Mount Pleasant. Construction of the golf course was privately funded but also received some federal New Deal aid. The Civilian Conservation Corps planted much of the grass for the course, and the WPA provided the labor to build the original clubhouse. The original nine Maxwell-designed holes can still be played today, but an additional nine holes were added to the course in 2000. (Courtesy of the *East Texas Journal*.)

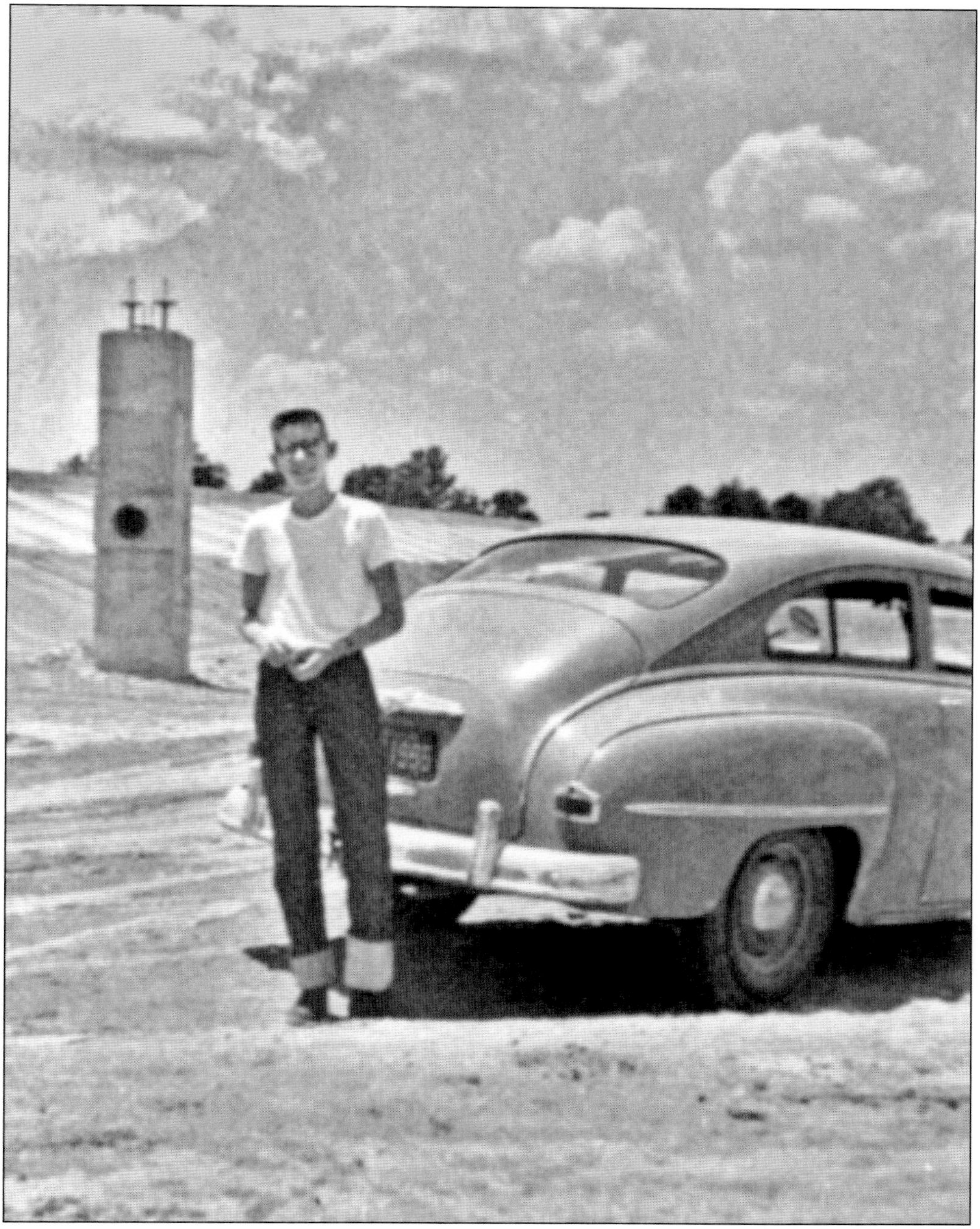

Mount Pleasant's original city water supply was Town Lake. Pictured here is Tankersly Lake, the second city water supply lake, while it was being built. (Courtesy of the *East Texas Journal*.)

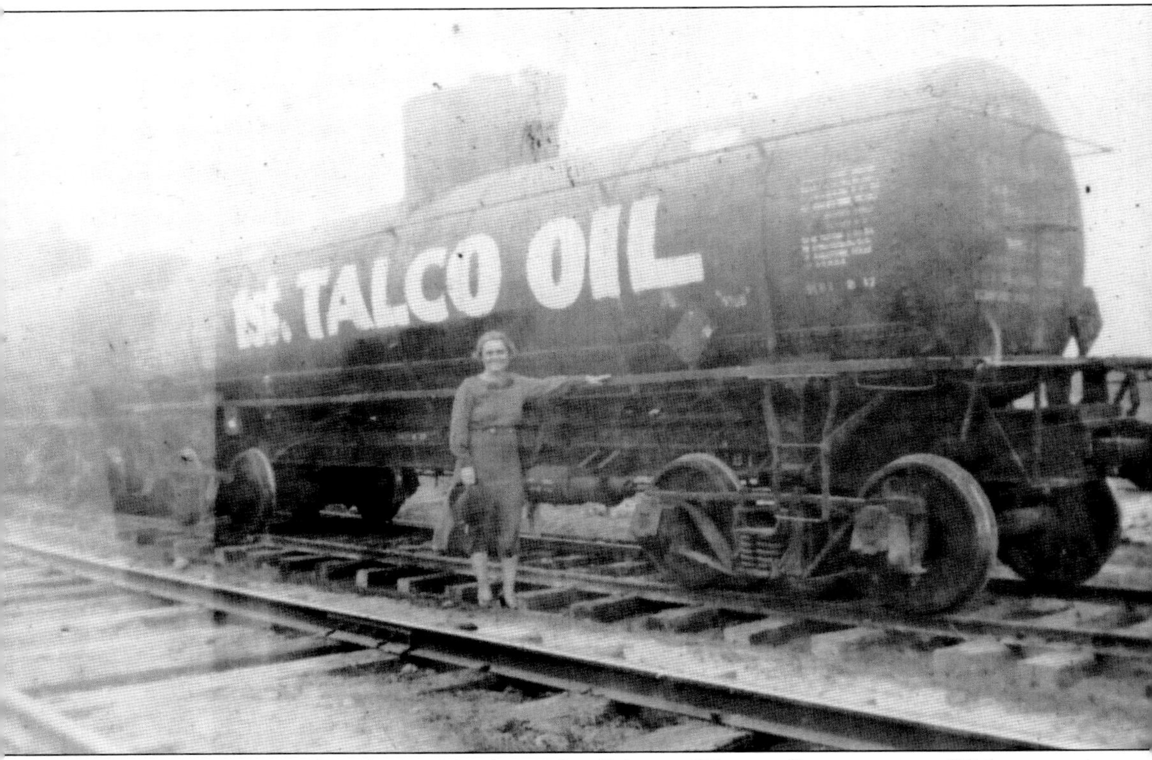


Ruth Ferguson stands in front of the first Talco Oil train. The small community of Talco came into being in 1912 after locals changed the name from Gouldsboro because it was too similar to other towns along the local mail route. The name itself was borrowed from a convenient box of candy. Big changes came to the sleepy town with the discovery of oil in 1936. Talco soon incorporated and boasted paved streets, a water and sewer system, and a city hall. Shortly after, a refinery was built outside Mount Pleasant that operated into the 1980s. (Courtesy of Mount Pleasant Public Library and Historical Museum.)

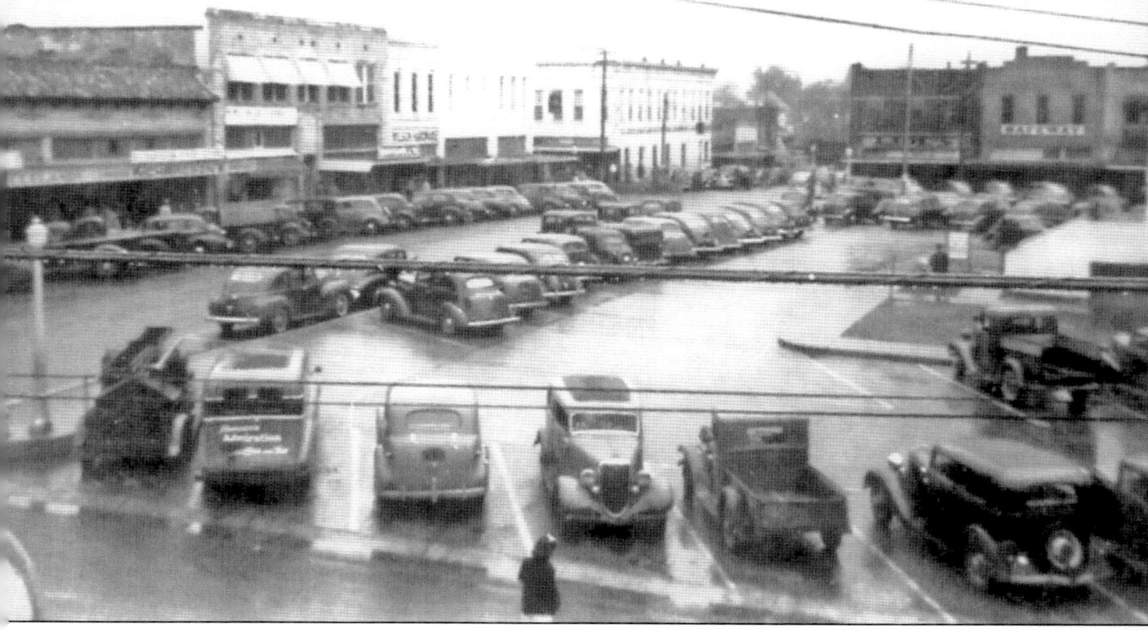

Looking east down Second Street on a rainy Mount Pleasant day in the early 1940s, only a small portion of the Titus County Courthouse can be seen on the right, but the First National Bank is clearly visible in the center of the photograph at the corner of Jefferson Avenue and Second Street. Judging by the number of parked vehicles around the square, the merchants of Mount Pleasant had a busy day despite the rain. (Courtesy of Barry Hamilton.)

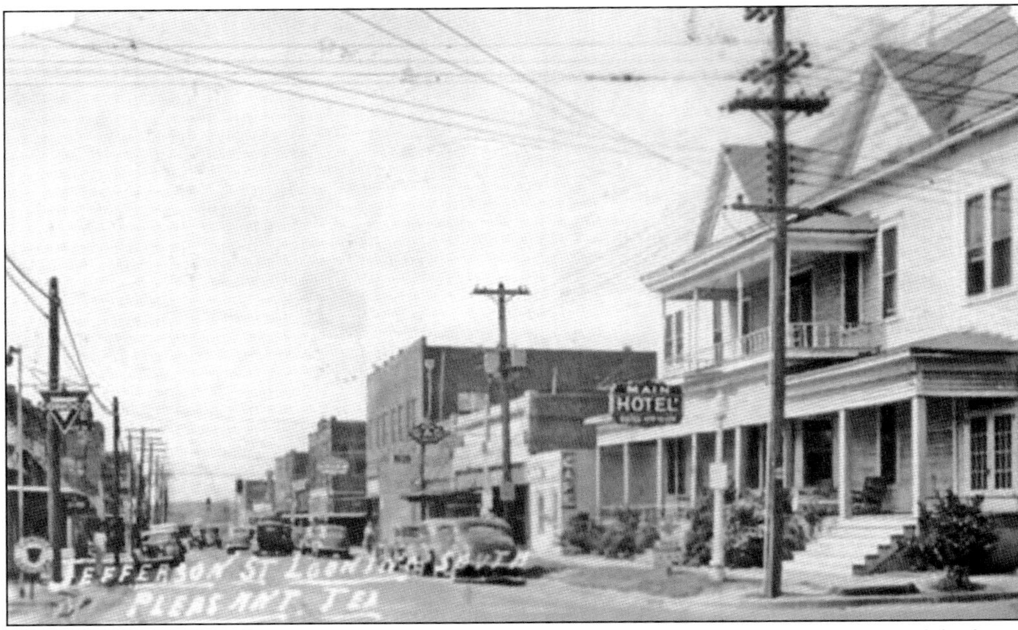


The Main Hotel, on the right, overlooks Jefferson Street during the 1940s. Just south of the hotel is the Main Café, owned and operated by Claude "Shorty" Alexander. This image is looking south. (Courtesy of the *East Texas Journal.*)

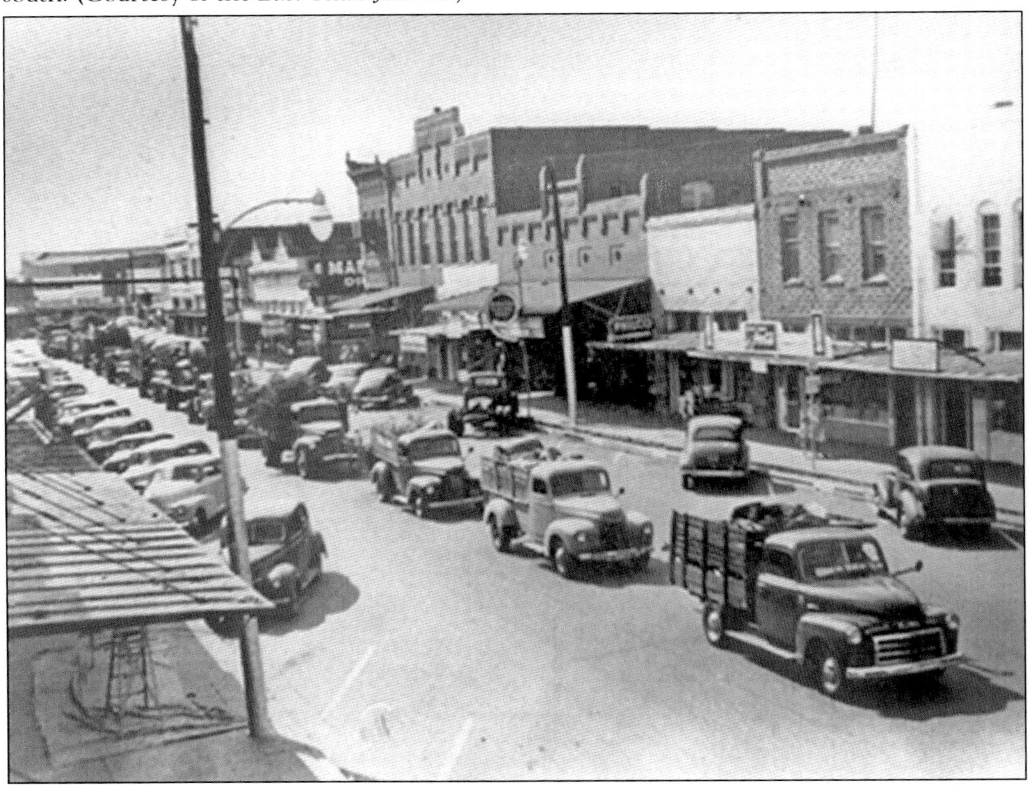

This street view of Madison Avenue in downtown was taken in the 1940s. (Courtesy of the *East Texas Journal.*)

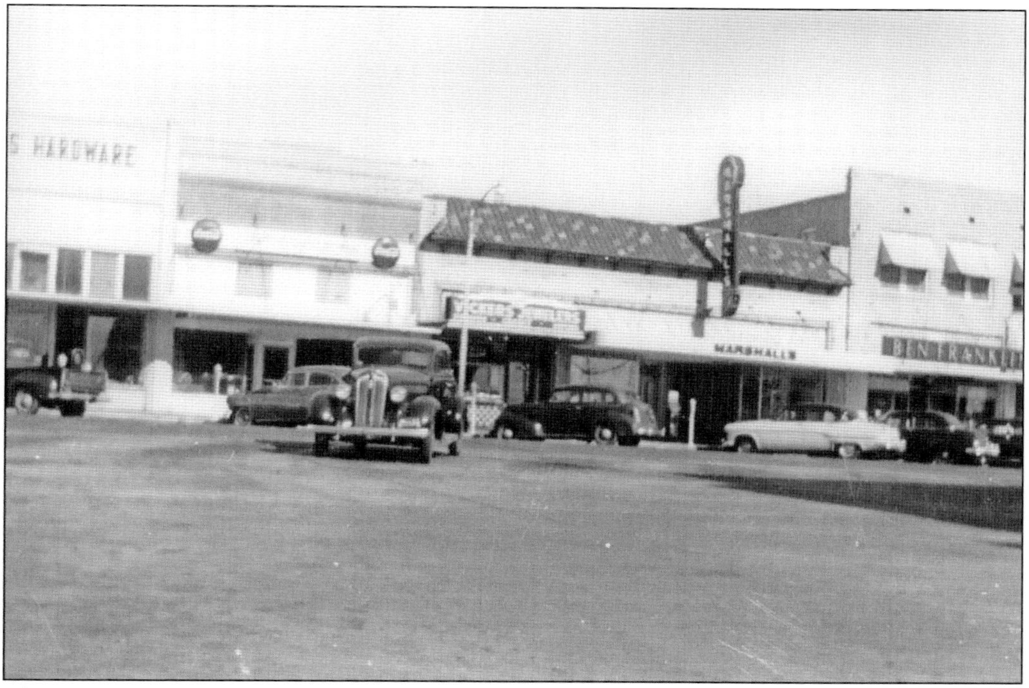


The Ben Franklin Five and Dime store and Marshalls were attractive options for Mount Pleasant shoppers on Second Street across from the Titus County Courthouse in the 1940s. (Courtesy of the *East Texas Journal*.)

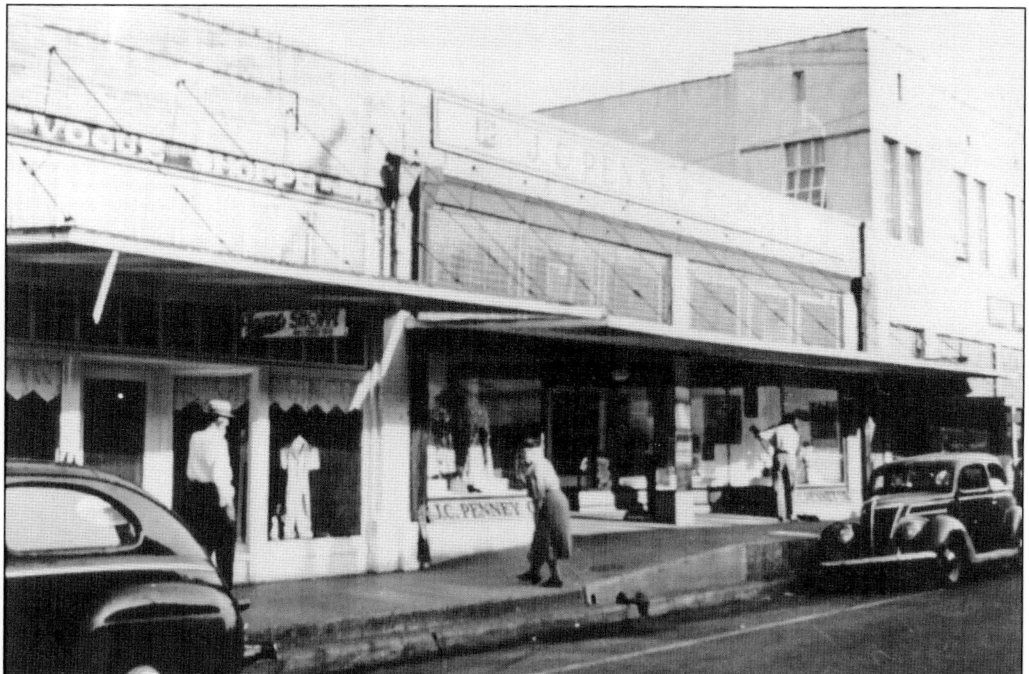


The J.C. Penney department store was located on Jefferson Avenue between Second and Third Streets. The building was home to Lide's department store during the 1920s. This image was taken in 1943. (Courtesy of Mount Pleasant Public Library and Historical Museum)

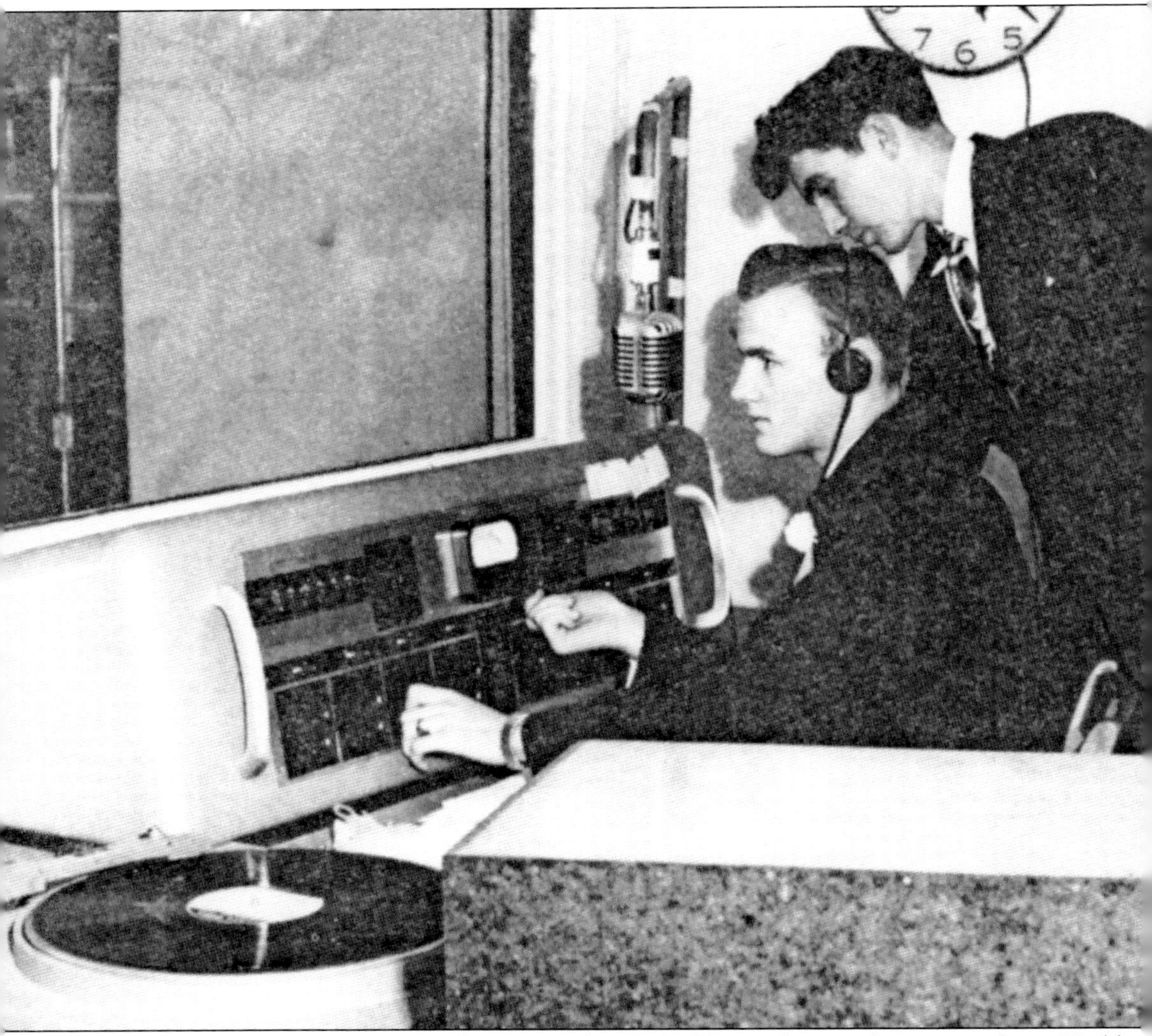

Radio stations came to Mount Pleasant in the 1940s. Here radiomen share news about World War II. (Courtesy of Mount Pleasant Public Library and Historical Museum.)

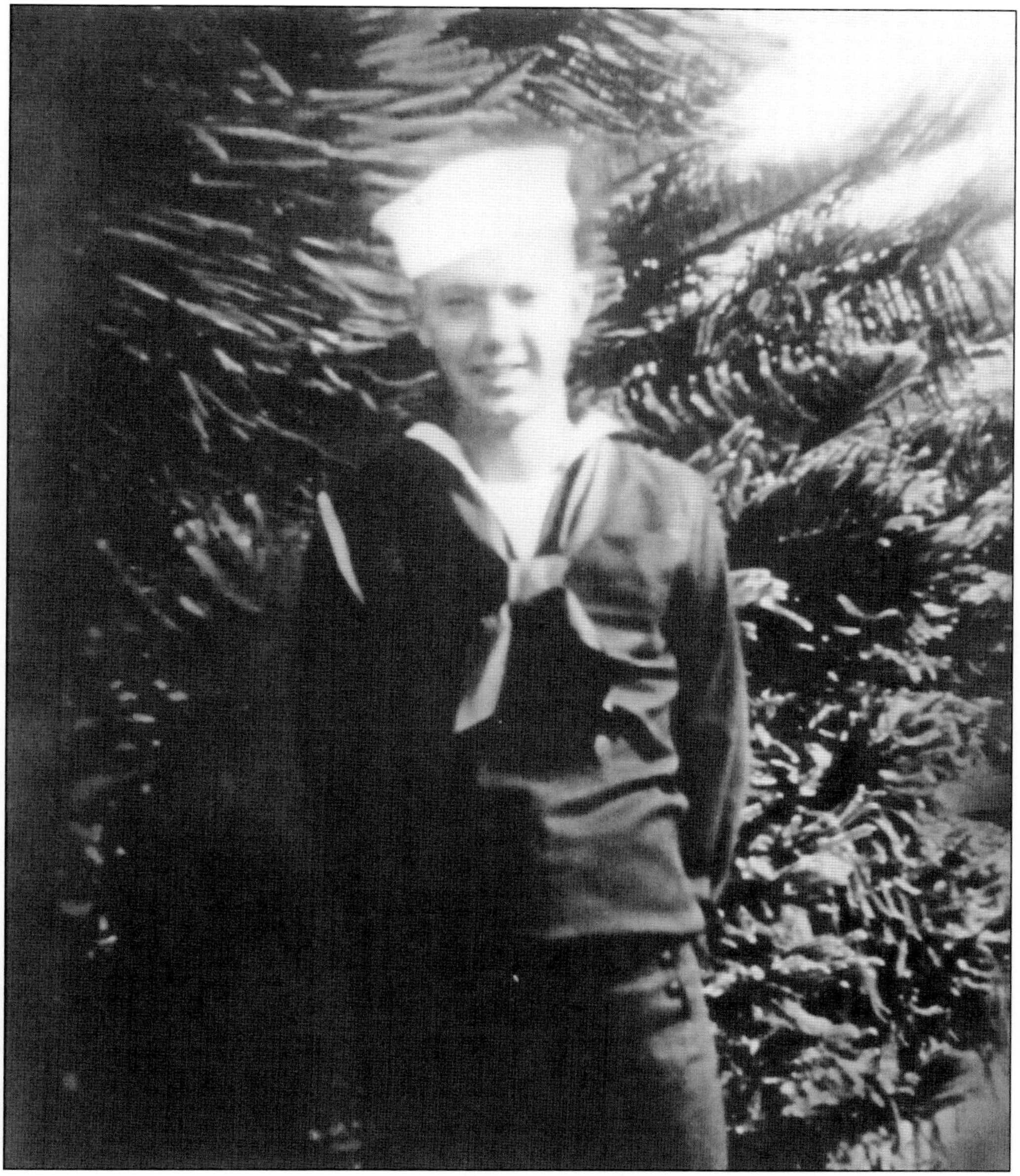

James Buchanan Reed Jr. enlisted in the US Navy in 1939 and served on board the USS *Arizona*. He was among the 1,177 crewmen who lost their lives on that ship on December 7, 1941, when the Japanese bombed Pearl Harbor. (Courtesy of Mount Pleasant Public Library and Historical Museum.)

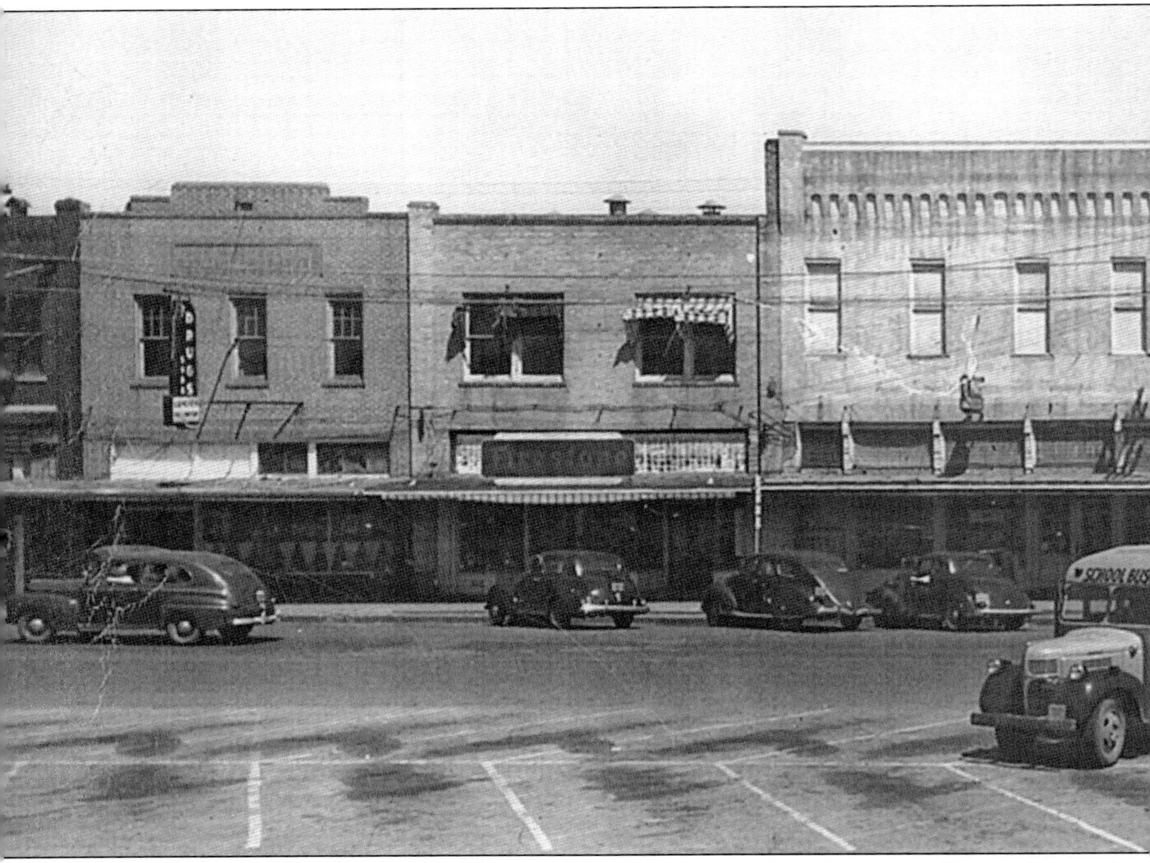


Mason Hardware was located directly east of the Titus County Courthouse on Jefferson Avenue. It is still is business today but is presently situated north of its 1940s downtown location at Jefferson

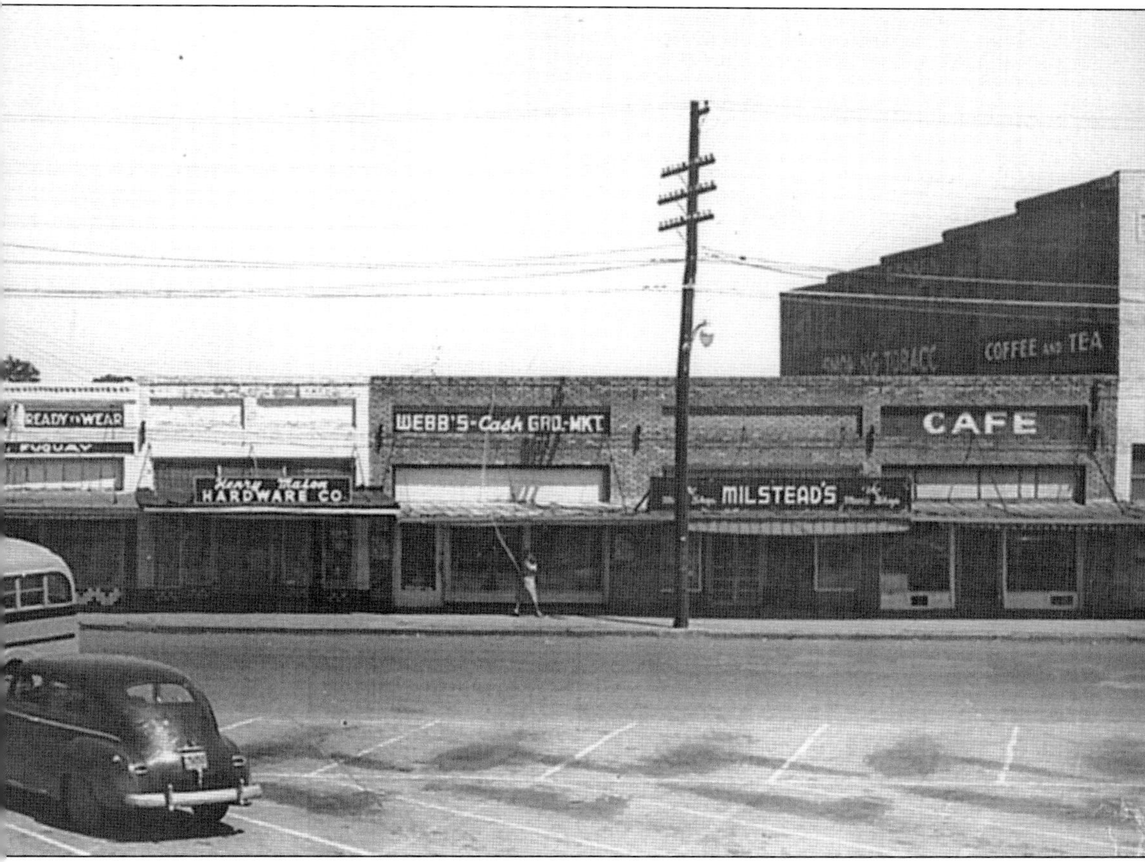


Avenue and Twelfth Street. (Courtesy of the *East Texas Journal*.)

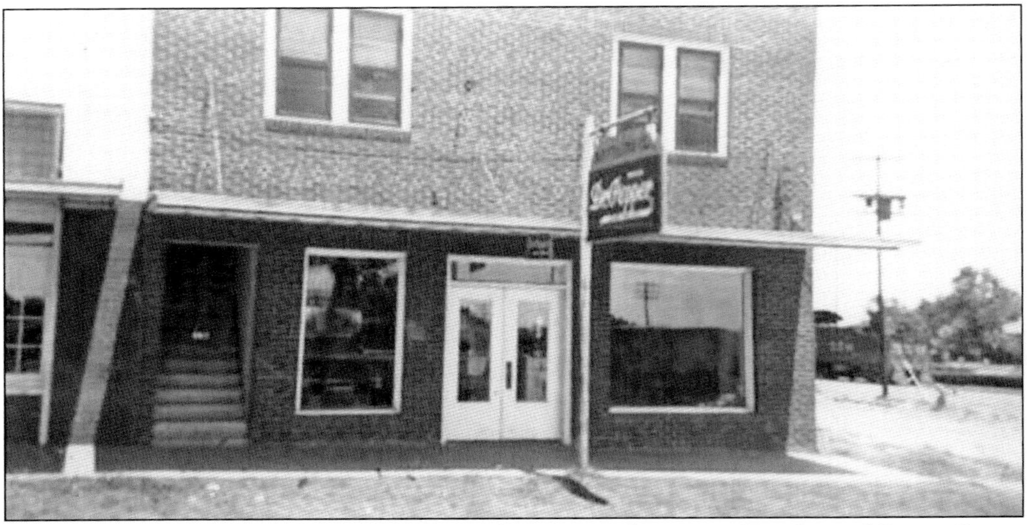

Dr. Pepper opened a bottling plant in Mount Pleasant on what is now East Second Street. Begun in 1928 by Otis McMinn, the facility met the increasing demand for carbonated beverages. The federal government declared such beverages a "liquid food," and thus they avoided the sugar rationing the nation faced in World War II. In addition to Dr. Pepper, the Mount Pleasant company bottled Delaware Punch and Nugrape at its Mount Pleasant facility. Young customers at the nearby Redfearn Bakery could enjoy eating their baked goods while watching the bottling through the large windows in front of the plant. This is the building that once housed the Dr. Pepper plant. (Authors.)

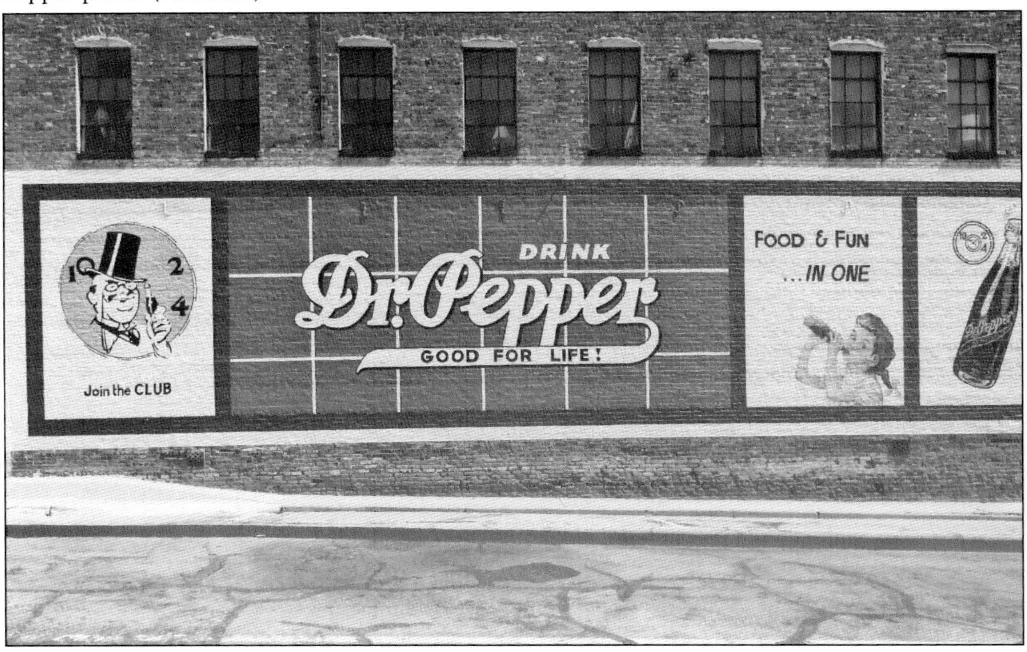


One of the largest Dr. Pepper murals in the country is painted on the south side of Jo's Antiques, the oldest remaining building in downtown Mount Pleasant. Although the soft drink is no longer bottled in the city, Dr. Pepper periodically restores the mural in honor of the company's history in Mount Pleasant going back to the 1920s. The mural is located on the corner of Jefferson Avenue and First Street. (Authors.)

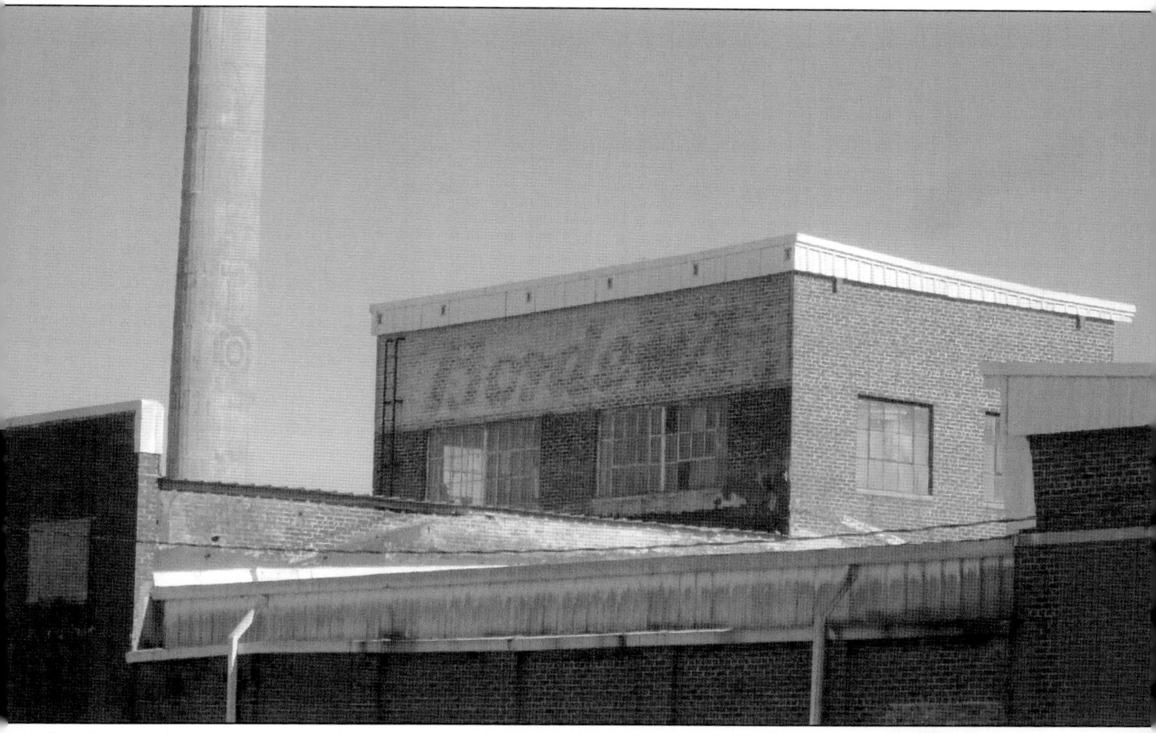

The first milk processing plant came to Mount Pleasant in 1929. The Texas Milk Products Company provided a market for all the milk the local dairy farmers could produce. It was turned into butter, powdered milk, and other products. Borden's Dairy purchased the plant in the 1930s. The availability of the processing facility encouraged the growth of the dairy industry in Titus County. Dairy cows became increasingly common on local farms. However, by the time milk production surpassed cotton production in the area, beef production had become the number-one agricultural commodity in the region. In 1960, the plant closed down. It can still be seen a few blocks southeast of the courthouse along the railroad tracks that once busily transported milk products. The concrete stack reveals the molded letters T, M, P, and Co., while the word "Borden's" can still be seen painted atop the north-facing wall. (Authors.)

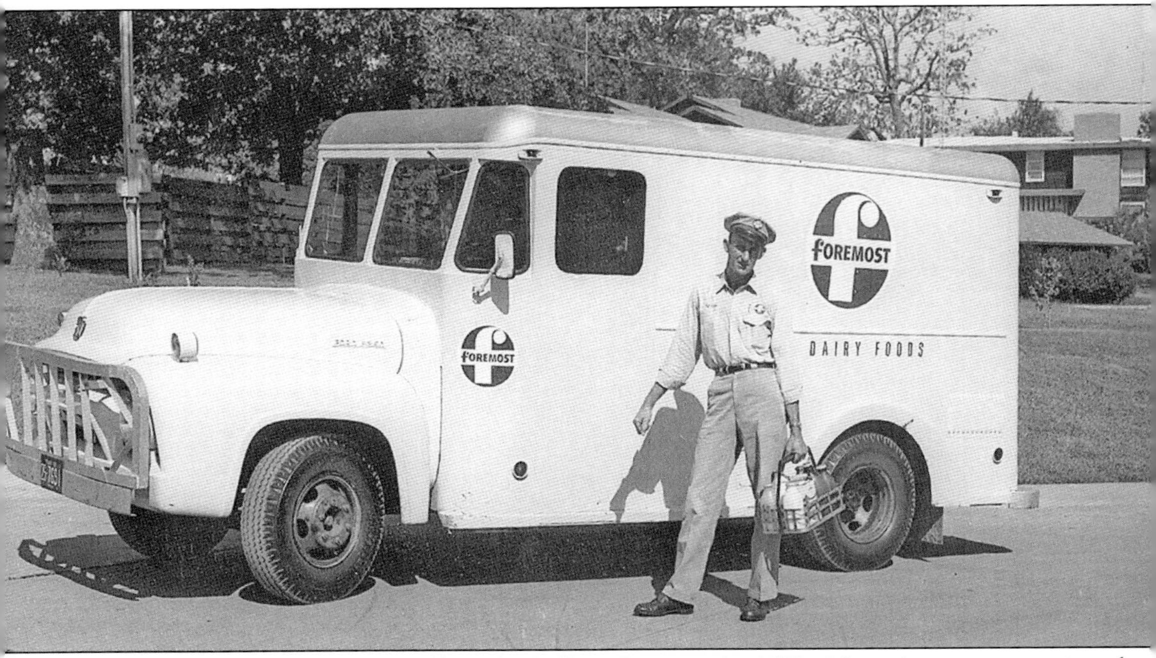


The Foremost Man delivers milk to the Dellwood area in the 1950s. Many Americans continued to have milk delivered directly to their homes well into the 1960s. (Courtesy of the *East Texas Journal*.)

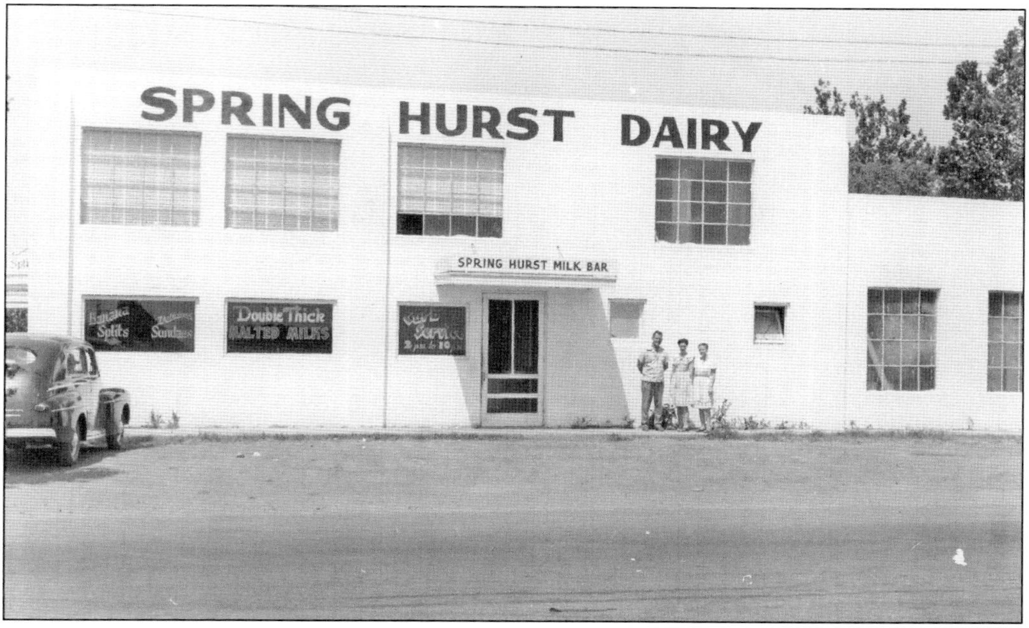


The Spring Hurst Dairy sold purebred Jersey pasteurized milk provided by local dairy farmers. (Courtesy of the *East Texas Journal.*)

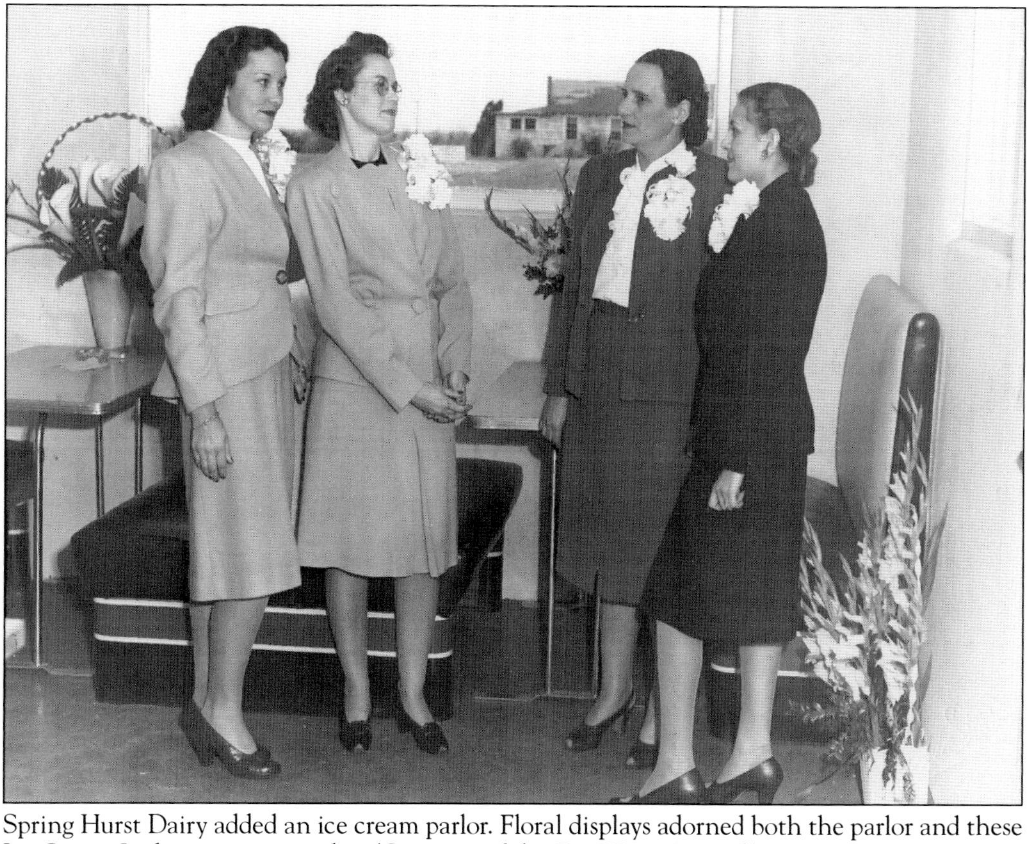

Spring Hurst Dairy added an ice cream parlor. Floral displays adorned both the parlor and these Ice Cream Ladies on opening day. (Courtesy of the *East Texas Journal.*)

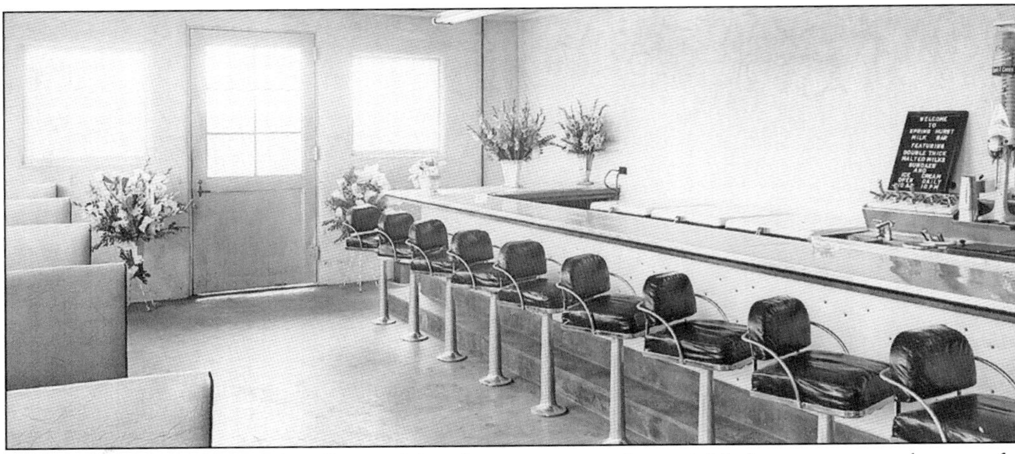

Shown here on opening day, Spring Hurst's ice cream parlor quickly became a popular spot for Mount Pleasant locals. (Courtesy of the *East Texas Journal.*)

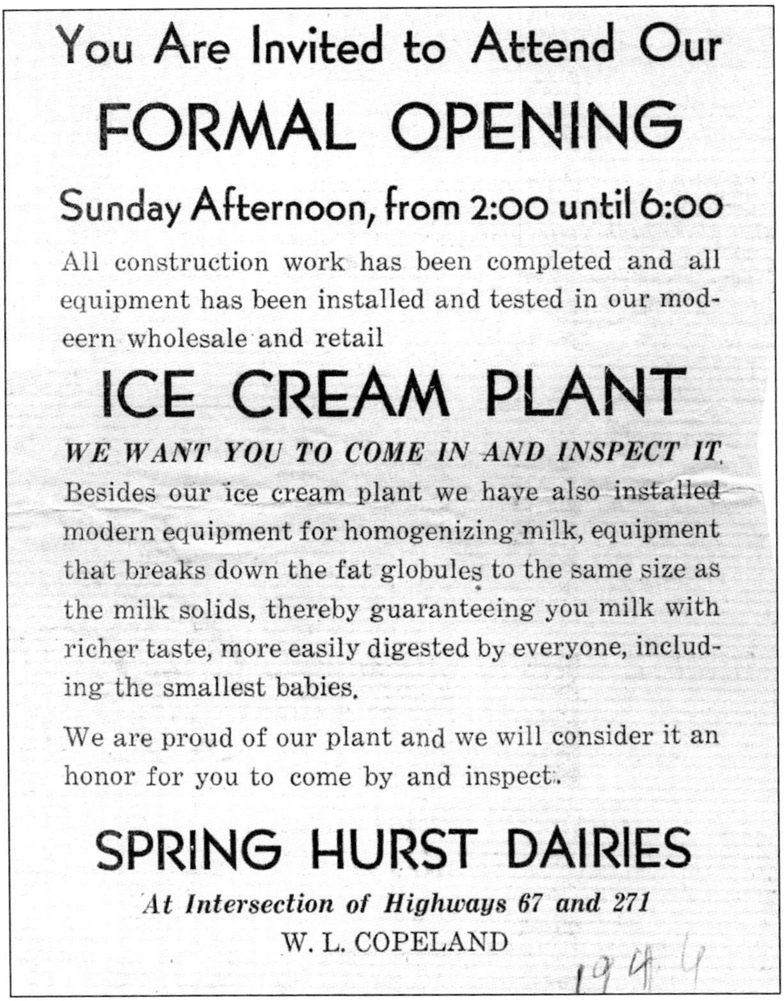

You Are Invited to Attend Our

FORMAL OPENING

Sunday Afternoon, from 2:00 until 6:00

All construction work has been completed and all equipment has been installed and tested in our modeern wholesale and retail

ICE CREAM PLANT

***WE WANT YOU TO COME IN AND INSPECT IT***

Besides our ice cream plant we have also installed modern equipment for homogenizing milk, equipment that breaks down the fat globules to the same size as the milk solids, thereby guaranteeing you milk with richer taste, more easily digested by everyone, including the smallest babies.

We are proud of our plant and we will consider it an honor for you to come by and inspect.

SPRING HURST DAIRIES

***At Intersection of Highways 67 and 271***

W. L. COPELAND

1944

The Spring Hurst Creamery opened in 1946. The dairy was located north of downtown Mount Pleasant at the intersection of US Highways 271 and 67. (Courtesy of the *East Texas Journal.*)

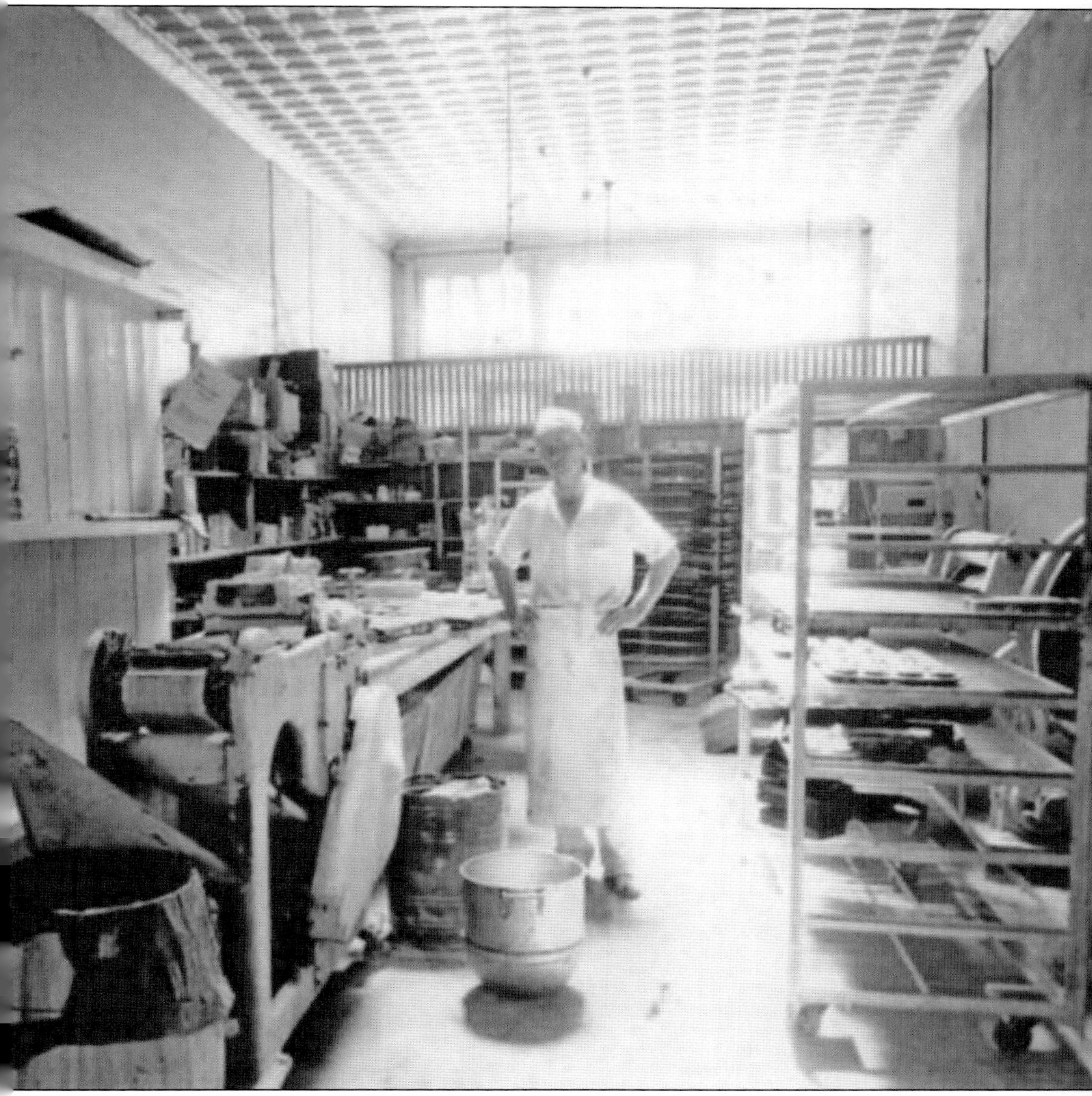

P.D. Marshall, pictured here, operated a bakery in Mount Pleasant during the 1940s. (Courtesy of the *East Texas Journal*.)

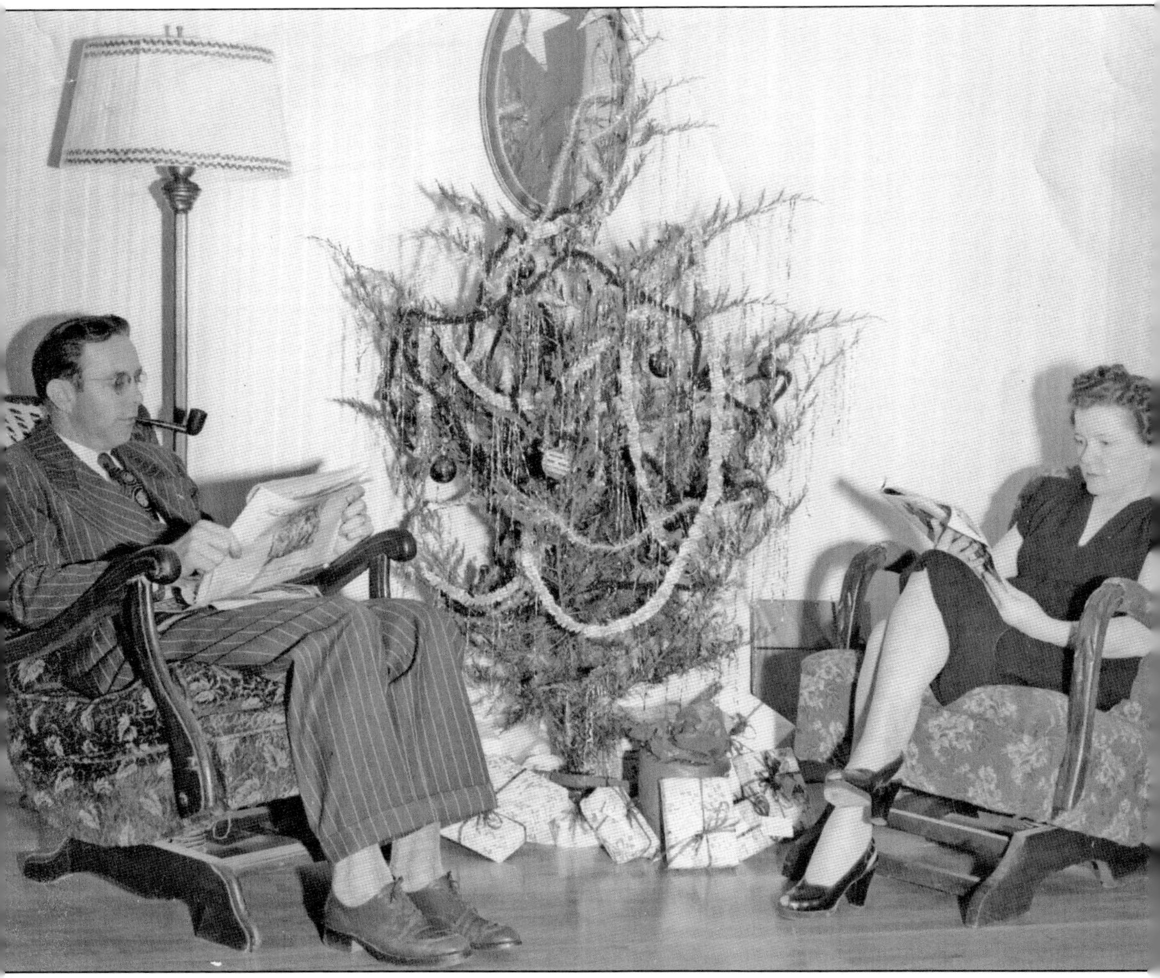

This image of an unidentified Mount Pleasant couple is typical of the 1950s. The overwhelmed Christmas tree at center was most likely harvested locally. (Courtesy of the *East Texas Journal*.)

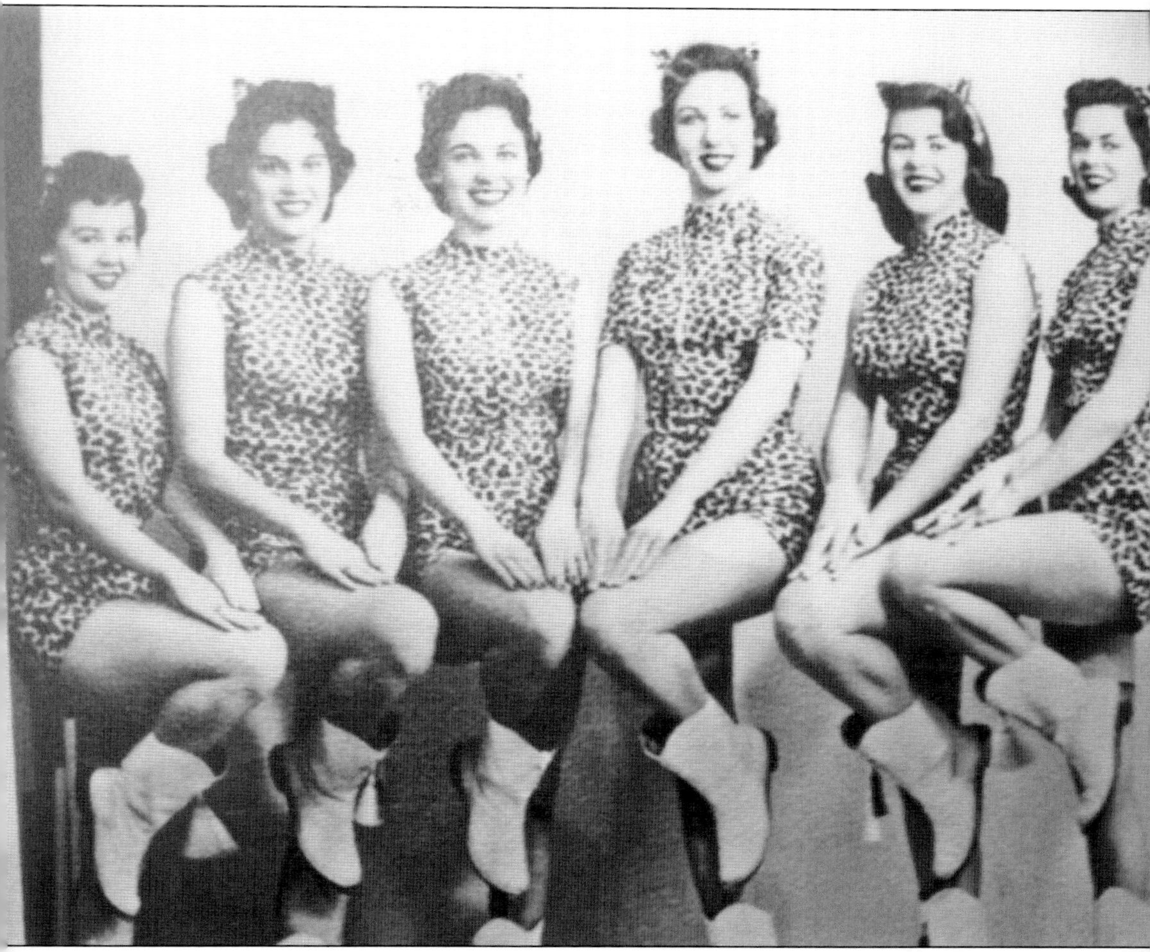

The 1959 Mount Pleasant High School majorettes are pictured here with drum major Ernestine Anders third from right. (Courtesy of the *East Texas Journal*.)

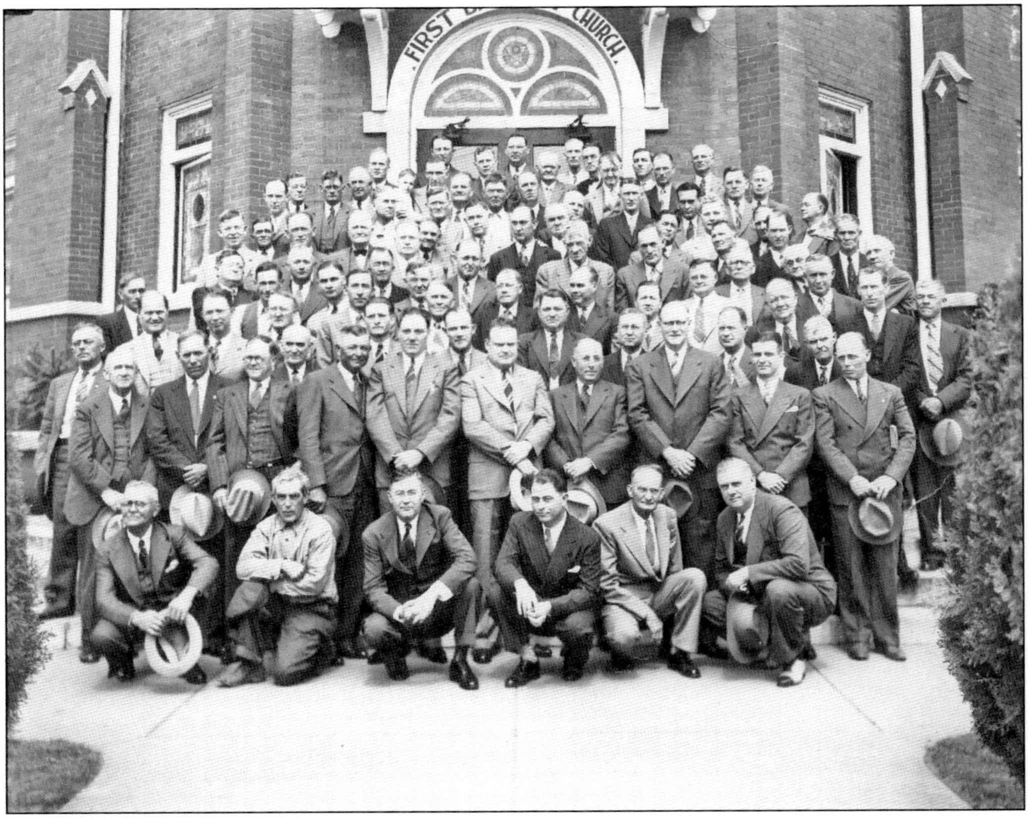

The Men's Bible Class of the Mount Pleasant First Baptist Church is pictured here on the front steps of the church around 1940. Founded in 1850 as a missionary Baptist church, the original church was a frame structure on North Jefferson Avenue. (Courtesy of Mount Pleasant Public Library and Historical Museum.)

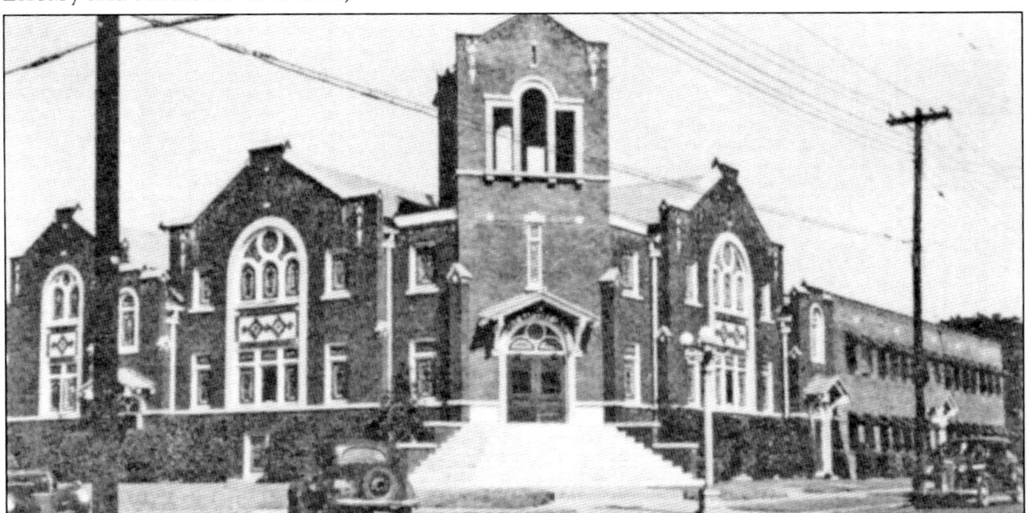

The First Baptist Church pictured here was completed in 1920 but was remodeled in the 1950s. Today, it is located east of town on State Highway 49. (Courtesy of Mount Pleasant Public Library and Historical Museum.)

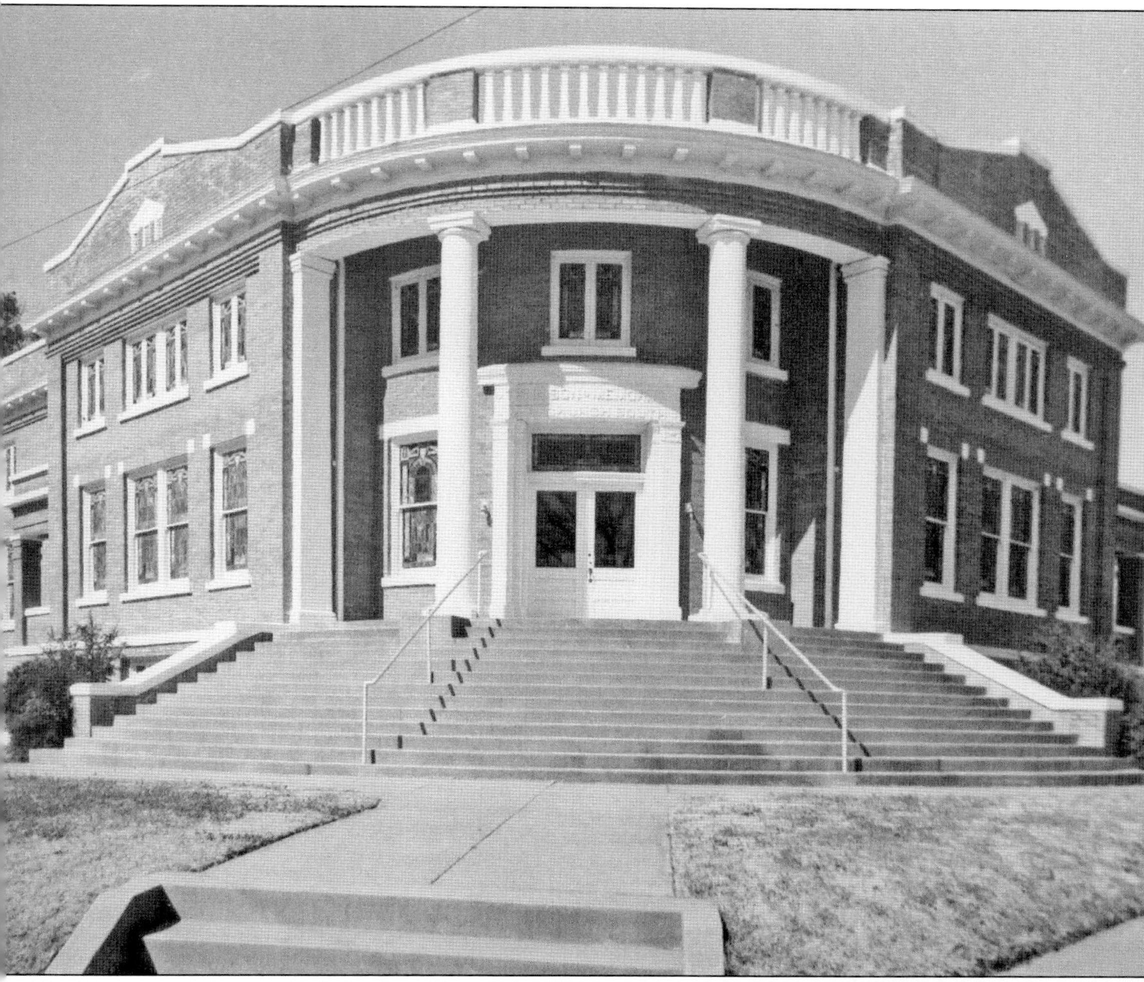

The Tennison Memorial Methodist Church building pictured here on East Third and Church Streets was completed in 1924, but the church dates back to the mid-19th century. Initially, the Methodists and Baptists shared a building on Jefferson Avenue and Third Street, holding services on alternating Sundays for a number of years until both congregations moved to separate locations. The church incurred a $25,0000 debt on its new facility in 1924 that was paid off by Booker Tennison Jr. The church has been called Tennison Memorial since then. This photograph was taken of the structure just before it was demolished in 1966–1967. A rebuilt Tennison Memorial is still located on Church Street just east of downtown Mount Pleasant. (Courtesy of the *East Texas Journal.*)

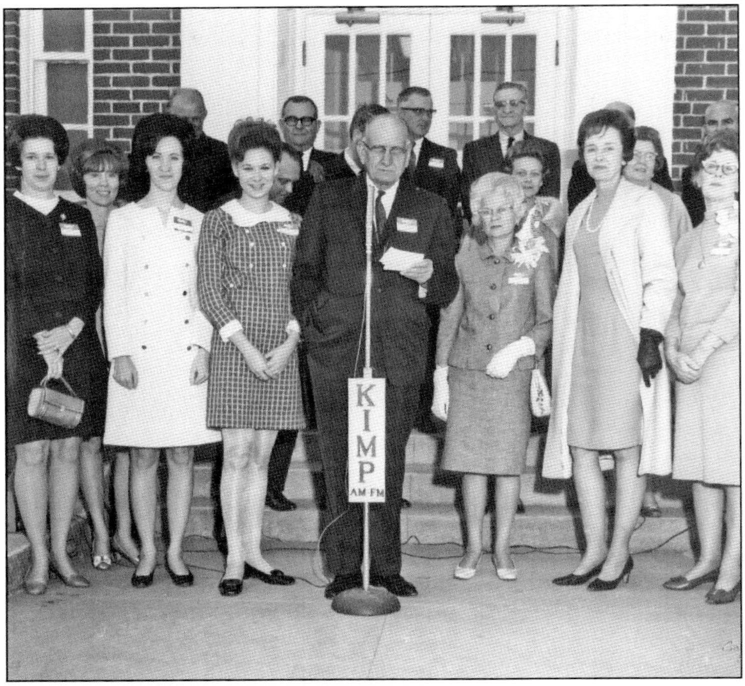


Mount Pleasant radio station KIMP broadcast the ceremony surrounding the dedication of the Mount Pleasant library in 1969. In this photograph, Traylor Russell stands behind the microphone. Russell researched the history of Mount Pleasant and Titus County quite extensively and is responsible for many of the items currently in the Mount Pleasant Library and Historical Museum. (Courtesy of Mount Pleasant Public Library and Historical Museum.)

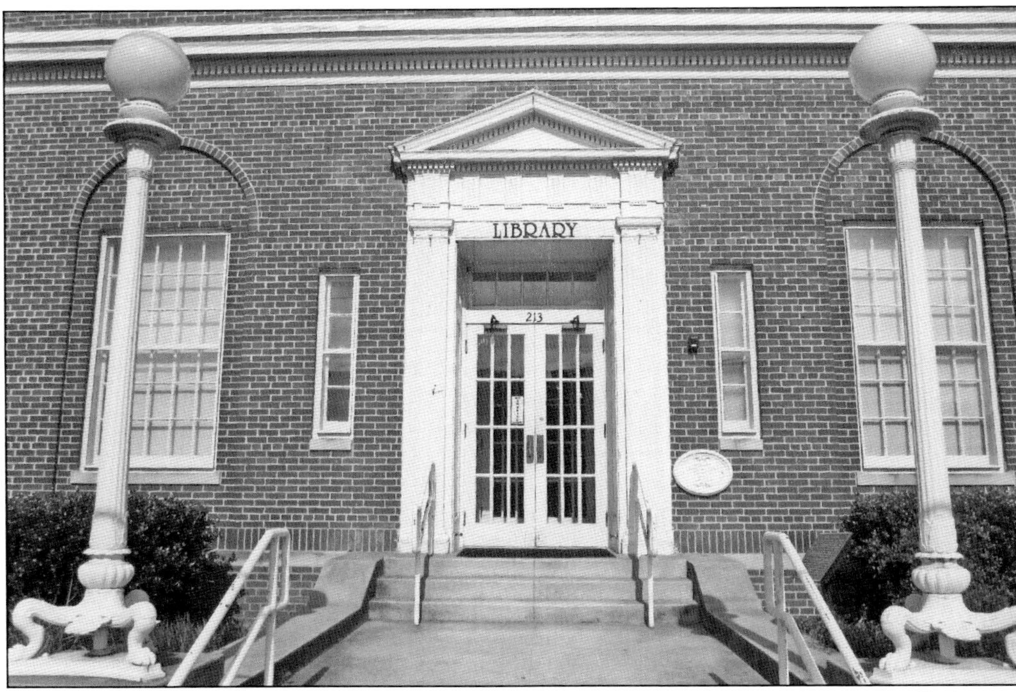


The Mount Pleasant Library was established in 1949 with 350 donated books. Originally housed on the second floor of city hall, the library moved to a new location on South Jefferson Avenue in 1964. The historic Mount Pleasant Post Office on Madison Avenue, remodeled in 1967, became the new public library at a dedication ceremony in 1969. In 2012, a new public library that also houses the city's historical museum opened a few blocks north of the old location. (Courtesy of Mount Pleasant Public Library and Historical Museum.)

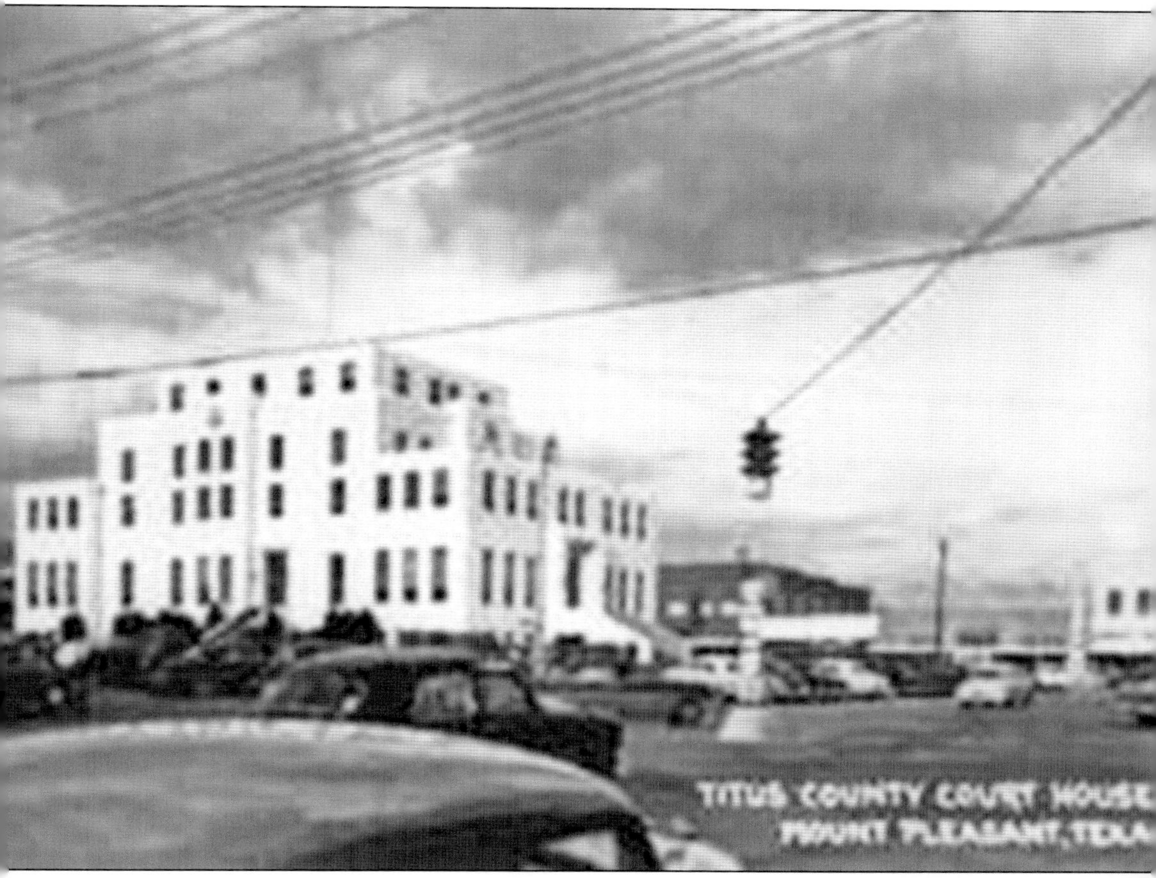


The Mount Pleasant courthouse has perhaps the most unique and interesting history of any courthouse in the state of Texas. Fire destroyed the first four Titus County courthouses. The current courthouse, which was originally built in 1895, can be seen in the image at the start of chapter two. That courthouse looked considerably different than the one pictured here in the early 1940s after the first of several remodeling efforts. Because it was less expensive than building a new courthouse, the county simply removed the bell tower, added a fourth floor, and remodeled the courthouse in what was then the modern style. (Courtesy of the *East Texas Journal*.)

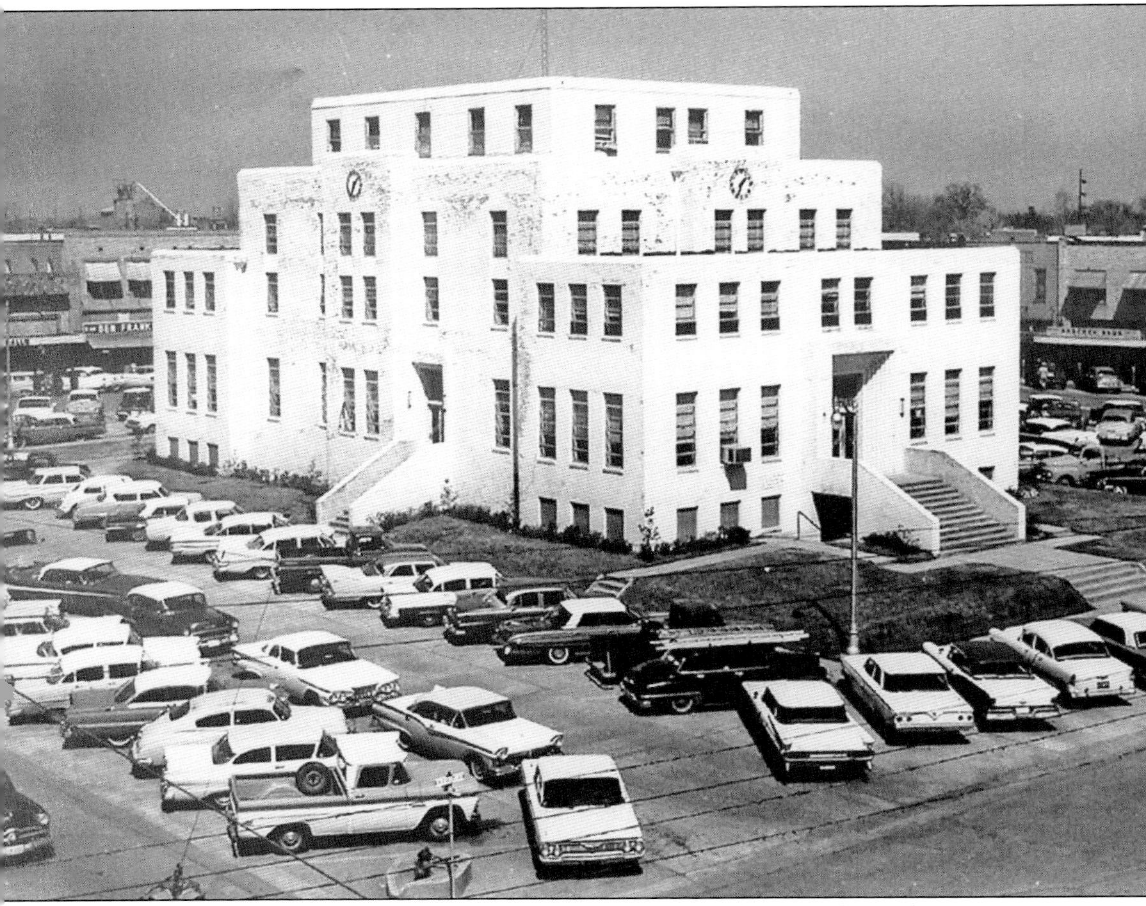

This photograph of the Titus County Courthouse in the early 1960s shows the worn appearance of the courthouse two decades after its facelift. The concrete facade was badly in need of repair, and the building itself required modernization. (Courtesy of the *East Texas Journal*.)

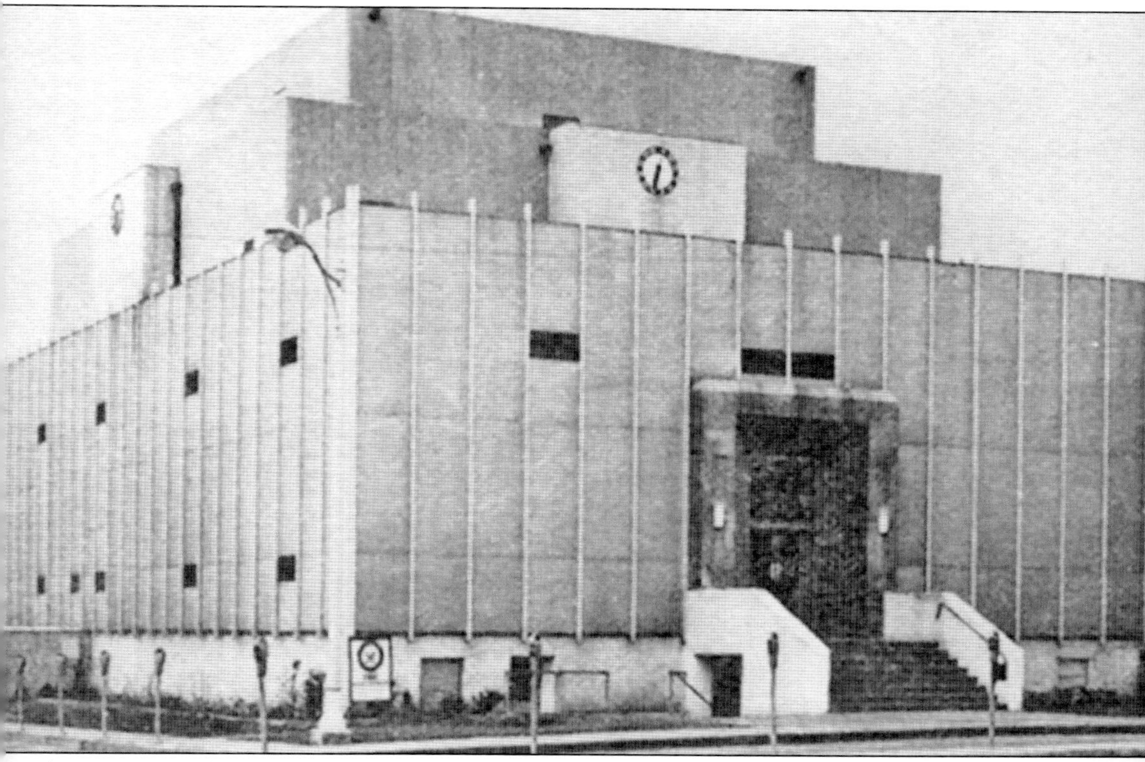

The 1960s remodel followed the same strategy of the 1940 remodel. Rather than building a new courthouse, the county placed a nearly windowless shell over the lower portion of the structure. This photograph shows the result of that remodel as seen in the 1970s. (Courtesy of the *East Texas Journal.*)

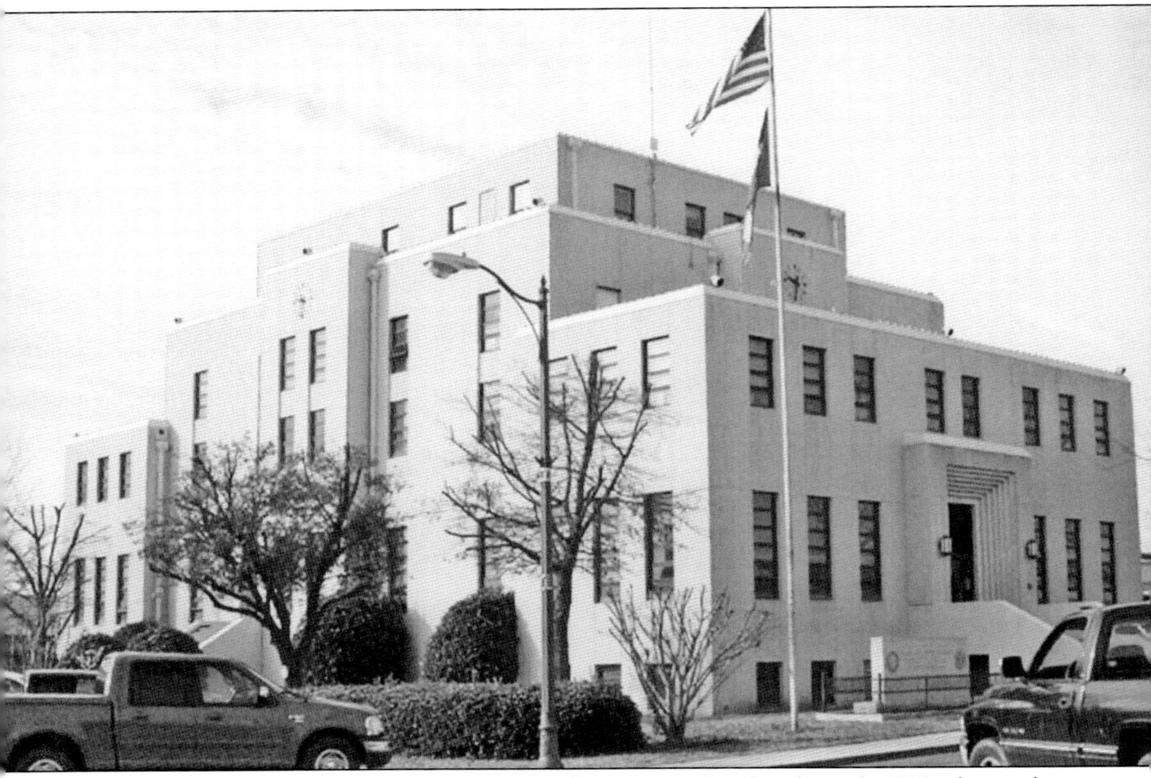

The final redesign of the Titus County Courthouse, completed in the early 1990s, featured a return to the Art Deco style of the 1940 remodel. Despite its age, the courthouse still serves as the center of government in Titus County. The astonishing thing is that visitors walking through the Titus County Courthouse are walking through the actual 1895 structure, just refaced on the outside. The building today does not look anywhere near as old as it actually is. Although the structure may be called by some the ugliest courthouse in Texas, it is definitely the most interesting and unique. (Courtesy of the *East Texas Journal*.)

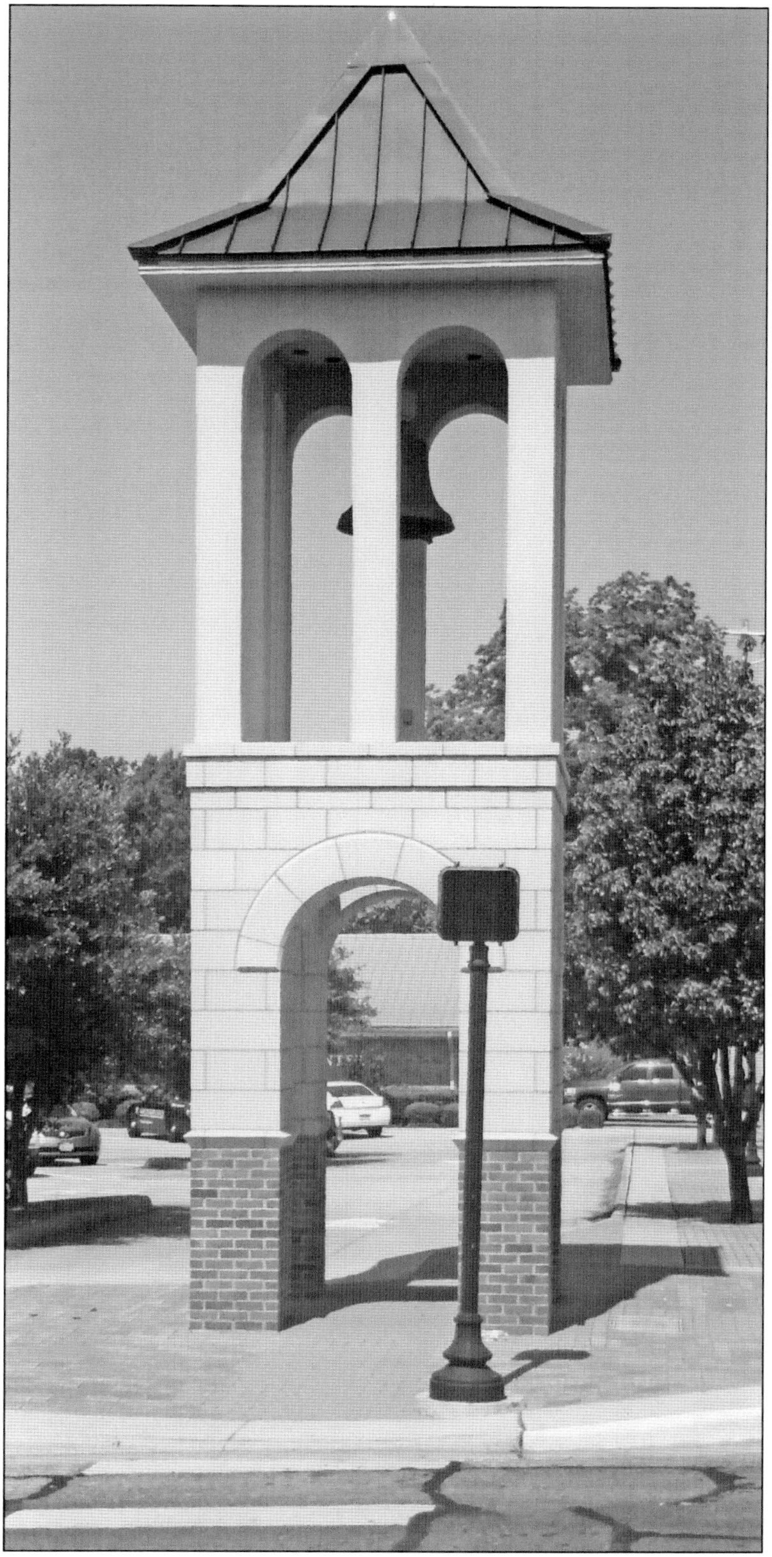

The 1940 remodel of the Titus County Courthouse resulted in the original 1895 bell tower being demolished to make way for a fourth floor. The towerless bell found a new home on display inside the courthouse. As part of the 1992 redesign of the courthouse, a new bell tower was constructed on the southwest corner of the square with the original 1895 bell as its centerpiece. Mount Pleasant citizens can now hear the bell every hour on the hour. (Authors.)

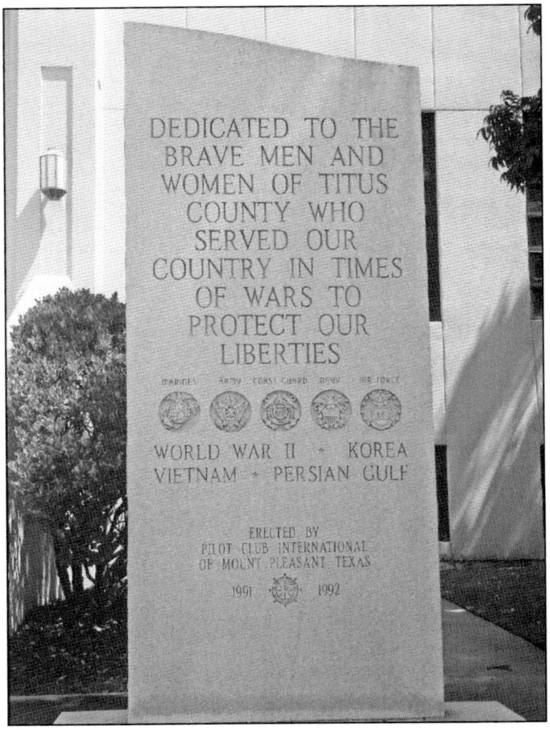


The Pilot Club of Mount Pleasant added this veterans' memorial to the grounds of the Titus County Courthouse in 1992. The monument commemorates the men and women of Titus County who served in all the branches of service from World War II to the first Gulf War. (Authors.)

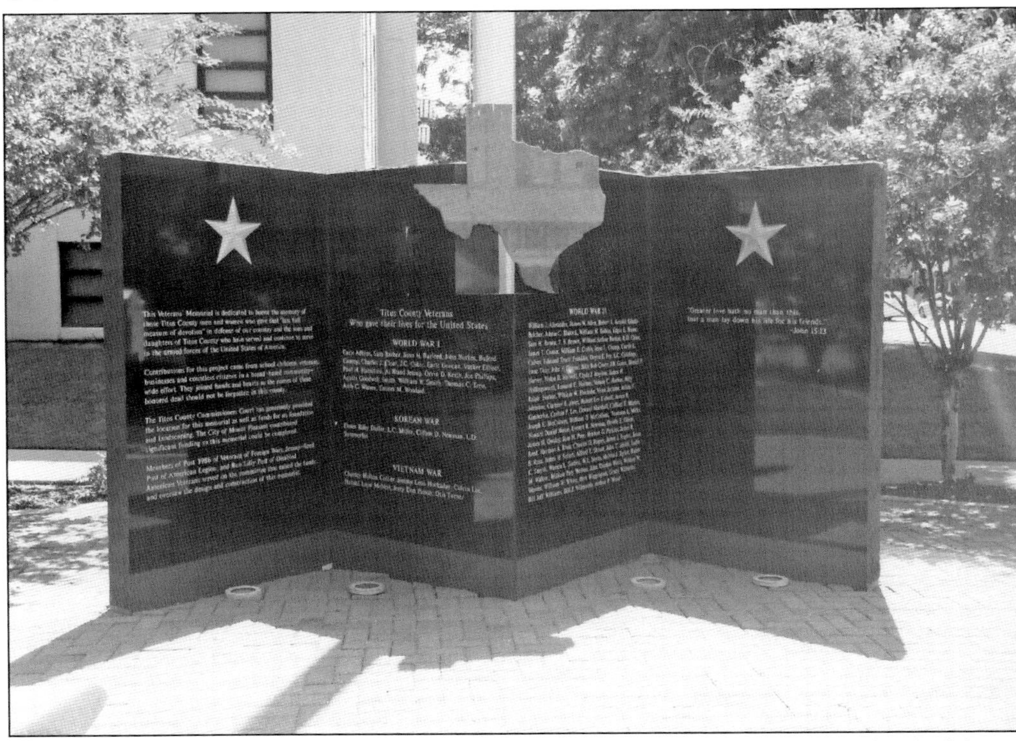

This veterans' memorial is dedicated to all the men and women of Titus County who died during American conflicts going back to the First World War. The monument is located on the southwest grounds of the Titus County Courthouse and was erected in 2006. (Authors.)

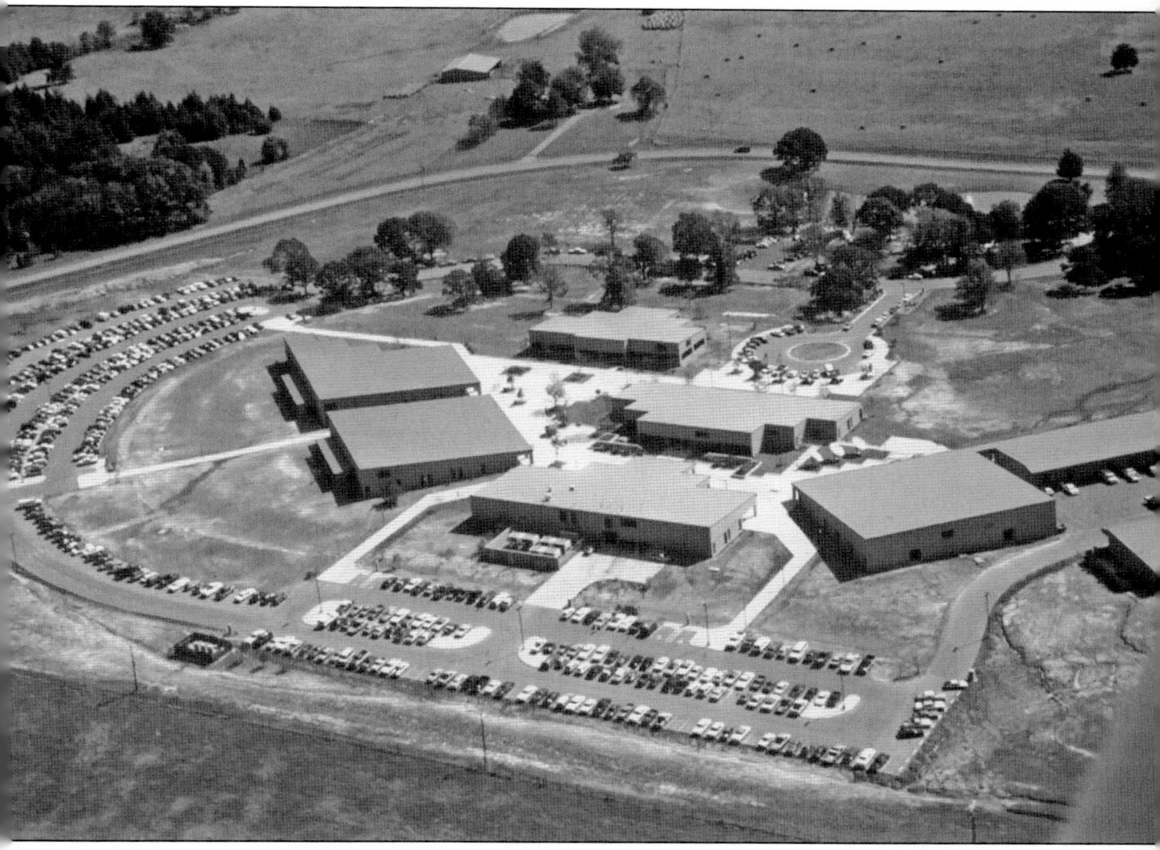

Mount Pleasant continued a long-standing tradition of offering varied education opportunities for its citizens when Titus County, in conjunction with neighboring Camp and Morris Counties, voted in support of a new community college. Taken in 1985, this aerial photograph of Northeast Texas Community College shows the school situated on 375 acres just east of Mount Pleasant in the Chapel Hill community on FM 1735. (Courtesy of Northeast Texas Community College.)